* * * * * * *

LEADERSHIP
Fitness

★ ★ ★ ★ ★ ★ ★ ★

LEADERSHIP
★ ★ ★ *Fitness* ★ ★ ★

Developing and Reinforcing
Successful, Positive Leaders

HOMER RICE

LOOKING GLASS BOOKS

Published by
LOOKING GLASS BOOKS

ISBN: 1-929619-26-X

Printed in the United States of America

Cover and book design by Burtch Hunter Design

FOREWORD

by BILL CURRY

Among Georgia Tech people there was something of a woe-is-me attitude about our facilities and our future in collegiate athletics in 1980.

The locker room at Grant Field was the same one I had stepped into as a Tech freshman in 1961, and the same one Tech players had stepped into in 1943. The jokes were constant, and they weren't funny. "Do not take prospects into the locker room under any circumstances. The rats are bigger than our linebackers."

Our strength facility consisted of three Olympic sets surrounded by chicken wire outside underneath the north stands.

Discussions were underway to consider moving the program to nonscholarship athletics, Division 3, and possibly do away with the athletic department.

Dr. Joseph Pettit, who was president, had said when he interviewed me as a candidate for head football coach, "I left the job as dean of engineering at Stanford to come to Tech. At Stanford no one said a word to me about football. Now something that is 2 percent of my budget is occupying 98 percent of my time. If I hire you, will you take this thing off me?"

"I will do my best," I said.

It was going to take a strong commitment from the president and the athletic director to turn the athletic program around. Then two weeks after Dr. Pettit hired me, our athletic director, Doug Weaver, accepted an opportunity to take the same position at his alma mater, Michigan State. Dr. Pettit called asked if I had any ideas about who might be right for the job.

"There's one man," I said, "but we can't get him. He's running the Cincinnati Bengals right now."

"Homer Rice?" Dr. Pettit said. "He's the only one on my list too."

Five years earlier, in 1975, I had just retired as a player in the NFL and was working as a scout for the Green Bay Packers. My job was to go all over America to observe the athletic abilities of college football players. When I arrived on campus at the University of North Carolina, the athletic director, Homer Rice, invited me to dinner at his home.

I had known Homer by reputation as an innovative college coach who had developed powerful offenses at Kentucky and Oklahoma as an assistant, and as head coach at the University of Cincinnati. I had also met him a time or two at Fellowship of Christian Athletes events. But this was the first time a college athletic director had invited me into his home while I was scouting on campus. I was utterly smitten with Homer and his wife, Phyllis, and Homer's way of doing things as athletic director.

Three years later, Homer was head coach of the Cincinnati Bengals and I was an assistant coach with the Packers. At the end of a game between the Packers and the Bengals, Homer made the effort to come across the field to find me and say hello. Not a lot of head coaches would have done that.

Those encounters, combined with Homer's success as A.D. at North Carolina, convinced me he would do great things at Georgia Tech. Dr. Pettit went to work recruiting Homer and convinced him to accept the challenge.

In my football career as a player, I was fortunate to have been thrown in with many of the great leaders from my walk of life. I reported to the Georgia Tech campus where I played for Coach Bobby Dodd. As an NFL rookie I reported to Green Bay where Vince Lombardi was coach of the Packers. Two years later I re-

ported to the Baltimore Colts and Don Shula. I snapped the ball
to Bart Starr and Johnny Unitas. Willie Davis was my mentor.
John Macke was my mentor.

By actual record these men are among the very best of all
time at what they did, yet each had his own manner of expres-
sion. Vince Lombardi, for example, said it in a ferocious way.
An intimidating way. He was extremely honest and let you know
he was about to use fear and intimidation. That worked for
Vince, but I didn't like it, and I didn't like Vince.

On the other hand Bart Starr, though he probably never
heard Homer's message, lives it and takes it another step. The
day I reported to the Green Bay Packers, I had been drafted in
the twentieth round—out of twenty rounds. I reported late because I had played in the College All Star Game and was
bumped off my flight from Chicago. I arrived at camp utterly
miserable, both physically and emotionally. Then I sensed a
presence at my side, and I turned to see Bart Starr, and he called
me by name.

"Bill, I don't know your faith," he said, "but we have a wonderful preacher at our Methodist church. Cherry and I would
like to invite you to join us."

From that day forward he has been the big brother I never had.

When I was traded to the Colts two years later, Don Shula,
who holds the NFL record for most career wins, was head
coach. His were the toughest training camps I had experienced;
practices were twice as long as Lombardi's. But Coach Shula
could spot talent nobody else wanted and get us to play for him.
He had a few great players and surrounded them with a bunch
of people like me. Then he believed in us so firmly, we learned
to believe in ourselves.

Homer Rice, in his leadership style, was unlike any of these
men, yet I sensed I was in the presence of greatness. Homer was
so quiet and reserved, yet utterly organized, he was intimidating

for someone who is not quiet. I immediately felt like I was sitting at the feet of a master, a great teacher.

Homer was transformational, by his example and by his actions. Soon after he arrived at Tech he gave me a new framework, which he called the Attitude Technique, to fit all the leadership qualities I had witnessed in Dodd, Lombardi, Shula, Starr, and Unitas, but could never have articulated myself. He gave leadership an orderly process, and he wanted me to teach that process to our players—not just talk to them about, but teach them for an hour a week in class. "But first," he said, "you have to learn it."

Here was the basic framework of the Attitude Technique:

1. Make a commitment.
2. Set a target date.
3. Assemble the ingredients.
4. Learn to give sacrificially.
5. Visualize the end result.
6. Articulate and speak as if the desired result were a *fait accompli*.
7. Expect the results you desire.

Over time Homer would confirm my earliest impressions in a thousand ways: he lived the Attitude Technique even as he taught it to me. He didn't tell what he hoped. He told me, "We *will be* at the top of the ACC academically and athletically."

My challenge, then, was to begin living out the message and then teach it, because if you start teaching and you don't live it, it's a joke. Certain personal habits had to change, particularly my language. I had fallen into the NFL language, where certain things came out of my mouth that I wouldn't want my mama or my wife to hear. You can't do that in college.

I'm sure he had to correct me on many occasions; two of

those corrections stand out in my memory.

I looked up into the south stands at Grant Field one day and saw what appeared to be a weed growing up from the concrete. I walked up for a closer look, and sure enough, the weed was as big around as my wrist. We couldn't build a winning program if the maintenance staff didn't do a better job in our stadium than that, so I marched into Homer's and told him what I had seen.

Instead of joining me in my fury, Homer simply said, "I'll tell you what, you work with the football team, and I'll work with the weeds. Anything else you want to discuss today?"

"No sir," I said.

He called me in a little later, after I had gone into several press conferences and confronted the media about some of the things they had written. He said, "You are critiquing the sportswriters?"

"Yes sir," I said, "that's exactly what I'm doing."

"Well, you're going to stop," he said. "Furthermore, you're going to stop reading the sports page."

I protested, "I've read the sports page since I was six years old. I'm not going to stop now."

Then Homer spoke very quietly and said, "Let me put this another way. That was not a suggestion."

So I quit reading the sports page, and my attitude changed for the better. Five years later I convinced Carolyn, my wife, to quit reading the sports page, and life has been better every day since.

Homer understood the transformation of the athletic program would take years, would require more than just a change in attitude, and the process at times would not be pretty. We were transitioning into the Atlantic Coast Conference, yet our non-conference games included Alabama, Auburn, Tennessee, Georgia, Florida, and Notre Dame. There was no disagreement that Tech had the most difficult schedule in the nation. Homer called me into his office and assured me, "I'm going to do something about this schedule. Teams that win a lot of games play teams that lose a lot of games."

Despite his assurances for the future, whenever we lost I would go into apoplexy. I hate losing. It's like a disease. I got on the airplane coming home and I stared at people who tried to be encouraging. I spread a funk all over the environment.

Once again, Homer called me in and asked, "Tell me what's going on with you after games?"

"What's going on," I said, "is I'm sick in my heart. It kills me to lose."

"What you're doing," Homer said, "is displaying a poor attitude, and I want it to stop now."

I said, "Yes sir," and I did try, but I didn't obey that one very well.

After two years we had won two games, and my friends started telling me about alumni meetings where people were saying I needed to be fired. Homer would speak to alumni groups, and somebody would stand up and say, "What are we gonna do about Curry?"

"What do you mean?" Homer would ask, knowing exactly what he meant.

"Well, he's a nice boy and a Tech man and all that," the person would say, "but it's obvious he doesn't know how to coach football."

Then Homer would answer calmly, "As long as I am the athletic director, Bill Curry will be our coach. Next question."

That's the kind of support you have to have, and nobody gets it in today's world. No matter who you are, your athletic director is not going to stand up for you like Homer did year after year. He stood up for Bobby Cremins, for Jim Morris, and for me. That's the acid test. And we accomplished exactly what he predicted we would accomplish. After six years of gut-wrenching work we became a Top 20 team, won a big bowl game, and graduated every senior off that team.

When Tech alumni realized Homer had this thing going in the right direction, a groundswell of support arose. The Edge Building happened. The weight room was built. We got new locker rooms for ourselves and our visitors. Homer made it clear that ours would be the kind of crowd that killed visitors with kindness. He constantly reinforced that idea.

Then after one more season, Alabama called, and I took off. Whether I should have taken that job is a matter for people who have opinions about that sort of thing.

When Alabama called, I called Coach Dodd to ask his opinion, thinking I knew what he would say. He stunned me.

"If they interview you," he said, "they will offer the job, and you have to take it."

Then he said words I will never forget: "I love Georgia Tech, but I love you more. I know what you are and I know what you have to do. You must go."

So I called Homer and told him I was going.

That was not the right way to do it. I was egotistical and stupid. I should have sat down with him, explained the situation, and listened to him. I don't know what would have happened if I had done that, but what I did was incredibly unfair to Homer.

For you to understand what happened next, you need to know that Homer and I share a similar theology. Two weeks after I had moved to Alabama, I was knocked to my knees. "You fool! You get yourself to Atlanta and humble yourself before that great man!"

So I got in my car and drove to Atlanta. I walked into Homer's office, and though I did not literally drop to my knees, I did so figuratively, wept, and apologized.

That was Homer's chance to tell me, "You had your chance to do this the right way."

But he did not. Instead, all he did was to forgive me.

In his seventeen years as athletic director at Georgia Tech, Homer Rice led a remarkable transformation of won-loss records, facilities, with more than $100 million invested in improvements, and attitude. His Total Person Program, based on the Attitude Technique, became the model for the NCAA Life Skills program at schools across the country.

Through *Leadership Fitness*, Homer continues his lifelong commitment to the development of positive leaders.

INTRODUCING HOMER RICE

by PAUL J. MEYER
Founder of Success Motivation® International, Inc.

Even as a youngster, Homer Rice was gathering information that would help him write *Leadership Fitness: Developing and Reinforcing Successful, Positive Leaders.* As a twelve-year-old, Homer read a compelling book on goal-setting his father gave him for his birthday. This book challenged its readers to consider how to approach life and to search for the secrets of success. Homer took the mandate seriously and began a life-long habit of writing down goals for every area of his life. And thus began the rich life experiences that make Homer Rice uniquely qualified to write this outstanding book.

Achieving goals early in his life convinced Homer of the power of goal setting. These early successes also made him aware of the wellspring of wisdom in good books. He continued his search for the keys to success by reading the best books ever written on the topic. Homer's quest for knowledge resulted in his becoming an even more fervent advocate of committing one's goals to writing.

In addition, Homer identified from his comprehensive reading the significant elements of success: attitude, desire, belief, visualization, spaced repetition, habits, and focus. Homer's studies also led him to believe that true and lasting success comes only to those who set and achieve goals in all areas of life.

Investing life in studying, teaching, and practicing success principles created the opportunity for Homer and me to meet decades ago. I had been on an intense journey quite similar to Homer's in search of the keys to a life of positive achievement.

Like Homer, I had a burning desire to share this phenomenal "secret" with others. In 1960 I founded my flagship company and dedicated it to "motivating people to their full potential." I began writing and marketing information on how to set goals in every area of life and how to reach them by marshaling the powerful forces of a positive attitude, desire, belief, visualization, and all the other elements of success Homer and I had identified independently in our own journeys.

Our mutual zeal and commitment to learning more about success and sharing this information with others created an instantaneous bond. We enjoyed doing some writing together and kept up with each other over the years. Homer earned phenomenal success described more specifically elsewhere in this book. I also earned personal and financial success as my company and its affiliated companies spread throughout the United States and to more than sixty countries speaking twenty-three languages.

I believe my business background qualifies me as a credible judge of this book. While I treasure my friendship with Homer, that relationship is not the sole reason I recommend his book. I encourage you to read it because it is based on valid principles that have worked for me for more than five decades.

In a book full of invaluable truths, my favorite is, *In order to lead others, you must first become the person you want to be.* Homer never challenged anyone to be anything he was not willing to work toward becoming himself. I admire him for taking this stand, along with many others he has taken in his life. Homer, for example, never rested on his laurels. Although decades ago he reached countless pinnacles of success, he kept setting new worthwhile goals—and reaching them. What is even more gratifying is how his goals always seemed to be driven by the best interest of others. Homer Rice is a true leader.

The language of *Leadership Fitness* is straightforward and reader friendly. The anecdotes and examples are interesting, and they add validity and credibility to the message. Embedded within these compelling pages is nothing short of a full-blown Ph.D. course of study. Homer Rice has distilled into one great book the important success and leadership principles of the ages. This book is a culmination of Homer's extraordinary life and career. I congratulate him for writing it, and I commend you for reading it. When you put into action the powerful content of Homer Rice's book, your life will never be the same.

Someone once said that success is not measured only by your climbing the ladder to success but by the number of people you helped climb that ladder. If this is true, and I believe it is, then Homer Rice is certainly one of the most successful leaders I have been privileged to know or even know about.

Read *Leadership Fitness: Developing and Reinforcing Successful, Positive Leaders* and join the legions of others whom Homer Rice has led to success beyond their wildest dreams. You will be astonished at what you can do.

ACKNOWLEDGMENTS

After authoring *Lessons for Leaders* (Longstreet Press) in 2000, I received letter after letter from people seeking more information on The Attitude Technique Philosophy, a Total Person-Total Success concept. No doubt, this stimulated me to think in terms of another book. I made the decision to include another manuscript on positive leadership development in my next five-year plan of goals. My "commitment" began the task. As I explain in this book, accomplishing a goal begins with "I", but actually making it happen requires others, which means the goal ends in "we." The team does it!

I needed a complete "squad" to work through and complete *Leadership Fitness*. The key was a disciplined approach: writing every day. It may have been ten minutes or several hours, but I did something each day. Once a lesson was completed, my long-time administrative assistant, Ann Harrell, typed the notes into a clean copy. As with *Lessons for Leaders*, I then turned to Elizabeth Haven Hawley, an astute doctoral student and American history instructor at Georgia Tech. While working on her own dissertation, Haven used her experience as a former journalism major and typesetter to edit my writing, helping to bring the manuscript from rough copy into a cohesive form. She again worked miracles, and the book took shape with positive results. Chuck Perry later edited the final version to make it book-ready.

Input from many people helped influence the final shape of the message of *Leadership Fitness*, and they are listed in Appendix "I" and on pages 153-166 of the Afterword (the latter focusing on the Leadership Fitness class of 2003). Corrections, additions, interviews, articles, and research by all of these people made this book happen. I thank them for their sincere efforts. As with the last book, I asked Bob Harty, executive director of Georgia Tech's

Institute Communications and Public Affairs department and an expert on publications, to critique the final copy. When Bob gave his blessings, I knew we had passed the test.

Before the completed copy was ready for the publisher, Ann Harrell became ill and passed away on October 4, 2003. What a wonderful human being she was—loved by everyone who knew her and a pillar of strength in the Georgia Tech Athletic Association. Surely she is in heaven smiling down on us as we struggle on without her tender, loving care. She will be sorely missed but, knowing Ann as I do, she would be disappointed if we did not carry on to do our very best. She was *always* at her best.

The final stage: Is the book worthy of publication and distribution? I sent a pre-press copy to the top people in various fields for their assessments. I asked Paul J. Meyer, founder of Success Motivation® International and a *New York Times* best-selling author, to review the material and, if so inclined, to consider writing the Foreword to the book. Paul is a pioneer of the motivation and leadership industry. His program materials have sold more than $2 billion worldwide—more than any other author in this field. Paul is a true "giver" (read *The Joy and Responsibility of Stewardship*) and a dear friend for more than forty years. He taught me the principle of the Total Person that shaped my life and gave me the idea to begin and implement a similar program for student-athletes throughout the colleges and universities in America and foreign lands. I certainly owe him much for his influence upon my work through the years. I knew Paul would be totally honest in his evaluation of *Leadership Fitness*. I was excited and extremely happy when he gave his approval and agreed to contribute the Foreword.

From the business world, I gained assistance from J. C. "Bud" Shaw, founder and past chairman of the board of Shaw Industries, the world's largest carpet industry. Bud is the ultimate leader in the business world, yet he has made time in his schedule through the years to visit my Leadership Fitness Class and to offer his positive advice to the students at Georgia Tech. During my years as director of athletics, he always supported programs benefiting student-athletes. His involvement usually assured the success of any program.

In writing *Leadership Fitness*, multiple memories popped from my human computer for suggestions and thoughts. One day I thought of Danny Lotz, a good friend and former outstanding athlete at the University of North Carolina. Danny became a prominent dentist in Raleigh, NC, after graduation. When I was director of athletics at UNC, I invited Danny to a football game and to sit in my box. He came accompanied by his wife Anne and her distinguished parents, Dr. and Mrs. Billy Graham. My wife's mother was visiting us at the time, and we were all ecstatic that this great spiritual leader would be seated in our box. Billy asked me to play a part in his crusade, which was taking place in nearby Raleigh the following week. I was honored by his request. Afterward, whenever my wife Phyllis and I attended the Fellowship of Christian Athletes conference each summer in Black Mountain, NC, we were always invited to visit the Grahams' home nearby. As time went on, their daughter Anne also became a prominent spiritual leader. Her books, lectures, TV and radio appearances brought belief in God to millions around the world through her "Angel Ministries" programs. I am convinced that successful, positive leaders must incorporate a spiritual aspect into their lives. Belief in God is a foundation of Leadership Fitness. I wondered if Dr. Danny Lotz would read *Leadership Fitness* and endorse its contents. A quick call to Danny confirmed that he would.

It finally was time to seek out those in the professional world who knew of my work over the years as a coach, teacher, administrator, and person. This would be the true test of the validity of *Leadership Fitness*.

From the coaching profession, who could be better than

Grant Teaff, executive director of the American Football Coaching Association? Grant was National Coach of the Year while coaching at Baylor University, where he had phenomenal success and currently provides tremendous positive leadership for football coaches at all levels. Grant provided the Foreword for *Lessons for Leaders*. Next I turned to athletic administration, calling Mike Cleary, long-time executive director of the National Association of the Collegiate Directors of Athletics. NACDA represents all colleges and universities on every level throughout the country and worldwide, and Mike's leadership has steered this organization to the top of the ladder. From the NCAA Divison-1 Athletic Directors came Executive Director Dutch Baughman, representing the top 117 universities in the United States. Dutch has provided the positive leadership to make good things happen for all of athletic administration. He has promoted the CHAMPS program that encourages the right ethics for intercollegiate athletics.

Colleagues such as Gene Corrigan—former director of athletics at the University of Virginia and at Notre Dame, commissioner of the Atlantic Coast Conference, and president of the National Collegiate Athletic Association—have also endorsed the book. My first collegiate administrative post was as director of athletics at the University of North Carolina, and the first visitor to my office was Gene Corrigan. We became instant friends and worked together for the betterment of student-athletes from that point forward. Gene is a super positive leader.

When I think of the giants in the field of preventive medicine, there is no one higher than Dr. Kenneth H. Cooper. This man may have saved many lives by developing the aerobic program for good health. No leader can be fit for the role without living a lifestyle that promotes good health. I have made many trips to Dr. Cooper's Aerobic Center in Dallas, TX. It's always a privilege to visit with Ken and get the latest news in good preventive health. His books are a must-read for aspiring leaders.

As I've noted in Appendix I on pages 215-217 and throughout these pages, this book was put together with aid from many people. It is an accumulation of notes, interviews, research, wisdom from speakers to classes, past writings, memories, and other people's recollections of the facts. This book reflects many of my own strong feelings, all backed by personal experience in finding the best approach to becoming a successful, positive leader. The good results have been overwhelming. To the best of my knowledge, all the data is accurate—and even my elaborations are based on true stories! I began jotting down notes for future use after my twelfth birthday, and later I decided to record my involvement in my profession. This book is my seventh to be published.

Successful seasons on the gridiron brought requests to speak at national clinics and to write articles for sports magazines, along with authors asking me to contribute to their books. Then one day a letter came from Prentice-Hall Publishing Co. to author a book for the Coaches' Book Club. That brought forth the *Explosive Short-T / Homer Rice on Triple Option Football*, and *The Air Option* (co-authored with Steve Moore).

When my football coaching ended and athletic administration began, I turned to writing books about leadership, such as *Leadership in Athletics* (Paul Meyer's Success Motivation® International, Inc.), *Leadership for Leaders* (MacGregor Sports), and *Lessons for Leaders* (Longstreet Press).

Leadership Fitness is the base for successful positive leadership. Whatever field you are engaged in or about to enter will require study and skills development in order to accomplish your goals in that area. But it is imperative to get your life into shape first. This program offers the ingredients to begin that project.

DEDICATION

Each book I have authored has been dedicated to my family. First, to my dear wife, Phyllis. We met in the seventh grade in 1939. I asked her for a date, my first date, and she accepted. We took in a Saturday afternoon movie. She claims she had to pay her own way, and I have been paying for that mistake ever since! Soon I secretly declared that she would become my wife. After high school, World War II, and college, we were married in 1950. We have been fortunate to have three lovely and talented daughters: Nancy Hetherington, Phyllis Ingle, and Angela Miller. They in turn have given us seven wonderful grandchildren: Ryce Hetherington, Leigh Hetherington, Drew Hetherington, Jamie Ingle, Brian Ingle, David Miller, and Andrew Miller. I dedicate *Leadership Fitness* to our wonderful and very close family.

There are others that I must recognize, including my parents, Dr. Samuel and Grace Rice, whose memories continue to inspire me; my older brother Robert Cecil Rice, whom I tagged after as a youngster; and my high school coach, Ewell "Judge" Waddell. Coach Waddell had a profound influence upon my career choice. Having him hire me as his replacment at Highlands High School in Fort Thomas, KY, was, at the time, my ultimate achievement. Many others had a tremendous influence upon my career and life, but to mention all of them would be a book in itself. I have been most fortunate to have received so much from so many.

PREFACE

Scientists tell us that billions of years ago a "Big Bang" occurred. Theologians affirm that a Supreme Being—God—brought this about, resulting in the cosmos: earth, moon, sun, solar system, galaxies, and an endless expanse of planets throughout the universe. The *piece de resistance* of this creative process is human beings, creatures with brains and the power to think, to choose, to control and to create. We have minds of our own, minds that function both consciously and subconsciously.

This mental activity operates incessantly, serving as the most sophisticated computer ever built. Our inner computer can be programmed for negative or positive responses, and designed to build or to destroy. It is precisely this cognitive capability that makes us human: to think abstractly; to reflect on ourselves; to govern our behavior; to make value judgments; to set goals; to organize; and to establish relationships—all for good or ill.

Leadership is the key to personal and social well-being. That is what this book is about: developing positive leadership that contributes to the common good. Robert Frost said we do not so much believe in the future as we believe the future in. The future largely becomes what the world's people believe and practice. *Leadership Fitness* is a study in human fulfillment and a wholesome society. Each of us is either part of the solution or part of the problem. My hope in these pages is to encourage and enable positive, effective leaders.

CONTENTS

PERSONAL NOTES

MY PERSONAL LIFE BLUEPRINT

NAME _____

DATE _____

Once you sign your name and date, this manuscript becomes YOUR guide to become a positive, successful leader. Utilize the information to fit your needs and style. May you become "fit" to be the Ultimate Leader in Charge!

INTRODUCTION

*As a student, athlete, teacher, coach, and athletic
administrator, I have learned it takes a leader
to shape a team into a successful unit.
This process starts with "I"
and transforms into "we."
The Team does it!*

In May 1997, I ended a forty-seven-year career in athletics by announcing my retirement as director of athletics and executive assistant to the president at Georgia Tech. Little did I know that another career was about to begin for me at the age of seventy. Georgia Tech President Wayne Clough invited me to consider serving as a development consultant for both the university and the Department of Athletics. That was not all. Dr. Gary Schuster, Dean of the College of Sciences, encouraged me to consider teaching. I accepted both invitations, and overnight I became an adjunct professor. I asked Dean Schuster the meaning of "adjunct," and he promptly replied that it meant **no pay**. The course would be one dear to my heart, however: It would explain the Attitude Technique philosophy, a total person, total success concept for leadership. The title for the course became "Leadership Fitness."

My book *Lessons for Leaders* was at that time being published by Longstreet Press. The book sold out in the first year.

Readers, along with my publisher, encouraged me to follow up with a book that delved more deeply into my philosophy of positive leadership.

My class, comprised mostly of seniors, became the laboratory for research and development of that next book, *Leadership Fitness*. Those bright, energetic young men and women were the challengers who kept me on my toes while together we explored this extremely important subject. That class energized me not only to continue teaching but also to seek other ways of promoting effective leadership and positive life skills. They told me that they would probably forget many of their class assignments from Georgia Tech, but "Leadership Fitness" would give them something to carry with them for the rest of their lives. That message made me realize the importance of my involvement in educating leaders. I learned that the great effort I'd taken to develop a high-level version of the program was appreciated. The positive feedback has been overwhelming.

One feature that I added to class meetings was exposing students to individuals who were highly successful in many fields. These people visited and spoke to students on their respective subjects of expertise. Several of the people whom students found most engaging have been asked to contribute to this book.

During my years at Georgia Tech, the Athletic Association began a program for student-athletes that became known as the Student-Athlete Total Person Program. Started in 1980, the program was very effective at preparing young men and women for the transitions they faced as they migrated from the world of college sports into their adult lives. It was so successful that it became a model for a national program that expanded to the athletic departments of more than 200 colleges and universities across the country. The Total Person Program was subsequently offered to all students at Georgia Tech. Will that program also expand to the full student bodies of other colleges and universities? We shall see!

During class, groups discussed compelling questions such as, "Which is more important, our willpower or our imagination?" The section about the human computer (Lesson One) helped to clear up this question. The students then wanted to know how society defines success. They concluded that success is the realization of a worthy idea, from attempt to completion. That led to a stimulating discussion about whether we should be considered failures for not living up to society's expectations. Life should not be viewed in terms of failure, we found, but in degrees of success.

SUCCESS is not a grand-slam homerun. Success is consistently hitting those dependable singles every day. Individual or groups that make it to the top concentrate on staying at bat and avoiding mistakes that detract from their performances. Once in a while, the perfect pitch comes across the plate. You will be ready to knock it out of the park if your hitting has been consistently solid.

The principle to grasp here is **PREPARATION**. Get ready for the big pitch by concentrating on singles until the right opportunity comes along. Ted Williams of the Boston Red Sox, the greatest hitter of all time, said that out of the twenty to fifty pitches that came his way every game, he expected only one perfect pitch. He had the self-discipline to wait and to be prepared when that pitch came.

A thin line divides success from failure. A determined person will not quit even in the darkest moment of tremendous strain. Training yourself to use your human computer to its fullest potential can propel you across that thin line, allowing you to make the jump from attempt to achievement.

PERCEPTION is another key to success. Many people live in an unreal world. They create a cosmos in their own minds based on the way they would like it to be, rather than the way it actually is. We must see the world of everyday life as it really is and know the difference between what is real and unreal, between fact and fiction, and between what works and what doesn't work. God has endowed us with a human computer that permeates our entire being and allows us to develop a clear and truthful perception.

There are four basic realities to understand:

1) We will always have **Problems.** If we don't, we have set our goals too low.

2) **There is a Natural Law of Balance.** We see it each day: electrons and protons; night and day; male and female; hot and cold; life and death; the two sides of a coin. Nothing is one way. For every positive, there's an offsetting negative; for every negative, there's an offsetting positive. To gain something, you must give up something. Always look quickly for the offsetting positive in every negative situation, which is what positive mental attitude is all about. Always look for the half-full glass rather than the half-empty glass. Look for the positives as soon as something goes wrong. This is a success force.

3) The **Law of Averages cannot be ignored.** Insurance companies use it to compile actuary tables. Gambling casinos use it to take your money. In sports we keep innumerable statistics. All things being equal, if you attempt something twenty times with the correct preparation, your chances of succeeding are twice as good as if you tried it only ten times. Why doesn't everybody apply this basic law? Most people do not believe the Law of Averages will work for them. Colonel Sanders approached more than a thousand restaurants before a single one bought his chicken recipe. Thomas Edison tried an immense number of techniques for creating a light bulb before he made any that worked. If we never quit, we will eventually succeed. We may

have temporary setbacks, but we will never be defeated.

4) Through the power of the mind, we can control our destiny. The principle of the **Subconscious Mind**—our subjective imagination, our human computer—will be thoroughly explained in a lesson to follow. Dr. Karl Pribram, a Stanford University neurosurgeon, has demonstrated convincingly the direct correlation between what the mind visualizes and what a person achieves. Develop the habit of imagining that you are already successful.

ATTITUDE should follow perception. After we comprehend that a situation is real, we need to position our minds for success. We can accomplish almost any task by applying a positive attitude, but a negative attitude will prevent us from succeeding. You've never seen a bookstore carry a title like *The Power of Negative Thinking*!

The American philosopher William James summed it up when he said, "The greatest revolution of our generation is the discovery that human beings, by changing the inner attitudes of their minds, can change the outer aspects of their lives." To acquire a true and positive mental attitude, we must analyze and understand exactly what a positive mental attitude is, and how and why it works.

CONCLUSION

The more positive your system of beliefs, the more you will believe in your ability to control your destiny. You will be able to accomplish specific tasks when others have said, "It can't be done."

Sometimes we may not get a solution that allows us to achieve our original objective. We may find an alternative that takes us in an entirely different direction. That direction more often than not turns out to be superior to the one in which we were originally headed.

WE ARE FREE TO CHOOSE OUR ATTITUDE

Can we motivate other people? We can help them to become motivated by guiding them to the source of their own power. Whether they move forward from there is a personal matter. Where is this power? It's inside everyone. It's the human computer, the starting place for developing positive and negative leadership.

We discovered in class discussion that an individual's personality is the sum total of all that person's habits and characteristics. Brainstorming, we came up with a list of positive words and phrases that describe a positive approach in an individual's personality. The positive leader often is most or all of the following:

- Trustworthy
- Moral
- Ethical
- A servant leader
- A leader by strong principles
- Unselfish
- Treats employees, followers, or customers with fairness
- Good listener and communicator
- Strong
- Friendly
- Uses common sense as necessary
- Positive
- Master of skills appropriate for a position
- Hard and smart worker
- Quick problem solver
- Master of tough decisions
- Has a vision for the company or program
- Surrounds himself/herself with positive and smart people
- Self motivated
- Effective leader

We usually find these types of leaders at the heads of nations, militaries, governments, corporations, companies, teams, religious organizations, medicine, education, families, and almost any field or group. Although styles may be different, in the final analysis, the positive leader has the best and sometimes the only chance to succeed.

By contrast, a negative leader may be some or all of these:

- Untrustworthy
- Immoral
- Unethical
- Corrupt
- Greedy
- Selfish
- Evil
- Poor communicator
- Unfair
- Negative
- Disloyal
- Weak
- Unfriendly
- Lazy
- Not respected by employees
- Surrounds himself/herself with people who can be controlled
- Will not listen to others
- Arrogant

During World War II (1941-1945), the media reported positively about America's involvement in the war to save the free world. We understood from reports in newspapers, in films, and on the radio that Germany and Japan had to be unconditionally defeated. As a seventeen-year-old young man, I wanted to join the military. The Navy admitted me and soon I began serving my country in the South Pacific theatre. Positive-ness was the key attitude that pulled everyone together. We were united.

During our class, a similar attitude developed. It's clear that being unified makes our nation stronger than the sum of its parts. Add to that our moral fiber and belief in God and His creation, and we have the foundation of strength that can overcome any obstacle. This program emphasizes how spirituality forms the base that we all work from to become a truly successful person, group or nation. Character, integrity, determination, and drive to overcome the many obstacles one may face are crucial for long-term success in sports, business, and in life! The power of prayer can enhance all of these things. God has given us the freedom to choose our own thoughts.

Especially in America, we have the freedom to choose how we experience life and its many opportunities. We can make those thoughts focus on prosperity, health, work and relationships. We are free to choose from the wonder of God's unlimited creation, the universe. In spirituality, people of all faiths—Christians, Jews, Muslims, Buddhists, and others—must respect each other's beliefs and communicate with each other to promote peace in the world. Otherwise the world will destroy itself. The more we bless others, the more God will bless us. Helping others and not dwelling on our own problems will multiply God's miracles and build bridges of understanding. The spirit of God within us gives us a vision that perceives the good that can become a reality. Before a great invention can take shape, someone with foresight and imagination steers it from idea to reality. That person unites spirit, mind, and body with God to form or create something. God is with us, as described in Acts 18:9-10. One night the Lord said to Paul in a vision, "Do not be afraid, but speak and do not be silent; for I am with you." God supplies the energy throughout our bodies to overcome any obstacle. He gives us vitality and strength of spirit, body, and mind. That mind is our human computer.

It is clear to all of us that the world today needs positive leaders. We have been shaken by numerous tragedies of late, from terrorism to corporate scandals. These issues make forming a positive plan even more important today.

This book builds a case for how to produce those positive leaders. *Leadership Fitness* will work for anyone, regardless of faith or career path. Whether used in education, religion, government, business, medicine, military, large groups, or small groups, *Leadership Fitness* presents a clear route to achieving that goal.

NOTE

Georgia Tech is a state-supported institution. This curriculum has been developed to demonstrate how I apply the principles of leadership fitness to my personal life. Where references to God, spirituality, and bible verses appear, one should understand that these are my personal opinions and beliefs. They do not reflect the individual views of class members or of the University. I encourage members of this class to apply the principles of leadership fitness to their own life perspectives. By integrating the lessons that follow into your own value system, you will gain the greatest amount from this course.

ARE YOU FIT TO BE A POSITIVE LEADER?

THE HUMAN COMPUTER

*You must **want** to become a positive leader, and you must follow a plan of action to become one.*

Positive leadership requires many elements. First, you must understand the intricacies of your position. You have to master knowledge, wisdom, fundamentals, strategies, techniques, and leadership nomenclature necessary for your situation. Then you have to be able to demonstrate, teach, and implement these requirements. Finally, you must provide the positive leadership that will produce success. Are you fit to be a positive leader?

A positive leader will guide the members of his or her team to a resource that will empower and motivate them to success. Leaders come in all types, however, and some are evil, corrupt, greedy, selfish, or untrustworthy. These types are capable of generating successful results, but at some point in time, they will fail miserably. Their demise can harm people severely, causing teams, corporations, or even governments to break down.

The *Leadership Fitness* plan focuses on the positive person who is trustworthy. That leader is strong, unselfish, fair, friendly, and has both common sense and excellent communication skills.

1

These traits gain respect from employees and make a leader known as a giver rather than a taker. With these characteristics, you can train yourself and then those around you to be capable of mentally motivating themselves. This internal drive is the difference between winning and losing, between success and failure. But first you, the leader, must become that self-motivated person.

Let's explore the facts. A person who is self-motivated is prepared to understand the mental element of life. We have resources within us that provide the power to do practically anything. Belief is the way of focusing our power onto a goal. To realize our beliefs, we need to exercise several principles. We must understand the functions of our brain, part of which operates at the sub-conscious level. Like a computer, that segment operates as an information processing mechanism. That computer, and hence our attitudes, can be changed and improved by our actions. Each of us can develop a technique that gives us full access to and control over our built-in personal computer.

Understanding our brain allows us to control and use its power. Having this power at our disposal can motivate us, energize us and give us control over how we intentionally behave to reach specific goals. Computers compile, sort, and correlate data, solving problems by virtue of how they respond to input and output. Input refers to information inserted into the machine. That information is converted into a code. The computer processes and acts upon that information in accordance with instructions and other information that make up the program. The resulting information, returned to the user through a paper printout or on a display screen, is known as output.

Human memory works the same as any manufactured computer. Input enters our brains in the form of information. We process that information through a variety of programs that we carry within us. Those programs are diverse, and they include

1

sophisticated ways of thinking or behaving that we have picked up through a lifetime of experience. Processing input through those mental codes results in the output—the actions we take, conclusions we draw, and emotions we feel. Human beings are programmed much the same as man-made computers: input, instructions, information sorting, and output.

Randall W. Engle, research scientist and chair of the School of Psychology in the College of Sciences at Georgia Tech, recently explained how performance on measurements of working memory capacity predicts performance on a wide range of real-world cognitive tasks. In other words, we have the ability to focus on a task and block out other distractions. The objective imagination of our conscious mind can control our thoughts for either positive or negative results.

The human brain weighs about fifty ounces, or just over three pounds. It is comprised of tens of billions of nerve cells. Computer chips would have to be at least 10,000 times larger than their current capacity to approach that number. Think of this incredible source of power that each of us is blessed with. That power came to us as a gift from God. Our responsibility, in return, is to thank Him for this gift and to use it for worthwhile achievements, and after achieving success, to thank Him again.

The brain has two minds: the conscious and the subconscious. The conscious mind accepts our thoughts and passes the information on to the subconscious, which records, sorts, and produces our thoughts. I call this the human computer because of its similar functions to the manufactured computers we use every day. This process is the key determinant of the actions that we will take.

There is a simple secret that makes this computer analogy valuable. By controlling what comes into your conscious mind, you can influence your own actions. If a thought is negative, unworthy, evil or corrupt, stop for one full minute and change that

1

thought into a positive, worthwhile one. By practicing this action over a period of time, you can become the person and leader you aspire to be. This process is the Attitude Technique. By learning this lesson and passing it on to our followers, we will spark motivation for success throughout our team. Through years of research, study and moment-by-moment practice, I have developed a philosophy from this concept that has literally changed people's lives—including my own—for the better.

This is the source of true motivation. The human computer accepts as input whatever the conscious mind allows it to receive. Our subconscious does not know the difference between what is real and what is imagined; it only processes the input passed to it from the objective imagination. Give it clean, wholesome and positive information, and you will act as a person motivated by those traits. Convey this to your team, and they, in turn, will become believers and winners.

A magnetized piece of steel will lift twelve times its own weight, but if you demagnetize the same piece of steel it will not even lift a feather. Similarly, there are two types of people—the magnetized person, who is full of confidence and faith, and the demagnetized type, who is full of fears and doubt. When opportunities come, the demagnetized person says, "I might fail." And failure will come because his or her human computer has been instructed to execute those thoughts. By absorbing and teaching the Attitude Technique philosophy, we can change the negative to the positive, and bad to good, through self-motivating actions that will produce successful results. Our imagination is stronger than our willpower—if it is directed through the human computer.

The practice of the Attitude Technique will undoubtedly produce positive results. Ralph Waldo Emerson said, "Man is what he thinks all day long." William James, the father of American psychology, said, "The power to move the world is in your subconscious mind." And the Bible says, "If you believe, you will receive whatever you ask for in prayer." (Matthew 21:22) We literally become what we think about and plan. By repeating positive affirmations over and over again, we ensure that our subconscious, or subjective imagination, accepts this as real and performs positive actions. We bring things into being through self-imaging.

Careful planning is important to success. You have probably heard the story of the two men hiking in the Rocky Mountains when they see a grizzly bear in the distance coming toward them. Immediately, one of the men pulls his running shoes out of his backpack and begins putting them on. The other man looks at him and says, "You know you can't outrun the grizzly." The first man replies, "I don't have to. I just have to outrun you." For the game of life, we need a game plan. Do you have a plan for your life and for your leadership role?

Once we get our own thinking straight, we are ready to teach our staff or team members the simple secret. We then can set goals both for our personal life and for the organization.

Positive attitudes lead people to the winner's circle in all areas of life. All of us experience problems or troubles in life. But more important than the difficulties is how we react to them. People who have positive attitudes still face disappointments, frustrations, and pressures, but their reactions are different. Problems can cause unhappiness, and they can defeat you if you allow that to happen. But if you never give up, you will eventually win!

We may experience temporary defeat, but if we persevere, we will win. Babe Ruth struck out more times than any man in baseball history. Ty Cobb was thrown out trying to steal more than any man in baseball history. Jackie Robinson overcame mental and physical abuse to become the first African-American to play Major League Baseball. Vince Lombardi, one of the most

1

successful football coaches of his time, was line coach at Fordham University at age 43. His great success came years later. Paul Brown, a man who coached successfully at all levels of football—from high school to college, from military to professional—had many setbacks. But his will was stronger than any temporary defeat.

Albert Einstein flunked courses in math. Henry Ford was broke at age 40. Andrew Young, a frequent speaker to my Leadership Fitness classes, overcame racial discrimination to become the United States' representative to the United Nations. Thomas Edison's teacher called him a dunce, and Edison later failed more than 14,000 times in his efforts to perfect the incandescent light. I have seen many athletes become stars who once could not make the team—even some who were advised to drop out of their sport. Archie Griffin was told he was too small to play football on the college level, let alone at powerhouse Ohio State; "You'll never play. You'll be lost in the shuffle," critics said. But Archie not only played, he became the only two-time Heisman Trophy winner in history. Later on, I was fortunate to coach Archie as a productive running back with the NFL Cincinnati Bengals. The examples go on and on. The lesson to learn is that we are created for a purpose. You are here for a reason. You only need a direction. The Attitude Technique philosophy will lead you to become whatever you desire to become.

As you set your goals, first of all, think wisely. "What do I have, and what can I do with what I have in order to reach where I want to go?" Put your goals into writing. When a goal is written, it is crystallized. You know exactly what you want to do. Booker T. Washington said, "I have begun everything with the idea that I could succeed." Committing your goal to paper impresses it upon the subconscious mind. This will guide the human computer to work 24 hours each day to reach your desire. If you plan wisely, if you do it step-by-step as you experience similar successes on the way toward ultimate success, good things will happen because you will make them happen. Remember: A winner is always aware of what he or she doesn't know, and works to improve in those areas.

As leaders, we can make a difference in the future of our countries by becoming self-motivated positive leaders for the betterment of mankind and passing on to our followers the proper use of a powerful tool—our human computer. In my own search for a higher goal, I often use the Bible. For me, God is the source for all our needs. The seventh chapter of Matthew, seventh and eighth verses, offer the familiar words, "Ask and you will be given what you ask for. Seek and you will find. Knock and the door will be opened. For everyone who asks, receives. Anyone who seeks, finds. If only you will knock, the door will be opened." (*The Living Bible.*)

An organization that is making a difference on college campuses across the country is Omicron Delta Kappa Society (ODK). Students, faculty, administration are recognized for their positive leadership. I asked my friend John Morgan, Executive Director of the Omicron Delta Kappa Society, to share the ODK Leadership Development Program (Appendix B).

You may decide to stay right where you are and to make your job and your life meaningful and successful. You may decide you want to move to a higher or different position in another location. Whatever path you decide upon can become a happy, exciting adventure. You don't need to delay or hold off. Start now—the rewards are waiting for you. The architect of the universe did not design a ladder leading nowhere. The carpenter from the plains of Galilee gave us the only tool we need—the advice of his teaching: "As you sow, so shall you reap." We become what we plan. We are at this moment exactly what we have planned to be: nothing more, nothing less.

1

All the philosophers, prophets, teachers and wise men through-out history have disagreed on many things, but on this one subject they are in complete and unanimous agreement. Marcus Aurelius, the great Roman emperor and philosopher, said, " A man's life is what his thoughts are made of." In more modern times, Dr. Norman Vincent Peal said, "If we think in negative terms, we receive negative results. Conversely, if we think in positive terms, we receive the positive results." We can control our lives by controlling our thoughts. Remember: We become what we plan. This is the human computer in action.

I have applied this principle first to my life and then to the young men I have coached. Through writing and public speak-ing, I have shared it with thousands of others. It all began when I realized that it was possible to reach positive success in any task I decided to undertake, whether in education, coaching, administration or business—with the right approach.

As the years passed, there were times when my control seemed less strong or in doubt. Those were the moments when I simply reread, restudied, and readjusted to regain my objective and subjective thinking with the practice of the Attitude Technique. Each and every time, this set me back on the right track.

The Attitude Technique might be considered a success force. As my life continued through the years, I sometimes realized that I was slipping downward. At those times a force of energy caught me, as if to remind me of the direction I had set. This en-ergized me to put my force into forward motion again, and to apply the technique to regain a forward and upward path. It al-ways worked.

This is an affirmative, scientific approach to becoming a win-ner—a complete winner. Your future will result from your plan. It is difficult to predict the future. Problems will always exist in the world, and predicting the future is presumptuous. Nevertheless, a

1

positive, planned, personal program is still clearly necessary and viable. A person can control his or her future. Success can be yours as it has been for others. Striving to become the successful, positive leader of the organization or a small group can be the most exciting adventure you will ever undertake.

A true positive leader brings people together for the common goal of achieving positive success. This type of leadership unites; it does not divide. United we stand—divided we fall! Once you have begun practicing self-motivation through using your human computer, other people will notice. They will want to be around you. And they will follow you.

What better time to exercise this achievement than now, when the world needs our positive-ness more than ever before?. Everyone wins!

KEEPING SCORE

Before moving on to Lesson Two, rate your assets (strengths) and liabilities (weaknesses). Darrell Royal, a famous University of Texas football coach, once made the statement, "If the game isn't important, why do we keep score?" In other words, it is important to keep score in order to decide who wins and who loses. The same applies in life. Are we winners or losers? If your life is important, then we should keep score!

The Keeping Score chart must be filled in for you to see where you stand. After you complete the nine lessons, you will be asked to score yourself again. You should work on this process throughout your life, not just in this class. The feedback you will gain from this exercise will help you change liabilities (weaknesses) into assets (strengths).

1

KEEPING SCORE

Rate: Superior, Excellent, Good, Fair, or Poor.
Then Go Back and Write in Your Remarks.

Subject	Assets (Strengths)	Liabilities (Weaknesses)
Spiritual Values		
Family Relations		
How I Perceive Myself		
How I Think Others Perceive Me		
Social Life		
How I Get Along With Others		
Health Status		
Aerobic Fitness		

Subject	Assets (Strengths)	Liabilities (Weaknesses)
Relaxation		
Recreational		
Rest		
Mental Stimulation		
Self-Discipline		
Self-Motivation		
Self-Confidence		
Controlled Visualization		
Goal Setting		
Career		
Financial Planning		

1

THE BIRTH AND DEVELOPMENT OF THE ATTITUDE TECHNIQUE PHILOSOPHY

A TOTAL PERSON-TOTAL SUCCESS CONCEPT

People continue to ask me, "Where and how did the Attitude Technique begin?" My answer is always the same. For my twelfth birthday in 1939, my father presented me with a book entitled *I Dare You.* That book by William Danforth, chairman of the Checker Board Square in St. Louis, MO, was one of the first books written on goal setting. This masterpiece challenged me to spend effort considering how I approached life. It stimulated me to search for the secrets to successful living. The book instructed readers to write goals in every area of their lives. I began this "dare." Throughout the years, each goal I have written has come true. This made it simple for me to become a believer in the practice of setting to paper the things I wanted to achieve.

Later on, when I entered my career as a high school coach, I began using the term Attitude Technique. I don't remember the exact time and place, but the basis was this: in our coaching drills we referred to various methods of teaching each player

2

skills in his position. These were physical techniques. Realizing there must be a mental skill to initiate each physical practice, I at first called this "the mental technique." A player's thoughts must be perfected before he can carry out his assignments. I later changed the word mental to "attitude," thus resulting in the Attitude Technique.

There are many degrees of attitude, so excelling at the process required further analysis. I knew that attitude had to be positive to produce successful results. Then my curiosity, study, and research moved toward finding a simple way to develop and maintain a positive attitude. While some people may be more optimistic than others by nature, I discovered a specific technique for developing optimism in oneself. I found that secret, and I have used it throughout my life and career. As positive results occurred, I began sharing the system with others—with my family, my teams, in seminars and workshops, in articles, and through books. The feedback was unbelievably positive. Because of that response, the Attitude Technique philosophy became my high purpose in life, and sharing it became my goal. Through the years, I worked on this personal project almost daily despite ups and downs, victories and defeats, good times and tough times. Nevertheless, the Attitude Technique program kept me going. Here's my story.

My career started as a high school coach in a small, rural area. During my initial season, only seven players reported to the first practice. I will never forget running all the way home (we did not own an automobile at the time) shortly before the first game and hugging my wife Phyllis with joy because the eleventh player had finally reported. I finally had enough players to start the first game. That was a special team. We were united to do our very best. And they succeeded, accomplishing an undefeated season— the only one in the school's history. They followed instructions perfectly, and that year jumpstarted my career as a football

2

coach, providing me with self-confidence. The positive approach actually worked. However, to follow up I needed more study, more information—so the story continues.

During the early years of my career, I needed to take an additional job to supplement my income. I accepted a part-time position with a life insurance company. During a sales program, I learned the basic principles of management and motivation. Before six months had elapsed, I led the company in sales. In fact, the insurance job potential was so lucrative that I soon faced the difficult decision of which career path I wanted to follow—professional sales or athletics. I now know that the program I developed would have allowed me to be successful in any profession. By faithfully practicing the Attitude Technique philosophy, I advanced from that first, small high school to a prominent, larger one, then to the college ranks, on to the National Football League, and finally to positions as the director of athletics and executive assistant to the president at two of the leading universities in the nation. This trajectory did not come by accident. It was planned. I trained myself, and I was prepared for each opportunity when it came.

It's impossible not to notice that as I write this narrative, the personal pronoun "I" appears frequently. That's because it is imperative for me to show how the Attitude Technique lessons have worked in my own life in order for you, the reader, to embark upon your own successful path to positive success. I believe strongly in the team system—a united group working together for a common cause, finishing with a victory. But the leader, who has the ultimate responsibility, stands alone. That person must be a positive force.

The word positive has many meanings: confident, certain, affirmative, among others. In this book, positive means the ultimate form of worthiness, goodness, ability to inspire trust, and many other qualities that represent what is *good*. The positive

2

leader is fit, on many levels, to be the ultimate person in charge.

Utilizing written goals and plans, I found it possible to achieve exactly what I wanted. The results have been amazing. More importantly, while finding the pathway for my own journey, I developed a program that could be shared with others. What are these management and motivation principles that I learned and practiced? During the early 1950s, top executives of large corporations studied the scientific basis of success. The private sessions and seminars they sponsored yielded spectacular results, but the findings were kept secret until companies specializing in teaching motivation began to merchandise the information. The material then became available to anyone. Only a few took advantage, however.

In the life insurance field, I was introduced to motivational material for business executives. Along with reading the book *I Dare You*, I began studying, researching and applying those corporate principles to my life and work. To completely understand the management concept, I began translating the executive language into everyday lessons. Little by little, I developed a guide that produced almost unbelievable results.

As I continued my studies, I wondered why some people were successful and others were not. My curiosity about this was keen. I wanted to understand why and how successful people got where they were. At first most of my concern revolved around the field of athletics. Why were certain athletes better than others? When I myself was a young athlete before my work career began, I had sought out ways to become a better player. This desire to understand the nature of achievement continued as I grew older. During my college years, I read anything I could find that dealt with success and motivation. The works of Andrew Carnegie were among the first I came across. Later on, someone gave me the book *Think and Grow Rich* by Napoleon Hill. From it I learned to rank the ideas that I could use to challenge myself in my pursuit.

2

When I began my coaching career on the high school level in 1951, my inquisitiveness was even stronger. I made a trip to Massillon, OH. At that time Massillon High School was considered the best high school football team in the nation. After going over their program from top to bottom, I realized they were winning because of one thing—a planned positive attitude. They actually believed they would win each and every contest. That made an indelible impression upon me. Shortly after my return from Massillon, I listened to a record by Earl Nightingale titled, "The Strangest Secret." It wrapped up the works of Andrew Carnegie, Napoleon Hill, and Norman Vincent Peale all in one package. It was inspiring and led me to read Peale's works: *The Art of Living*, *The Power of Positive Thinking*, and *The Amazing Results of Positive Thinking*. I analyzed Dr. Peale's Philosophy and integrated it into my own.

Later I met Paul J. Meyer, founder and president of Success Motivation® Institute. He encouraged me to further my study in the field. I began taking the management and goal-setting courses offered by his company. I started early each morning and studied for only thirty minutes, but it was worth every minute. In just thirty minutes a day, I gained something that probably has made the difference in my life today: I developed an attitude with which to start the day, direct my thoughts, and eventually control my life. I went through several cassette tape programs offered by Paul Meyer's company. They were sensational. Each tape emphasized space repetition. Each time I listened to the tape and read the text simultaneously, I received an idea that I could incorporate into my work that particular day. The idea was always a positive, worthwhile gesture that facilitated progress in some area. When you begin to add up one idea each day, you can see how the suggestions multiplied and amazing results began to flow.

With an enthusiasm that seemed inspired, I continued to read other books throughout the early years: *The Magic of Thinking*

Big by David J. Schwartz; *Psycho Cybernetics* by Maxwell Maltz; *On Becoming Human* by Ross Snyder; *Life is Tremendous* by Charles E. Jones; *Secrets of Mind Power* by Harry Lorayne; *Successful Living* by Nelson Boswell; *The Magic of Believing* by Claude M. Bristol; *You Can Become the Person You Want to Be* by Robert H. Schuller; *As a Man Thinketh* by James Allen; *The Success System That Never Fails* by Clement Stone; *The Greatest Salesman in the World* by Og Mandino; *See You at the Top* by Zig Ziglar; *The Blueprint* by Carl Stevens; *Positive Books* by Jack Kinder; and hundreds of additional books on the subject of success. As the years passed, each book contributed to my thinking. I researched and digested them until I adopted their common tenet: "Control your mind and, in turn, control your life in a positive mental attitude."

After I began my personal program, I wanted to test the technique on young men in athletics. With my advanced research and my own work in athletics, the stage was set for me to apply success theories to a particular football coaching situation. The experiment would be a live test because the result would be judged by thousands of people and measured by the direct effect it had on members of the squad.

My first attempts were a bit discouraging, and it would have been easy to be cynical and give up. I had learned that most people do not take full advantage of their opportunities in our country.. Despite the fact that the United States is the richest land on the face of the earth, only about five to ten percent ever achieve complete success. Why is this?

The secret of all successful people starts with setting a predetermined goal. The fact that the odds may be as high as ninety-five percent against a person's becoming successful means that the field is wide open for those with the desire to achieve their goals. The potential is present in each of us, and we only have to know how simple it is to use our valuable resources. The great majority of people don't even try, however. Only one in one thousand will thoroughly attempt this plan. Will I be that one, I wondered? I was recommitted.

Anyone can reach a plateau of mediocrity, but achievers will decide how high above that plateau they want to rise by setting goals. The amount of success a person achieves is the direct result of how well he or she plans each and every moment. So long as the thinking is good, worthy, and clearly defined in the mind, the individual is on the way to some very satisfying experiences—on the way, in fact, to total success.

Each goal must be a simple ambition without other complications. This literally means that you must decide what you want in life. The goal must fit into a plan and be something to bounce out of bed for every morning. And you have to set your sights high. Thinking big creates its own magic. It is absolutely necessary to reach for the sky and to command all the resources available.

This means we have to have a commitment: What do we want? We must then decide when we want to reach our goal and determine the ingredients necessary to achieving that goal. Follow that with an assessment of what we are willing to give in return for what we will receive. The final step is self-imagery: Visualize the goal already accomplished and start believing it will come about. With this formula, you can use the power of positive prayer by asking God to guide you toward your worthy goal.

Write these steps and read them aloud each day. This brings about the action component. We can plan a lot of things, but unless we act upon them, our total efforts will fall hard and fast. After the plan works the first time, we begin expecting it to succeed each time.

As we control our thinking in a positive and worthwhile manner, we can achieve whatever we want. If our thoughts become negative, we will have negative problems. It means starting over again until we learn to accept and believe.

2

In my first application of the Attitude Technique, I asked each member of the squad to work out his personal plan for life. Then we set our goal for the football season. Our goal was to establish the best record in the history of the school. We made the plan. Then we began the action.

It wasn't easy, but the Attitude Technique soon caused changes in the lives of our players. Very few people really believed we would achieve the success we were shooting for, because not many people understood our plan. It was our secret, and we had pledged not to reveal our team goal to anyone outside the squad family. As the season opened that year, we had no doubt in our minds that we would play each and every minute with the precision of the plan. We thought of each member as a link in a chain. A single link doubting our goal could break the chain. Each member of the squad became very important. This put tremendous responsibility on each person, for the failure of one jeopardized the organization's success. Our plan involved the entire squad, not just the first eleven, demanding a strong sense of dedication and concentration.

After the first game, the final score indicated that our plan would work. This was a great feeling. Our season had a fine start, but the battle had only begun. We realized that to continue, we had to improve each day. This is the essence of motivation— growing as an individual and improving as a player each day. It is a plain fact in any test of skills that we are either getting better or slipping backwards. We never stand still. After a single accomplishment, it is common to let up on a large goal. That's how upsets happen in sports. Our team had taken the first step. Now it was time to dig in and work even harder to prepare for the coming opponent. During the next week, we worked for improvement. Each day we strove to be just a little bit better than the day before. We knew we had to do this to accomplish our task, and that we had undertaken a continuing process.

Although the first season started fine, it had downturns. At times we were frustrated, fearful, and worried. Several players developed a negative attitude. A number quit the squad—not because of the hard physical work, but because they would not allow themselves to accept the positive mental attitude each individual had to assume to succeed in our undertaking.

The practice of controlled thinking sometimes reminds me of an illustration. If you placed an iron plank six inches wide and fifty feet long on the ground, anyone could walk its length without difficulty. But place the same plank a hundred feet up in the air, braced between two buildings and over a street, and hardly anyone would ever attempt to cross it. And why is that? The plank is the same, whether lying on the ground or as a bridge across a street. The people who walk its length on the ground have the same muscles, the same mind, and the same will. But the person who sees the board suspended in mid-air typically thinks about falling. Great leadership is the capacity to develop the will to achieve and accept a positive mental attitude toward the attempt, rather than focusing on failure.

The next season brought back several young men who were dedicated in their willingness to think positively. We also gained several new players who were ready to learn. It was a fresh year. We capitalized on the mistakes, trials, and tribulations of the past season and once again started our work for the new season in the same manner as the previous year. However, we worked and thought positively even more than before. The season rolled on. When it was completed, we found ourselves just one point and 30 seconds short of our goal. Although we had not reached the perfect season, we had had the best season yet. This proved to the players and coaching staff that our goal could be obtained. It truly was possible. We were becoming believers.

All we needed was just a little more effort. We had come so close to our goal, yet hardly anyone was satisfied because we realized we could have made it if only we had believed strongly enough. The chain, with each of us as a durable link, was forming and becoming stronger. When the following year arrived, our athletes were ready. They had talked about their intentions with one another, and they had worked very hard over the summer to be in the best physical condition possible. When fall practice opened, these players were not going to be denied their victory. They parked their automobiles and began riding bicycles. They were off the streets at 8:30 p.m. and in bed each night by 10:30, living the life of a true athlete.

The chief of police remarked to me the effect this program had on the entire community. He related how peaceful his job became when football season began. When classes opened, our players were leaders. Many of our young men held offices in their classrooms and in student government. They not only went to church each week, but they also influenced their parents to go. This squad had found the key and gone to work.

That year we became the state champions. We achieved that best season. The squad received numerous accolades. While they were flushed with this success, I took the opportunity to remind them that this was just the first step toward a complete life of success. They had accomplished their goal as a result of their planning. They had simply decided to be something in life. The ones who stayed with it realized fully that they could continue and achieve their life ambitions. They understood the secret. And it was so simple.

Why only a few actually make the grade is difficult to understand. We can stumble around as we attempt success, but if we never pinpoint our objectives, we will allow negative thoughts to creep in and we will give up easily. An individual finds out about himself or herself through participating in sports. He or she learns to win the battle over self, to submit to self-discipline, and to believe.

2

This approach to football for the high school team was amazing. It brought about a season considered the best in the school's history and a claim to the state championship. Remember, however, that this did not happen in the first season or even in the second.,. It happened in the third season, when it was clear that the staff and players would not quit. They persevered and became true winners. After that remarkable year, could the program stay on top? Could it improve? The first players would be graduating and new young men taking their places. The Attitude Technique still existed. And the graduating seniors had planned beyond the football season. Their careers for life had been designed. They carried with them the benefits of what they had learned and, in addition, built the foundation for those who came after them. It was always an exceptional experience for me to follow their budding careers, which made me realize even more that this program works!

The "program," as it was often called, was highly respected in our area and gained prominence in other places. I was asked to lecture at many clinics and to write articles on our football techniques for national sports magazines. Attendance at our games began to soar. An undefeated regular season carried through to fifty consecutive victories. It wasn't easy, but the next four seasons each produced championships. Each year critics predicted the fall of the empire, but we confounded skeptics by repeating the previous year's success. The new team not only believed they could win but they also expected victory—and they won!

Looking back to that first year, I can see it would have been easy to give up on our goal. Sometimes we nearly did. There were frustrating moments, just as in any climb to gain excellence. But we knew we would never find out what lay inside of us if we did not strive to do our best and then some. At times we held on by only a thread. But we proved that we had to hang on together in order to regain the momentum to carry us to the top. Each contest in life must be approached this way.

In sports, there comes a time when one team experiences frustrations and the members have to decide whether they will give up. At that moment, the opposing team finds it easy to take control and claim victory. But if we hang on, never lose our composure, and strive for excellence even through the darkest moments, we can win. It may take until the last second, but even that final part of the contest is what we must prepare for. We are in it for the entire game—for an entire life.

You must be a giver. A person gets back from life what he or she puts into it. In business, a person's earnings are measured by service. To earn money we must provide more and better service. Conversely, earnings will fall if we give poor service. This principle holds in every form of human endeavor: it is true in our spiritual life, in marriage, in athletics, in business, in everything. The return is in proportion to the personal investment.

My test with this particular high school football program proved that the Attitude Technique theory was valid. Each player now had the chief ingredient to become successful in his coming life. He understood it was easy to reach success by following this plan. Yet at least 90 percent of people do not apply themselves fully to reaching their goals, leaving the field wide open for those who will.

This experience was only one example, but it inspired me to continue the study and research of the mental principles that ensure happiness, fulfillment, and achievement. I learned that a person cannot be forced to do something he or she is not willing to do voluntarily. The way to get people to choose success is by understanding that they respond to challenges and quality leadership. People can be stimulated by fear and incentives, but their responses will not be consistent or permanent. Each person emotionally responds to commands with either gratitude or resentment. Attitude creates a personal and effective motivation that can be accomplished only on an individual basis.

As the years passed, the Attitude Technique philosophy came to be utilized numerous times. Given enough time to be implemented, the plan never failed.

What I am talking about, and the ultimate objective of the philosophy, is having a winning career, living a vibrant life, developing inner happiness, and retiring financially independent. As you will see, the Attitude Technique can lead to a complete life.

The following chapters will spell out the steps to total success. As a positive leader, you will be energized to jump up and move forward!

2

LESSON THREE

TIME MANAGEMENT
PLANNING OUR THOUGHTS

3

Warning!
Lack of planning may be hazardous to your future!

—

The bad news is time flies. The good news is you're the pilot.
MICHAEL ALTSHULER

—

*In coaching, it is important to have a game plan
for each game. However, it's more important
to have a game plan for your life!*

To become a positive, successful person who leads a group, one must be highly organized. We control our lives by scheduling our time. Efficiency is the result of attention to detail. To become an effective leader, the first step is to manage your time well.

In my early years, I struggled with details and working out time schedules. After studying Paul Meyer's Success Motivation® program, I learned to organize my time to become effective as a leader. Later on I was tested on the "right brain-left brain" theory. I turned out to be a big picture person—a visionary. That's why I had difficulty with the details of time. By utilizing the time study program,

I learned to excel in both the large picture and the details.

Before we move on, it is important to write down your thoughts. This program is about you. Start by writing the thoughts that will shape your life and future. Those thoughts precede our ability to schedule time properly. In order to lead others, you first must become the person you want to be. The following charts will help you define your goals.

MASTER DREAM LIST

Write everything you've ever wanted, every place you've wanted to go, and everything you'd like to become or achieve. Date each item when you enter it.

In compiling the list below, remember to take off the judge's robe and let your imagination run free. Give no consideration to limitations, money, education, ability, or what may seem illogical. This is a completely unrestrained list.

_____

_____

_____

_____

_____

_____

_____

_____

_____

_____

_____

_____

_____

3

_____
_____
_____
_____
_____
_____
_____
_____
_____
_____
_____
_____
_____
_____
_____
_____

The Master Dream List is an important exercise in seeking your goals. This is *where* and *how* starts. Don't hold back. Let the human computer explore all avenues. And remember, the sub-conscious mind (human computer) does not distinguish between what is objective and subjective. It will record whatever your conscious thoughts feed to your subconscious mind. By writing these thoughts into the master dream list, you are actually applying another sense to your memory bank.

We learn and comprehend by way of our five senses: sight, smell, hearing, speech, and touch. The more senses we use at one time, the more we comprehend. By writing our thoughts on the Master Dream List, then reading them aloud to send that information to the brain, we have exercised multiple senses for recording those thoughts.

3

After working with the Master Dream List for several days, turn to the next chart, "Where I Stand in My Present Job." A top leader should know exactly where he or she stands. You may be an employee or staff member without leadership responsibilities but aspire to move in that direction. You may already possess a high leadership position but need to improve by understanding the qualities necessary for attaining that goal, wherever you rank on the scale. Begin by describing your professional status.

Once you have a good start on where you currently stand, turn to the next chart, "Where I Want To Go in My Profession." Perhaps you may want to stay exactly where you are. But if you see yourself moving up the ladder of success to a more demanding and rewarding position, this chart will prepare you for your future climb.

WHERE I STAND IN MY PRESENT CAREER

Your description of your present professional status should include a list of your strengths, talents, abilities, and accomplishments, as well as your weaknesses and needs. Rewrite the description when significant change or personal growth occurs.

Date: _____

_____

_____

_____

_____

_____

_____

_____

_____

3

_____

_____

_____

_____

_____

_____

_____

_____

_____

_____

_____

_____

_____

_____

_____

_____

_____

_____

WHERE I WANT TO GO IN MY PROFESSION

Make your description specific. Include exact duties, type of organization, and details of the position you desire.

Date: _____

_____

_____

_____

_____

_____

3

_____
_____
_____
_____
_____
_____
_____
_____
_____
_____
_____
_____
_____
_____
_____
_____
_____
_____
_____
_____
_____
_____

How do we build a successful and happy life? Thomas Edison once said, "Genius is one percent inspiration and ninety-nine percent perspiration." It is certainly true that fortune favors the prepared.

Time is our most valuable possession. Proper time control motivates us to succeed. How you use each moment will determine how far you climb in any area.

Nature's treasures can be tapped easily if you understand how to use your time intelligently. Remember: once we waste time, it is gone forever and can never be replaced. Each day is of the highest importance because we exchange one day of our lives for it. With each day that passes, we are running out of time. The wasted hours you spend are the very ones that you could have used constructively to win victory.

Use your time wisely and you will be repaid in multiples. Bob Richards, the former Olympic pole vault champion, began the groundwork for his future success at age thirteen. From that age, he spent more than 10,000 hours in preparation for his event, with the result that he became a world champion. Wisely invest 10,000 hours into any task, and you will become the champion of what you desire.

Time control, planning, and motivation are closely related. Motivation is planning—planning your career and your life. Planning does not mean daydreaming. It means written planning, or setting up the design in advance—for one year, one month, one week, or one day.

Write a daily plan to follow. By following it, you develop the self-discipline necessary to become motivated.

How does one organize time? First you must find out how you are presently using your time. You are going to be surprised. We often say, "If only I had more time," or, "I just can't do it—I don't have the time." But when you discover how you are using your precious time ... well, get ready for some fun!

For starters, list in descending order on Your Task List everything in which you are involved. Each of us has different responsibilities, activities, and everyday duties. Some of the differences are slight; others are substantial. There is no typical example, but as an illustration, I have indicated on the following chart my own list from when I was a NFL head football coach. I call it a task list. It includes an outline of the demands upon my time during that period of my career, including my personal life, my civic life, my church life, and the responsibilities of my position.

TASK LIST (EXAMPLE)

1. Major goals for team and plans to accomplish these goals
2. Structuring of program to achieve top performance
3. Organization and management of staff
4. Out-of-season, in-season fitness program
5. Technical aspects of the game (film study)
6. Motivation program for staff and players
7. Scouting service and preparation for the college player draft
8. Public relations for club
9. Leadership program—"Attitude Technique, Inc."
10. Staff personnel selections
11. Calendar planning
12. Daily correspondence
13. Everyday folder
14. Meetings involving league
15. Speaking engagements
16. Individual conferences and letter writing to players
17. Personal fitness and recreation activities
18. Bible study, prayer, and meditation
19. Personal goals
20. Family activities
21. Civic, charitable, and national organizations
22. Reading
23. Writing
24. Meals, personal hygiene
25. Telephone
26. Interruptions
27.
28.
29.
30.
31.

YOUR TASK LIST

1. _____
2. _____
3. _____
4. _____
5. _____
6. _____
7. _____
8. _____
9. _____
10. _____
11. _____
12. _____
13. _____
14. _____
15. _____
16. _____
17. _____
18. _____
19. _____
20. _____
21. _____
22. _____
23. _____
24. _____
25. _____
26. _____
27. _____
28. _____
29. _____
30. _____
31. _____

3

3

I listed twenty-six items on my task list. I also left plenty of open spaces at the end because I know from experience that as I review the list, I will become aware of tasks not listed that I didn't realize I was doing.

Once you have made a list of everything you think you are involved in, break your day into three parts—morning, afternoon, and evening. Then divide your tasks among these sections. This is the basic document for a "test of time."

Next, start recording each day from the moment you wake up. Record the minutes you are actually engaged in an activity (no matter what it is) under the hour it occurs. When the day is over, total the number of minutes. You will discover how much time you are spending on each item on your Time Task list. No matter how thorough you believe your list to be, it is likely that other responsibilities, activities, and surprises will arise that you did not anticipate. Be sure to list telephone calls and interruptions on your task list. They consume an inordinate amount of time. When I first used the "Test of Time," I found I was allowing the telephone and other interruptions to rule my day. At first you may forget to record certain elements, but stay with it for one full week to get a good test.

Once you find out where your time is going, you can begin to work out plans to use your minutes and hours in a productive manner.

TIME STUDY ANALYSIS

DATE_____

3

TASK LIST	MORNING						AFTERNOON						EVENING						TOTAL MINUTES
	6	7	8	9	10	11	12	1	2	3	4	5	6	7	8	9	10	11	
1.																			
2.																			
3.																			
4.																			
5.																			
6.																			
7.																			
8.																			
9.																			
10.																			
11.																			
12.																			
13.																			
14.																			
15.																			
16.																			
17.																			
18.																			
19.																			
20.																			
21.																			

3

TASK LIST	MORNING						AFTERNOON						EVENING						TOTAL MINUTES
	6	7	8	9	10	11	12	1	2	3	4	5	6	7	8	9	10	11	
22.																			
23.																			
24.																			
25.																			
26.																			
27.																			
28.																			
29.																			
30.																			
31.																			
32.																			
33.																			
34.																			
35.																			
36.																			
37.																			
38.																			
39.																			
40.																			
41.																			
42.																			

After completing and analyzing the "Test of Time," begin writing a basic plan to follow. First list the standard procedures you need to follow each day. If you maintain an office as an administrator, consider these eight items to be checked every day:

- Everyday folder (keep current items available)
- Meetings (time)
- Appointments (time)
- Correspondence (in and out)
- Planning sessions
- Telephone messages
- Other details and surprises
- Interruptions (record and learn how to reduce this number)

3

If you have a secretary or personal assistant, instruct this person when to accept calls and when to allow interruptions. After establishing procedures for the office, write the priorities for other daily activities in which you will be involved—personal fitness, recreation program, spiritual life, family, social life, reading, writing, personal goals, personal matters, continuing education, meditation, relaxation periods—anything you desire to accomplish on a daily plan.

Now write the amount of time you need to sleep. A friend once told me that the verse in Proverbs 20:13 is interpreted, "If you love sleep, you will end in poverty." Stay awake, work hard and smart, and you won't go hungry. Many great people in history had one thing in common: they were early risers.

In the next chart, "My Ideal Time Plan," fill in the blanks for your perfect day. Then work for that perfection.

MY IDEAL TIME PLAN

Date: _____

6:00 a.m. _____	3:00 p.m. _____
6:30 a.m. _____	3:30 p.m. _____
7:00 a.m. _____	4:00 p.m. _____
7:30 a.m. _____	4:30 p.m. _____
8:00 a.m. _____	5:00 p.m. _____
8:30 a.m. _____	5:30 p.m. _____
9:00 a.m. _____	6:00 p.m. _____
8:30 a.m. _____	6:30 p.m. _____
10:00 a.m. _____	7:00 p.m. _____
10:30 a.m. _____	7:30 p.m. _____
11:00 a.m. _____	8:00 p.m. _____
11:30 a.m. _____	8:30 p.m. _____
12:00 p.m. _____	9:00 p.m. _____
12:30 p.m. _____	9:30 p.m. _____
1:00 p.m. _____	10:00 p.m. _____
1:30 p.m. _____	10:30 p.m. _____
2:00 p.m. _____	11:00 p.m. _____
2:30 p.m. _____	11:30 p.m. _____

12:00 midnight—lights out—the human computer takes over.

Prepare each day and you will become highly organized and very effective in your work and personal life. Always allow for surprises. They are bound to occur, so be flexible and learn to adjust.

Back in my coaching days, during one game a player came off the field shaking his head and said, "They are doing this and doing this and...." I interrupted and simply told the player, "Son, just adjust." That statement stuck with me from then on. When something happened that I was not prepared for, I thought about my response to my player. I began adjusting. It actually works!

3

By writing out your daily plan, you will be able to make adjustments and get back on schedule. Plan. Then relax. You will accomplish three times as much as you did previously. The greatest asset of this type of plan is promoting living by action—which requires less effort than living by reaction. It is amazing how effectively a written time plan organizes our minds and our work, allowing us to become truly positive, successful individuals.

Once you develop the habit of daily planning, work out your weekly plans. Planning in advance increases your effectiveness and decreases the amount of time necessary to spend on the daily plan. After mastery of the weekly plan, develop a monthly plan, then yearly or seasonal or other plans appropriate for your work. Eventually you will have planned your future success.

I strongly encourage you to give yourself the "Test of Time." Use this time study exercise to find out how you are spending time. Then plan how to best keep your time under your control. If you don't plan for distributing your own time, others will do that for you. If you have wasted time in the past through lack of organization, that can't be helped. There is no way to change what has been done. Nevertheless, tomorrow can be different. It isn't here yet, so you can plan the entire day. Remember—time is speeding away. Don't delay. The journey will be worth your life—a life of true happiness and positive success. This truth is motivation. Your goals can be accomplished, day by day.

NOTE

In the first three lessons, I described the magic of the human computer, how it came about, and a time plan to allow you to embark upon the adventure of becoming a positive, successful leader. Before we delve into the goals program in Lesson Eight that actually maps the way to accomplishing whatever it is we want to become, we need to explore the total person-total success concept. The total person program is divided into four components:

- Building a spiritual, positive self-image.
- Seeking optimum health.
- Achieving career success.
- Reaching financial independence.

Fasten your seat belts—we are ready to enter the most important dialogue of our future lives.

BUILDING A SPIRITUAL, POSITIVE SELF-IMAGE

SPIRITUALITY

4

Believing, accepting, and practicing the Attitude Technique philosophy will lead you to a plateau of success in your chosen career and throughout your lifetime. We start the action by building a positive self-image.

Your self-image controls how you feel about yourself, and it relates to how you perceive that others feel about you. By building a strong inner awareness, you will become self-confident, self-disciplined, and possess a powerful spiritual faith. In fact, a strong belief in God, permeating our lives, is the master key to the positive life we are seeking through the Attitude Technique philosophy.

It's clear to me that without a proper spiritual base we cannot become successful, positive leaders. "What profit is there if you gain the whole world and lose eternal life?" is one way of putting this. The only way we can be wise, successful, and happy is to begin with reverence for God. Our growth in wisdom comes from obeying divine laws. From the religious teachings I follow, I have come to believe that God intended for each of us to mature, excel, and live a vibrant life. This means being healthy, having the things we need to sustain our families and selves, and having careers we enjoy and a way to contribute to mankind. By putting God first in our lives, we can utilize our full potential and possess a strong positive inner self-image.

Millions of the most intelligent, learned, and scientific minds of today believe in God, strong faith, and prayer. Prayer is a spiritual exercise whereby we draw ourselves to God until we are part of God's plan and purpose. Understanding this will develop true happiness, which is the object of success. It will lead us to an enriching family and social life. It will nurture our ability to achieve smaller goals, such as the type of home we want, where we want to live, the things we want to do for our children, the friends with whom we want to associate, and many more.

Possessing a strong, positive self-image begins with true faith. Our families are the most important parts of our lives, and family is the single most important part of blending our spiritual faith into our everyday lives. This love is so strong that nothing should override its importance in our lives.

Following in the footsteps of our personal faith and family are our friendships. Having close friends and being a friendly person can add significantly to one's overall life success. People who are difficult to get along with and who deliberately avoid being decent to others will, at some point, phase themselves out of goal-oriented environments. More significantly, that type of person misses out on the happiness that can be achieved by anyone simply willing to make the effort. People may forget what you do, but they will never forget how you make them feel! An exceptional book on friendship to read is Stephen E. Ambrose's book, *Comrades*.

Along with needing a strong faith to develop a positive self-image, one also should possess patience. I really do not like using the word patience. Instead, I favor the phrase "relaxed persistence." Nevertheless, we all must develop patience, and this is another important key. Patience is a vital factor in reaching success.

Anything is possible if a person has enough faith and patience. You have probably heard the story of the man who said, "I am hungry enough to eat an elephant." Someone challenged him by saying, "How could you possibly eat an elephant?" The man replied confidently, "One bite at a time." There is almost no problem that patience cannot solve. You are never defeated until you lose your patience. When the situation looks hopeless, keep hoping. When everything looks impossible, refuse to accept defeat. Most people who succeed in the face of seemingly impossible conditions are people who simply don't know how to quit.

4

Great people are just ordinary people with an extraordinary amount of determination. No person will ever truly know that they have succeeded until they experience an apparent failure. The pole-vaulter cannot be certain of jumping as high as possible until he or she knocks the bar down. Reach as high as you possibly can.

Life is ten percent what happens to you and ninety percent how you react. Positive thinking people never quit. They simply adjust to a proper spiritual life, which is the foundation of the total person. A total person striving toward total success in all areas of his or her life is a free individual. That person has literally found God and no longer has a vacuum in his or her life. They follow God's command.

How did I find God? Here's my personal story:

~

I had an advantage while growing up. I lived in a loving Christian home. My father, Dr. Samuel Rice, a minister and district superintendent in the Kentucky Conference of the Methodist Church; my mother; and my older brother,

Robert Cecil, surrounded me with love and understanding. This was a proper and natural setting in which to find God.

My father gave me the right to choose my own life. Due to the influence of that Christian home, going to Sunday school and church became a pattern and then a habit in my life. I was careful of my behavior. Listening to sermon after sermon, it became automatic for me to do these things. But something was lacking. I wasn't sure just what, but there was a void in my life.

While in high school, I became captain of the football team and was named All-State quarterback. I was also a leader in student government. My plans included college, but World War II came along. I joined the Navy and was soon out to sea in the Pacific.

When we traveled over the ocean at night, all lights had to be off aboard ship. Often I went to the top deck to get some fresh air. One evening I found myself there all alone. I stood, with a light rain falling and a breeze blowing across the deck. I remember looking up into the sky and feeling that something was trying to reach me. This was my first interaction with our Father in Heaven. There were no sirens, no actual voice speaking, no special lighting effects—just a feeling and a realization that the Father was there. I sensed that I must follow Him. It wasn't strong or overwhelming, but more instinctual— that He was there and that I needed Him.

After the war, I finally went to college. Again I became captain of the football team and earned All-American honors as a quarterback. I pursued studies in social science, physical education, education, administration, and psychology. My ambition was to become a football coach and a leader. I did not really know why I wanted that life, but I thought and dreamed about it. A strong desire to do well filled me.

After marrying my beautiful wife, Phyllis, we began my coaching career. Starting in small high schools, I worked my way back to Highlands, my own high school in Fort Thomas, KY. I gained success as a coach, but my life was still incomplete.

Some time later, I was writing a book on technical football training while my family and I were on vacation. I returned home early, leaving my family to enjoy Florida for a couple of weeks longer while I spent time in isolation working on the book. Late one evening, while sitting in the living room going over some notes, I experienced the same feeling I had had years before aboard my ship at sea. I walked out on the front porch and felt a light mist and breeze. Again, I looked up into the heavens and again the Father was talking to me. I did not hear a voice. There were no bright lights or visions. There was just a feeling that He was talking to me. It became clear what I must do with my life. Somehow He had brought me into the coaching field. Now He was telling me to persevere and to devote my life to young people. From that point on, my life and my family gained a greater meaning. I had a direction. I had found God, and He was directing my life.

Many times I strayed, and doubts came; however, I only had to remember those two nights, and I was straight again—looking up, following Him. I knew that by believing in Him and depending on Him, I could do what He wanted me to do.

I sensed a positive life. He led me to realize that it was His will for me to be a very positive person and a successful individual. It was also clear that He wanted me to provide leadership.

Thinking, planning, and working took me from the

high school level into the college ranks as an assistant, as a head coach, as a director of athletics at major institutions, and eventually into the National Football League as a head football coach.

After twenty-seven years in the coaching profession, I received an invitation to become an executive in professional football. A few months later, Georgia Tech offered me a position in Atlanta as an assistant to the president and director over sports programs involving all the young people at that institution. It was a difficult decision. The financial rewards are much higher on the professional level. I had to weigh that against the opportunity to return to a position where I would be working with young people.

I kept remembering that evening when I sensed that the Heavenly Father wanted me to be involved with young people. I then realized that I couldn't decide this— that He would decide it for me.

I was tired on the night a few months later when the decision was due. Tension and pressure made me fitful, but I eventually fell asleep. The next morning, bright and early, I awakened refreshed, happy and excited because I knew what I needed to do. I was to go to Georgia Tech. Even today, I continue having a strong positive feeling that God sees me in this line of work.

In finding God, I was able to see that I have only one path: to follow Him and to accomplish the best that is in me. I have learned that God is the source of supply for all my needs. When I ask, I receive. When I seek, I find. When I knock, the door is opened to me. I believe in God, His Son, and the Holy Spirit. By allowing the Spirit to permeate my thoughts, my prayers, my work, and my very being every day, I am able to believe in myself, in my positive worth, and in my future.

~

As you strive to nurture a positive self-image, you will develop many good qualities. First of all, you will allow the human computer to assist in forming these qualities. As you move on toward the top step of this program, the human computer will begin reacting positively to any and every situation without your making any demands. This will require deep thinking.

Most importantly, you will become a giver. My father once told me, "Never judge anyone—that will be handled by the Supreme Being—but you will be able to recognize the grabbers from the givers." The giver gives time, service, talents, and possessions to God's plan. Only a giver can become a total person. Winston Churchill once said, "We make a living by what we get, but we make a life by what we give."

You may want to balance your life around a wheel of life with six spokes: God, Golden Rule, Family, Self, Job, and Country.

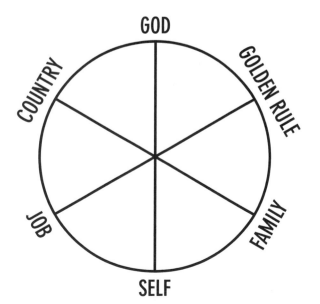

4

It is absolutely essential to blend a spiritual base into your life's plan. As an adjunct professor at Georgia Tech, I teach "Leadership Fitness" through the School of Applied Physiology of the College of Sciences. Primarily seniors sign up for my class each fall.

I teach many of the principles contained in this book. Georgia Tech is a state-supported institution, which requires the separation of church and state. I understand and accept this policy. Nevertheless, it is not possible to hide the spiritual component necessary for success. As a model to others in learning the relevance of spiritual faith to leadership success, I have explained how I personally believe. In class exit interviews, students occasionally ask me about my faith. Some are already strong believers in their own personal faiths; others ask for resources for their personal journeys. They want to know more about finding God and belief. A few years back, I read the book *The Case for Christ* by Lee Strobel. This manuscript is one example of how a person can go from being an atheist to a believer in a faith.

Strobel had been legal editor of the *Chicago Times* and considered himself an atheist. He decided to turn his investigative skills toward learning about Christianity in the same way that he had written about numerous criminal trials. Through that journey, he found a truth for his life and became a Christian. His book is an excellent example for both believers and doubters, and his findings will undoubtedly convince anyone of the power of true faith of God.

One of the highlights of my class is the range of outside speakers I bring to talk to students. These inspired people believe in the Attitude Technique approach to a successful life. The first speaker each year is my dear friend Bishop Bevel Jones.

I have asked Bishop Jones to contribute to *Leadership Fitness*: Bishop Jones, the Bishop in Residence at his alma mater,

The Candler School of Theology at Emory University, served several United Methodist churches over a period of thirty-five years. A teacher, author, and great friend to many outstanding people in the field of athletics, he is always a big hit with my class because of his approach to building a strong, spiritual self-image. His article to follow tells the story:

BUILDING A STRONG SELF-IMAGE

4

It is a privilege to have a part in this book. Homer is a great leader and a dear friend. He personifies all that he says in these pages and leads by example. I especially appreciate his sharing his own faith journey in this lesson, and I know how deep and genuine his spiritual life is. His relationship to God is the centerpiece of his character.

In the popular movie "City Slickers," Jack Palance exclaims, "Life is about one thing!" When Billy Crystal asks him what that thing is, he responds: "That's what you've got to figure out." How true that is for all of us. One of the marks of leadership is focus, a master motive. If we are to have a strong sense of our own identity, we need to be keenly aware of our Creator—the very source. St. Augustine realized after years of floundering that God has made us for Godself, and our hearts are restless until they find rest in Him. The key to Homer Rice's philosophy of the total person—and to his own life—is seeking and doing God's will.

In my late teens I came across a regimen for abundant and effective living. It consists of three principles that stand together like a three-legged stool. The first is *A Self Fit to Live With*. Fit to live with one's own self, and others also. We can be our own worst enemy. If we are at odds with ourselves, we will be at odds with other people. A positive self-image begins with oneself—attitude, spirit, self-acceptance, self-respect, self-discipline, and continual growth. The Psalmist's prayer fits all sizes: "Create in me a clean heart, O God, and renew a right spirit within me. Let the words of my mouth and the meditations of my heart be acceptable in your sight, my Strength and my Redeemer." (Psalm 51: 10).

Second, *A Purpose Fit to Live For.* A young boy missed a couple of days in school because of illness. His mother gave him a note for the teacher and told him it was his excuse for being absent. Not many days later the teacher asked her pupils to bring copies of their birth certificates for the school's records. The young lad went home and said, "Now they want my excuse for being born!" What's mine, and what's yours?

Mission is a word we customarily associate with church. Nowadays many individuals are writing personal mission statements. Corporations and institutions are doing the same. It's important to write, be specific, and keep always in mind what our purpose is and why we are doing what we do. If we are not thoughtful and careful, our actions become routine, and life is more like a treadmill than a worthwhile venture.

One of the finest men I know tells of his young adult years when he was raking in the money and thriving in his business. One day while driving home by himself from his lovely summer home on the river, the question arose like a specter in his mind: *Where are you going?* He couldn't answer that. He stopped his car on the shoulder of the highway and grappled with that issue. It marked a turning point in his life, a reorganizing of his priorities, concern more for persons than for material gain, and a primary regard for the things of God. He has moved from mere success to significance. Once he was filled full. Now he is fulfilled. The purpose has made all the difference.

Third, *A Faith Fit to Live By.* Without faith, life has no solid foundation. H.G. Wells, the historian, said that until we find

God and are found by God, we begin at no beginning and we work to no end. Scripture says that faith is the substance of things hoped for and the evidence of things not seen (Hebrews 11:1) Faith is not fanciful, having to do with fairy tales and make-believe. It is not trying to believe something you know isn't true. Faith is believing what you cannot prove but can't help believing. It doesn't go against reason, but beyond reason. Call it reason grown courageous. Better still, it is betting your life there is a God, a good and great God—one who is faithful and loving and will never let you down.

Faith corresponds with hope. I saw a bumper sticker the other day that said, "I sure do feel better now that I've given up hope." The truth is that where there's hope, there's life. We are not talking about optimism, but hardheaded hope: not wishing, but trusting. Martin Luther, the great reformer, said, "Faith is a living, daring confidence in God's grace, so sure and certain that the believer would stake his life on it a thousand times."

If we are to be strong, positive, and steadfast, we need hope born of faith. This means never giving up. Not that we are convinced everything will turn out well but because we are confident what we are doing is right regardless of how it turns out!

Recently I came upon a statement that strengthened my spirit and no doubt will yours:

Faith is hearing tomorrow's music.
Hope is dancing to it today!

L. BEVEL JONES
United Methodist Bishop, retired

Keep dancing.

Bevel Jones teaches us that having faith always gives us

hope. Without hope, we are defeated and never win. As believers, we have extreme hope. Without hope, we do not expect anything. Faith and hope set us free to think thoughts that lead us to life-enriching opportunities. With relaxed perseverance, we should persist in making full use of the ideas that flow into our human computer, in making the right choices, and in beginning action upon those decisions. Altering the word *patience* to *relaxed persistence* clearly fits our new life. We become free to believe, and gain faith that we have been created for life as part of a magnificent design of life and renewal. The story of Gen. James Dozier's faith and communication with God is a great example to remember.

In December 1981, the Red Brigade terrorist group kidnapped the deputy chief of staff for the North Atlantic Treaty Organization's Southern Region in Verona, Italy. Brigadier General James L. Dozier was kept chained and in captivity for forty-two days. During his ordeal he stayed in constant communication with God. He believed God would guide him and that the whole affair would work out for good ends. He believed others, including his wife Judy, his family, and his friends, were praying for him. Despite his situation, he visualized his release, the press conference, and the welcome by the authorities and his friends. He kept these positive thoughts throughout the time he was held. That visualization became a reality when a crack anti-terrorist unit freed him. His impressions, sustained in captivity, worked out in reality, producing the press conference and a welcome home, just as he had pictured them.

Your self-faith will lead to an experience of joy and fulfillment. As John Wesley said, "Teach faith until you have it yourself." I feel this way as I teach my class "Leadership Fitness" and speak about the human computer to students as well as other various groups. Faith is a powerful self-tool.

In sports, we hear and read a lot about the negatives. But one organization that is a positive influence is the Fellowship of Christian Athletes (FCA). My good friend Dal Shealy, a former successful collegiate football coach and now President of FCA, developed a program called "The Competitor's Creed" that embodies how this organization puts its faith into practice. He explains the purpose and details of "The Competitor's Creed" in Appendix C. That program helps to instill a commitment in coaches and athletes to provide positive leadership and to be role models. The result: it works!

God allows us to become whatever we decide to be. He allows us to live as we choose. Therefore, each individual is the sum of his or her thoughts. The human computer can aid you in building a positive self-image. Always remember that we are sustained by a higher power, regardless of our situation. It's simple to decide to be a self-confident human being who will succeed positively. Start now to become the person you should be and want to become. You will lead others to the winner's circle.

4

Taking one day at a time is an important step to living a life of health, peace, and fulfillment. We can alleviate regret about the past and fear about the future when we trust in God to guide us daily and we follow through with the right action.

We can plan for the future, but we do so only by living productively in the time we call today. Each prayer we pray, each divine idea we implement in our daily living, and each positive step we take today prepares us for tomorrow.

If thinking about an entire day of activity or inactivity causes you feelings of anxiety, then take one hour at a time, or even one moment at a time. We may need to affirm our faith, our strength, and our health in order to build on the truth of our affirmations. We are whole and complete in God, and today is a day of accomplishment and fulfillment. "This is a day which the Lord has made; let us rejoice and be glad in it." (Psalms 118:24)

Don Harp, the popular minister of Peachtree Road United

Methodist Church in Atlanta, recently made the following remarks about leadership in a sermon to his congregation. Don, a
dear friend and our minister, is a successful, positive leader in the
realm of spirituality.

He said that in becoming a good leader, it is most important
to set a good moral example. A simple and time-tested guide for
moral leadership would be the Ten Commandments. In our
halls of Congress, most of our laws are based on these true and
simple laws.

4

One easy-to-remember formula is,

1. Live by principles instead of feelings.

2. Associate with people of integrity. They will be great
    examples to you.

3. Reject anything that tempts you to lower your standards.

In every arena of life, we all look up to those who set good
moral examples. If you are striving to be a good leader, a fundamental quality to attain will be that of being a good moral leader.

As my wife, Phyllis, and I have found in our own involvement
in this church, one of the most rewarding aspects of taking part
in a religious community is the exposure it gives to positive leaders, especially through the Timothy Sunday School Class in
which we participate.

But wherever you live or worship, you'll find positive leaders.
Seek them out and learn from them.

LESSON FIVE

OPTIMUM HEALTH

5

In your efforts to become a positive, successful leader, you must strive for optimum health. If you don't feel well or if you have an unhealthy lifestyle, you will not be at your best. A positive leader must be fit for the job at many levels. This requires a medical and fitness check-up periodically to keep score on your health. Many elements make up a top physically fit leader.

- A planned fitness program
- Planned recreation
- Proper rest
- Relaxation techniques
- Proper nutrition
- Mental stimulation
- Solitude
- Laughter (humor)

One can survive a major illness if body, mind, and faith work in concert to lessen the chance of a bad outcome.

As a seventeen-year old high school senior and football player, I was in peak physical and mental condition. The time was 1944, when the United States was in the middle of World War II. I soon left for the Navy, and after basic training (boot camp), I was assigned to a ship bound for the South Pacific and eventually for a base in the Philippine Islands. At the time, the United States military was planning an attack—an unprecedented naval and aerial bombardment—on Kyushu, the southernmost of the Japanese home islands.

Fortunately, the war ended in August 1945, and I was reassigned for duty in the occupation of Japan. But before our ship sailed, I came down with an attack of malaria. Several of my shipmates died of that terrible disease, but I survived. My good fitness, condition, faith, and strong mental attitude helped me to overcome the disease. I knew I had to survive in order to fulfill my mission and purpose to return home, attend college, compete in collegiate athletics, and become a coach to prepare young men for successful careers. My mental state pulled me through that difficult period of my life.

Eventually I completed my plan to enter the coaching/teaching field. However, as years passed, even though I was involved in training football teams for competitive action, I somehow let my fitness program disappear. I paid very little attention to my personal health. Believing I could outwork my opponents, I slept only a few hours at night and became a workaholic. While undergoing a medical exam for a life insurance policy, my blood pressure went off the board. I could no longer ignore my unhealthy lifestyle.

During this period, I met the famous cardiologist Dr. Kenneth Cooper at a seminar where we were both scheduled to speak. His motivational speech about health fitness and preventive medicine probably saved my life. He gave me one of his early books, which I read cover to cover in one sitting. Dr. Cooper's advice convinced me at age thirty-eight that I had to begin a rigorous fitness program. Nutrition had to be a priority, and I needed to sleep at least six hours at night. I continued this program for many years.

In time, I had to face another dreaded disease when cancer struck my body. I underwent surgery for prostate cancer, then later for kidney cancer. In each case, the physician told me that my fitness and good health had pulled me through. As a two-time cancer survivor, I again had beaten the odds. As of this writing at age eighty-seven, I am in excellent health and continue the point program for good health.

PLANNED FITNESS PROGRAM

5

Dr. Kenneth Cooper developed the Aerobics Fitness Program. I am a strong advocate of his preventative approach. His work attacks the problem of disorders of the cardiovascular system, lungs, and nervous system through planned activities that include running, walking, cycling, swimming, and tennis, among other forms of exercise.

Dr. Cooper came up with the aerobic point score as part of a systematic program for our physical benefit. An aerobic program will improve the quality of one's life. Research proves that we can prevent illness by participating in this type of program. I heartily recommend Dr. Cooper's books about these issues.

PLANNED RECREATION

A health/fitness program must also include planned recreation. This can be tennis, golf, fishing, boating, or whatever activity you desire. The specific activity can include your family, thus serving two vital purposes.

PROPER REST

Proper rest is essential. Each person must find the number of hours needed for proper rest. Do not oversleep, however, because that can dull your senses and hold back opportunities. During the most productive years of my career, I managed to sleep six hours each night. Some health experts recommend seven to eight hours per night.

Whatever you can manage and still feel well rested the next morning is sufficient. Some of our great leaders have managed on a short nap of ten to twenty minutes several times a day. I believe that the objective is to achieve as much as you can during your hours awake. If you are dull and tired, you may make costly mistakes. A well-planned day is the key.

5

RELAXATION TECHNIQUES

Relaxation is also necessary for good health and productivity. Take one or two periods each day, of fifteen to twenty minutes each, to relax completely. This can be a time for meditation. Go to a darkened room where you will not be disturbed. Relax every part of your body. Do not think of anything. You might even drop off to sleep for a few minutes, and that can be your nap for the day. Start with your toes, working up to each part of your body and visualizing each part completely relaxed. Relax your hips, shoulders, and facial muscles. Experience quietness.

Relaxation also means taking a full, planned vacation.

PROPER NUTRITION

Proper nutrition is essential to a vibrant life. Work out a nutritional program that fits your body's mechanism. Dr. Chris Rosenbloom, Associate Professor of Nutrition at Georgia State University, is an authority on the subject. She offers extended nutrition advice in Appendix D.

A healthy, nutritional lifestyle must include a study of the vitamin-mineral story. Dr. Alexander Bralley, the founder of Metametrix Clinical Laboratory, has developed a program that should be seriously considered for a healthy life, preventing serious illnesses, and, in some cases, slowing down the aging process. The Case for Supplements is explained in Appendix E.

5

MENTAL STIMULATION

Mental stimulation is just as much a part of our well-being as any area of health. By studying and reading challenging books, we exercise the brain with deep thinking. Set aside a short time each day for reading to increase your mental capacity. You must have knowledge to achieve a successful life, and reading is the best way to acquire it. Some of our top leaders have exciting hobbies that keep them intellectually sharp and growing stronger mentally. One of my hobbies happens to be reading and studying American history. One part of our history that captures my interest is the Lewis and Clark expedition of 1804-1806.

SOLITUDE
(AND, THE LEWIS AND CLARK EXPEDITION)

In the early 1980s, I met William (Bill) E. Moore, a Georgia Tech graduate from 1938. Bill had been captain of the tennis team and became a highly successful entrepreneur. He expressed interest in helping me with my student/athlete total person program. His contributions were a tremendous aid for my work in exposing young people to "Leadership Fitness." With Bill and another close friend, Albert "Bud" Parker (also a tennis great from Georgia Tech), we formed a fishing trio. In the winter we traveled to my home in Marco Island for gulf fishing, and during the summer we visited Bill's Broken O Ranch in Montana for fly-fishing. We were serious fishermen and spent much time in the Sun River that flows through Bill's property. During our visits to the ranch, Bill introduced me to the journals of the famous Lewis and Clark Expedition. I became fascinated with that part of our American history. In time, I read many books on the subject, particularly Stephen E. Ambrose's *Undaunted Courage.*

In 1803, President Thomas Jefferson selected Captain Meriwether Lewis to lead an expedition to locate a water route across the continent to the Pacific Ocean. Lewis asked his friend, Captain William Clark, to join him on this trip. Their small party moved up the Missouri River to the Rockies but failed to find the much-desired water pathway.

They had to climb over the Rockies to eventually discover the Columbia River that led them to their destination. This journey through the new Louisiana Purchase territory opened up the west. On their return trip, Lewis and some of his men camped on the Sun River where Bill Moore's Ranch is located today. In a way, the Lewis and Clark journey became a hobby that led me to perfect solitude. Bill eventually set up quarters on the ranch so I could go out anytime and fish. I accepted this kind offer and began fly fishing the Sun River.

To be alone, wading the river, moving into position for a rainbow or brown trout to strike is *solitude* at the highest level. The water is cool and refreshing, the sky is big and blue, the Rockies in the distance display their snowcaps, an eagle flies overhead, perhaps a deer or antelope will run by on the bank, and there you are in a game with a trout. You land a rainbow, bring him in, kneel down, and he is released back to the stream. If I had problems in the real world to resolve, I forgot what they were when I was on that river. I thank God for this wonderful world He has created and that I am part of it. This is solitude, and it is an important ingredient to mix in with your health/fitness program. Time alone, away from the office and people, and, of course, away from negatives—that's one important step toward optimum health.

Successful people find solitude in many different ways. It might be a certain hobby, a trip to the lake or beach, or some other solitary activity. Solitude should be a planned part of your daily schedule. Without it we can be controlled by elements detrimental to our health, both mentally and physically. Solitude is powerful. It can erase stress and promote good health.

LAUGHTER

The final step to optimum health is laughter and good humor. Laughing can be a wonderful therapy. It will strengthen the body and pick up your spirits. When we laugh, invigorating agents called endorphins are released into our bodies. We become energized as the cells of our bodies are recharged through happiness. Laughter may be the hidden secret to good health. When we laugh—truly laugh, not with a forced outburst—we feel good, happy, and free of negative thoughts. Laughter is a positive reaction.

Even medical researchers are taking laughter seriously as a healer for illnesses. There are claims that a sense of humor has saved lives. Without humor, we live dull and unhappy lives. My friend Bud Parker consistently sends me humorous cartoons. He doesn't realize how many times his mailings have changed my negative thoughts to positive ones.

A good laugh gets the heart beating faster, brings in extra oxygen, and stimulates blood circulation. We feel better, our whole body relaxes, and disease-fighting immune cells go into production. Remember Norman Cousins' *Anatomy of an Illness*? He believed that laughter—along with hope, faith, the will to live, purpose, and determination—can assist medical science in its struggle against life-threatening diseases.

In the 1950s and 1960s, my wife Phyllis and our three young daughters (Nancy, Phyllis, and Angie) traveled with me each summer to the Fellowship of Christian Athletes Conference. The spiritually uplifting conference featured a minister, Grady Knutt, who was undoubtedly the funniest man in America. I would literally roll in the aisle. We all felt blessed and, indeed, healthy from his performance. Grady later joined the cast of the TV show "Hee-Haw."

I asked my good friend and cardiologist, Dr. John D. Cantwell—chief medical officer of the 1996 Olympic Games in Atlanta, medical director of the Homer Rice Center for Sports Performance at Georgia Tech, frequent speaker to the Leadership Fitness class, and also physician for the Atlanta Braves—to contribute a program of good health and fitness to *Leadership Fitness*. He shares his knowledge about "How to Be a Survivor: Guidelines on Living Well to Age 100" in Appendix F.

Following the plan presented in this lesson has kept me going with a high energy level. It is critically important to be physically, mentally, and spiritually fit in order to lead others to the top step and to be a positive successful leader.

Football coach.

Homer's plaque on Tech's Wall of Legends with John Heisman,
Bill Alexander, and Bobby Dodd.

How could I turn down Rice University when they named
the stadium "Rice Stadium?"

As an athlete!

Author of 7 major books as adjunct professor at Georgia Tech.

Director of Athletics at the University of North Carolina, with wife Phyllis and daughters (l to r) Angie, Phyllis and Nancy.

A victory interview after Homer Rice's Cincinnati Bengals defeated the World Champion Pittsburg Steelers 34 to 10 in 1979.

Retirement as Georgia Tech's Director of Athletics
and Executive Assistant to the President.

With Phyllis in front of The Homer Rice Center.

Phyllis Rice, the head coach in the Rice family.

Homer Rice providing leadership for the National Collegiate Athletic Association as Chairman of the NCAA's Football Rules Comittee.

(Top left) Steve Hatchell, President and CEO of the National Foundation and College Football Hall of Fame; Grant Teaff, Executive Director of the American Football Coaches Association.

(Bottom left) Bob Vecchione, Executive Director of NACDA; Homer Rice.

(Top right) Cedric Dempsey, Executive Director of the NCAA; Billy Joe, head football coach at Florida A&M.

(Bottom right) Bobby Bowden, head football coach at Florida State; Jim Host, CEO of Host Communications.

LESSON SIX

ACHIEVING CAREER SUCCESS

THROUGH SELF-CONTROLLED MOTIVATION

SELF MOTIVATION— CONTROLLED VISUALIZATION

6

The external world is intertwined with the inner world. Each is inseparable from the whole. A person's psychological state affects his or her day-to-day life and health, and likewise, a person's day-to-day life affects his or her psychological health. We now turn to a technique for organizing one's life to become a total person—a whole person—positioned for total success. That technique is the art of controlled visualization.

CAREER SUCCESS THROUGH SELF-CONTROLLED MOTIVATION

The key to a successful career is self-motivation. After we master this key, we can begin teaching staff/employees or whatever group we lead the art of self-motivation. I take the concept a step higher and call it self-written motivation. By writing your thoughts on paper, you will seal them in your human computer and call upon them when needed. Everything begins with an idea. If we can control our minds, we can control our future and our career success.

To become completely successful we must base everything on truth. If we are not truthful, we will fail. A lie cannot withstand the test of time. Truthful motivation is a spark that ignites us to do great things. We plan it. We write it. We may even record it on tape. We begin acting out the role we must play to accomplish our goals. Consistency and repetition pay off. The role becomes a ladder to climb. The higher we climb, the more aware we become of our potential.

Self-motivation, or self-written motivation, involves seven principles. Each principle represents a step up the ladder.

6 THE FIRST PRINCIPLE IS HAVING THE DESIRE TO ACCOMPLISH SOMETHING

Whatever it is, you must fix it in your mind in exact detail. Write it so it will become absolutely clear. This is the commitment and the beginning. Once you make the decision in writing, you then set a target date, giving yourself a deadline to work toward. Without a finishing point, you will never complete your desire. Once you establish a target date, you begin to write the ingredients necessary to achieve your goal. You may want to take it one step further and write a *plan of action* for gaining your desire. The next step is very important: You must declare what you're willing to give. Whatever your goal, you will never receive anything without first giving. It may be something as simple as your time or your effort, but you must give before you expect to receive.

After writing your desire or need, the target date, the ingredients and a plan of action, and what you are willing to give, you should begin to visualize your desire as already completed. Visualization is the beginning of the climb upward. The more you visualize the finished product, the closer you will move toward its realization. By reading your written statements each day, you bring that desire into focus. Then you must strive for its completion. The power of visualization will manage your life toward completing what you desire.

Desire is a prime motivating force in all of us. There are comparatively few people with great desire. Most are content to go along occupying the tiny niches in which they find themselves. They accept their positions in life as something that fate has fixed for them, and very seldom do they make either a mental or physical effort to extract themselves from those positions. Successful people realize that the greatest power is produced by desire. Whatever we fix our thoughts upon is the thing that we attract to us.

When you start, you may have no idea what the results will be. Don't concern yourself with this; leave it to the human computer. You will find that you receive assistance from the most unexpected sources. When you get an idea, follow it. Keep a note pad handy. When ideas come, even during the night, write them on the pad so they will not be lost. This is very important.

Edison kept a notebook, and his best ideas for many of his inventions came while he slept. Early in my career, as a young high school football coach, I awakened at 2:00 a.m. and diagrammed an offensive play on a pad by my nightstand. Little did I realize that this idea would become the triple option, one of the greatest innovations in the history of football. The person with a fixed thought, a clear picture of the desire, or an idea always before him causes it, through repetition, to be buried deep in his or her subconscious. That person is thus enabled, thanks to the brain's generative and sustaining power, to realize the goal in a minimum of time and physical effort. Pursue your thoughts unceasingly. Step by step, you will achieve your goal because all of your faculties and powers are directed toward that end.

Two objects cannot occupy the same space at the same time. Compare your mind to that space: it can't be filled with negative thoughts or doubts if you have it filled with positive, powerful, and creative thoughts. Whatever your desire may be, do not limit your thinking to a small area. Encompass broader fields of experience and action. Most people limit themselves to habits of thought that include their small, everyday happenings. Those patterns become chains that bind them to lives of inactivity, poverty, and limitation. Learn to think big. Your brain cells are aching for exercise in large visions. Everyone knows how to think small. It takes a truly expanded mind to think big.

How do you develop a desire, an idea? *Think*. Think inspired thoughts. Think creatively and dynamically. Think big. Think successful thoughts. Think wholesome thoughts. Think healthy thoughts. Visualize great things. Visualize achievement, perfection, and the situation you wish to be in. *Feel*. Feel your thoughts. Feel healthy and strong. Feel wholesome and successful, confident and poised. *Act*. Act with confidence, decisiveness. Be aggressive and have positive boldness in your actions. Play the part you wish to fill on the stage of life. Make your own decisions as to what you want to be, but set into motion the law of action by taking the first step.

Positive, creative thoughts, desires, or ideas lead to action and ultimately to their realization. The real power, much more than the action itself, is the thought. Whatever a person can conceive mentally, he or she can bring into effect. Desire is the first principle in self-motivation.

THE SECOND PRINCIPLE IS BELIEF

We must have a strong belief in the outcome. This is a state of mind that may be created by affirmation or repeated instructions to the human computer—the subconscious mind. Be persistent about attaining your desire. A mental image of yourself already accomplishing what you want, seen over and over again, will project the belief you need to achieve your goals.

Belief is related to faith. Our faith in God aids us in finding our identity with the Creator of the Universe. The world is filled with people who have worked hard but have little to show for it. Something more than hard work is necessary. That something is creative thinking and a firm belief in your ability to execute your ideas. Determine precisely what you want. You must have a mental pattern clearly drawn in your mind. Most people have a general idea that they would like to be successful, but beyond that everything is vague.

You must know precisely where you are headed. Keep a fixed desire or idea in view, and have faith, strong faith, that you will receive. Belief in yourself and in your destiny is an essential and important step in your climb up the ladder. "All things are possible to him that believes." We must work hard but we must also work smart.

6

THE THIRD PRINCIPLE IS IMAGINATION

A person can create anything he or she can imagine. Whatever we can visualize and believe in, we can achieve. All great people develop the power of self-motivation.

The power to create new ideas comes from combining previous experiences with vision. When you creatively imagine something, you are actually causing it to come into being. The process by which it comes to pass is a mystery, but the method for making it happen is this: Picture the things you want to do; hold them in consciousness; and pattern your actions in such a way that you are constantly working toward the fulfillment of the desires you hold in your imagination.

THE FOURTH PRINCIPLE
IS ORGANIZATION OF PLANNING

Whatever you desire in life cannot be done alone. Select one or more individuals to work with you in developing your plan. The more minds you can bring together working for a common purpose, the more related information is available. As a leader, you need to take into confidence a small team or group and listen to their ideas. Great ideas are a combination of related ideas. Pick the individuals or group with care. They must be hard and smart working, conscientious people you respect. You can have a lot of fun, and you will reach your desire much sooner.

Arrange to meet with your group at least once a week. Refine your plans until they are perfected. Each day you must know exactly what you are going to do and why. You must be a positive leader to direct your plan. Planning requires concentration. It is difficult to concentrate for any length of time. Our thoughts and ideas flow through our mind with astonishing rapidity.

You are constantly being swayed by what you read, see, and hear. As a result, the coordinating part of the creative force turns to the task of gathering these scattered elements into a confused mass, instead of developing itself to make a clear and dynamic picture of your desire. This is the primary reason we must write our desires and the plans that we will follow.

The mind must be held steady to the desire. Successful minds work to a single point. When concentrating, allow nothing to interfere with your mental concentration. Pick a definite time each day and sit quietly by yourself, concentrating your mental power on what you are trying to achieve. Organized planning will take you a step closer to your desired goal. By rearranging daily work so that we can succeed in little things, we build an atmosphere of success that will carry over into larger and more important undertakings.

THE FIFTH PRINCIPLE
IS TO BE ABLE TO MAKE DECISIONS

Decision-making is a necessary skill. Lack of decisiveness is the major cause of failure. Successful people reach decisions promptly and change them slowly, if there ever is a need for change. Failures reach decisions very slowly and change them rapidly. However, never make an important decision without getting all the facts. It is better to pause or hold until the facts are in and then to make a decision that is the best for the program—and stay with it. Most people are afraid to take on responsibilities, to make decisions, and to step out alone. That's why there are so few leaders and so many followers. When confronted with a problem, you will find that the longer you put it off, the greater it becomes, and the less confident you are of your ability to solve it. Learn to make decisions, because in not deciding, you fail to act; and in failing to act, you invite complete failure. All great people are people of quick decision. A quick decision ignites initiative, accumulated knowledge, and experience.

Abraham Lincoln once said, "If I were to try to react, much less answer, all the attacks on me, this shop might as well be closed for any other business. I do the very best I know how, the very best I can; and I mean to keep on doing so until the end. If the end brings me out all right, then what is said against me won't matter. If the end brings me out wrong, then ten angels swearing I was right would make no difference."

The important thing to remember is that mistakes are human. None of us can bat .1,000, but we bat zero if we never step up to home plate.

THE SIXTH PRINCIPLE:
WE MUST HAVE PERSISTENCE

When everything indicates it is all over, go the extra mile and succeed. This is the difference between success and failure. This is the separation of men from boys and women from girls. Persistence is a state of mind. It can, therefore, be cultivated. Persistence is the result of the habits we form. All successful coaches are persistent. They keep coming back against great odds, and they succeed. Paul Brown, Vince Lombardi, John Wooden, Paul Bryant, Eddie Robinson, Bud Wilkinson, and many other great coaches experienced defeat but would not give in. Their imagination and will power took them to the top.

Persistence creates a winning attitude. This means that you know what you want. Believe you can get it, work with all you have to achieve it, and refuse to give up under any odds.

THE SEVENTH PRINCIPLE—AND THE
ULTIMATE KEY TO POSITIVE LEADERSHIP,
SUCCESS, AND TRUE HAPPINESS
IS THE UNDERSTANDING OF THE HUMAN
COMPUTER, THE SUBCONSCIOUS MIND

Once you understand this personal machine and put it to positive, worthwhile, and constructive use, your life and your success can be, and will be, whatever you want it to be. In fact, there is no way it can be otherwise.

The human computer controls our minds, our thoughts, and our destinies. The scientific explanation is simple. By using the Attitude Technique, we control our thought process with positive, worthwhile affirmations. We may not understand completely the process of the brain and the two minds—conscious and subconscious—to which it is connected, but we do understand that it is the most powerful force the world has ever known. Think of all the miraculous things this human computer has given us: supersonic aircraft, spaceships to the moon, and the unbelievable power of the computer. Yet experts tell us that we use only a small percentage of our capabilities. Our potential is unlimited. This power is available to anyone who will only take the time to utilize its greatness.

I once heard a speaker tell the story of the legend of the creation of the universe: A committee held a conference and one member said, "Let us give to man the same creative power that we ourselves possess." The committee agreed, but one asked, "Where shall we hide this priceless gift?" Another answered, "Let us hide it where man will never think to look for it—within his own mind."

From a very early age, perhaps even in your mother's womb, everything you heard, saw, or felt was stored in your subconscious (human computer). Your conscious mind collects and your subconscious stores and performs. This is the exact process of a computer. The input (what we program into the computer) is our storehouse of information. The input subsequently determines actions, or output. Your human computer does not care what you give it. It will perform with whatever material is input. If you have given it negative, unworthy thoughts all these years, then you will perform as a negative person. When you do something you are sorry for later, it cannot be helped because this is your human computer performing as you have programmed it to do.

Our human computer is constantly at work molding our thoughts, feelings and actions. This computer is our inner power. It is recognized as the essence of life, and the limits of its power are unknown. It never sleeps. It comes to our support in time of great trouble. It warns us of impending danger. Often it aids us to do something that seems impossible. When properly employed, it performs so-called miracles. Objectively, it does as it is told. That is, it performs when and as it is commanded. Subjectively, it acts primarily upon its own initiative.

When this principle is fully comprehended, the result becomes breathtaking. Every student of the subject understands what can be accomplished by controlling our planned thoughts. Many have employed it to achieve fame and worthiness for the good of mankind. Its power is available to anyone. If you believe in its power and put it to work for you, it can and will shape and control your life. It can be used to solve a problem or achieve anything desired strongly enough by the individual.

How can you use it for your benefit? First, through positive prayer, be sure that you are asking for something that is rightfully yours to have and is within your ability to handle. The human computer manifests only according to the capabilities of the person.

Many people get into situations or positions that they cannot handle. It is better to wait for your desire until you are prepared. Second, you must have patience and absolute faith. Our computer will not work unless we believe it can. Start saying, "I believe, I believe." Say it 100 times. When you verbalize "I believe," your human computer responds and begins recording. This is the power of suggestion. You are not saying, "I do not believe."

Only one thought can occupy your mind. Therefore, if you keep that positive thought—"I believe"—in your conscious mind, your human computer will accept it, and you will begin believing. This is the Attitude Technique: training yourself toward successful positive leadership. You control your thoughts; there-fore, you begin controlling your performance. Your computer cannot tell the difference between negative and positive thoughts. The computer accepts whatever thought you give it.

Your need must be conveyed to the human computer as if the work has already been accomplished. Many times something happens that you feel has happened before. And often times it has, but only in your subconscious. While it is necessary for you to feel and to think yourself successful, it is important for you to go one step further and actually *see* yourself as a positive, suc-cessful leader. The final step is to wait patiently while the subcon-scious assimilates the elements of your problem and then goes about its own way to solve for you. The solution—the correct course of action that you must follow immediately and unques-tioningly—will be revealed to you. There must be no hesitation on your part, no mental reservation, no deliberation. Take the course of action. One day you will find yourself, through the aid of the human computer, in the position you sought.

All of us have seen and experienced how, in difficult situa-tions or sudden emergencies, our spontaneous action is always best. We have witnessed superhuman strength in individuals who were able to perform feats far beyond their normal powers. I remember watching a young basketball player only 5'8" dunk a basket to win a particular game. It was the only way he could have scored when heavily guarded under the goal by two giants on each side of him. Neither before nor since could he dunk a basketball. We have seen the 9.4 sprinter speeding toward a sure touchdown when suddenly the 10.5 defensive back comes from out of nowhere to overtake him. As one of Coach Bear Bryant's players once remarked, "He was only running for a touchdown; I was running for my life." We see it happen in the sports world often, and it's not uncommon in the outside world. An over-turned automobile pins a person underneath. His friend lifts the back end of the car, enabling the victim to roll to safety. Great rescues are related to the subconscious (human computer). So are heroic acts in war. This same power can give us whatever we want in our professional leadership careers.

The human computer always brings to reality whatever it is led to believe. Human imagination and concentration are the chief factors in developing the forces of the subconscious. Once you believe in your subconscious mind, you can utilize it for various situations. If you want to awaken at a certain time in the morning without using an alarm clock, just preorder your human computer to awaken you. If you have a problem, write it and then tell your human computer to give you the answer. It will never fail.

Repetition is a fundamental process. Repeated positive thoughts and suggestions can bring you success. Many people become confused and frustrated because they allow themselves to be influenced by the negative thoughts and action of others. Repetition of negative thoughts, if continued long enough, will discourage even the most powerful. We are all victims of suggestion. Get a clear picture of what you want, and keep telling yourself that you are going to get it. Then go to work, always keeping your goal in mind.

This program is not a ticket to fame and success overnight. It is intended only as a key to unlock the door that leads to the goal of your desire. Do not allow memories of past failures to affect your present performance. If you dwell upon them—"I failed yesterday, therefore, I will fail today."—you will assure that result. The moment you change your mind and stop giving power to the past; your past mistakes will lose power over you. "If you believe you can, or if you believe you can't, you are right."

Your human computer operates in terms of goals and end results. Once you give it a definite goal to achieve, you can depend upon its guidance system to take you to that end. You supply the desire by thinking in terms of the finished product. Your human computer supplies the means. The reason is simple: when you feel successful and self-confident, you act successfully. When the feeling is strong enough, you can literally do no wrong. In time, you will not only feel successful, but you will expect to be successful. You can train your human computer by building habits to perform any act you choose consciously. It will, in time, carry out any command that you give it.

You first must believe in its power, and then you must control your thoughts.

By constant repetition of positive thought, you will imprint it on your human computer, making it a part of the automatic reflex action of your subconscious mind. When you constantly report positive statements such as, "I am healthy, I have positive energy, I am happy," you actually raise the energy level of your body and release stored sugar in the liver, giving you greater vitality. On the other hand, negative suggestions such as, "I feel sick, I am tired, I feel terrible, I will catch cold," actually create the mental and physical atmosphere in which these negative conditions breed. When you act a part long enough, your human computer (subconscious mind) makes it a living reality.

Be certain, however, not to misuse your human computer. If it is employed for harmful or evil purposes, it will destroy you. The seven principles form an insurance policy against failure. They develop in you a sixth sense that comes from mastering the seven principles. It comes slowly by meditation, self-examination, and serious thought. The mind begins to work affirmatively and positively without any demands from the individual. It takes years of experience to develop this sense, but the minute you start your life takes on a new and different meaning. You begin to grow and mature a little each day. You become happy. Your health, your work, and your family and spiritual life improve. The change is so significant that you will wonder why you waited so long to grasp the new life. But it is never too late To go after the best.

6

We are the result of what we have thought. Your life is the result of your thought processes. The secret of success lies not without but within. Thought is the original source of all great things. Our thoughts make or break us. We become what we contemplate. We also are molded by the thoughts of others—by what we hear, read and see. If those thoughts are negative, we must learn to keep free of them. Our thoughts determine our conversation, our posture, and our facial expressions. Fear often tints our thoughts negatively. Fear is basically an imaginary factor. Changing from a fearful thought to a positive thought wipes out the imagination of a developed fear. The object of practicing thought and action is to make repeated trials and constantly correct errors until a hit is scored. A person is literally what he or she thinks, their character being the complete sum of their thoughts. Repeated positive thoughts and actions will develop the sixth sense.

Now that we have become self-motivated, we are prepared to teach others this power. First we must try to understand the other person. A motivated individual thinks of the work he or she does; the achievement on the job; responsibilities; advancement as a result of work accomplished; and recognition (notice, praise, or blame) in connection with work accomplished. A non-motivated individual thinks of: salary; supervision; working conditions; status; job security; staff policies, administration, and staff members. The employee or staff person who allows negative thoughts to rule the day is not focused on his or her responsibilities. That could be the fault of the leader for not building a positive attitude within the workforce. The most valuable asset in any organization is its workers. A leader must train, develop, and motivate people in a manner that wins confidence and gets results. An old adage says: "One percent make things happen, nine percent watch things happen, and ninety percent ask, 'What happened?'" The winning organization is united 100 percent to make things happen.

Our employees see their superiors as either
highly motivated or poorly motivated.
This chart illustrates how those you lead see you.

HOW THE WORKER SEES HIS OR HER BOSS

HIGHLY MOTIVATED	POORLY MOTIVATED
1. Easy to talk to, even under pressure	You have to pick carefully the time you talk to him
2. Tries to see the merit in your ideas, even if they conflict with his	Because he's the boss, he tends to assume his ideas are the best
3. Tries to help his people understand staff objectives	Lets people figure out for themselves how staff objectives apply to them
4. Tries to give his people all the information they want	Provides his people with as much information as he thinks they need
5. Has consistent, high expectations of staff members	His expectations of subordinates can change from day to day
6. Tries to encourage people to reach out in new directions	Tries to protect his people from taking big risks
7. Takes your mistakes in stride, so long as you learn from them	Allows little room for mistakes, especially those that might embarrass him
8. Tries mainly to correct mistakes and figure out how they can be prevented in the future	When something goes wrong, he primarily tries to find out who caused it
9. Expects superior performance and gives credit when you do it	Expects you to do an adequate job; doesn't say much unless something goes wrong

6

How can we aid our staff members to become motivated and to work effectively? We must give each one a challenging job, a feeling of achievement, a sense of responsibility and growth, a chance for advancement, an atmosphere of enjoyment of work, and an opportunity for earned recognition. Staff members become dissatisfied when opportunities for achievement are eliminated, and then they become insensitive to their environment.

More importantly, we motivate others by being motivated ourselves with the Positive Mental Attitude Technique. But it must be done in such a subtle way that it does not turn off others. Motivation of others requires good communication. Once you fully understand and begin applying the seven principles, you can begin teaching the principles to your group. Before you go into a competitive situation, close your eyes and say to yourself, "I'm as good as my competitor; as a matter of fact, I am better. I can win." Repeat this several times. Open your eyes and be amazed at the results.

Motivation is personal. It is not a system or formula but rather a way of life. Motivation is internal. A person can be stimulated but cannot be manipulated for long. Eventually he or she will respond only to a challenge and to quality leadership. Motivation involves change within the individual. When he or she is motivated, the person has a desire to improve, to create, and to do constructive work. We were born with motivation, but along the way we retreat or compromise with fear or weaknesses. Our creative impulses and desires to be constructive have been suppressed, restricted, or eliminated, but we can overcome fear by changing these thoughts to positive input for our human computer.

Throughout history, certain people have shown themselves capable of leading others to achievement. These people seemed to possess some strange, inner quality in their personalities that made them appear strong, steady, and in control of themselves. They had the courage to attempt seemingly impossible things, and they usually attained the goals they set for themselves and the group. The greatness of their achievements may be duplicated by anyone who has mastered the seven principles of self-motivation. When the principles are applied, the results are amazing. They come to understand that their actions are the result of controlling the information that is fed to the human computer.

Getting yourself ready to deal with details, as well as with the larger picture, starts with waking up each day and thinking positive thoughts that will condition your mind and body for that entire day's action. Believe what you are thinking. When you have faith in your thoughts, positive currents of energy flow in your brain and body and make your actions dynamic, worthy, and powerful for the good of mankind. In explaining to others this plan for becoming self-motivated, you will receive great inspiration and positive creative energy. Fulfilling the desire to help others is a tremendously satisfying ingredient of success. Winning is wrapped up in motivation. The lesson brings forth the same message each time—belief. It works because of actions performed by the human computer. People of all ages have known about it, and those with wisdom have used it. Socrates, the Greek philosopher, regularly took his class out to the country by a lake. One day a young student asked Socrates how to attain wisdom. Socrates led the student down to the lake, pushed his head under the water, and held him there for several moments. The young lad, pushing and fighting to pull his head out of the water, screamed, "I asked you how I could find wisdom and you tried to drown me!" To which Socrates replied, "If you want wisdom as bad as you wanted air, you will find it." Wisdom can be taught to others through sincere thinking, clear writing, and simple language.

6

WE LEARNED FROM OTHERS

How do you use self-motivation to achieve career success? Our class learned from a number of people.

Carolyn Luesing, president and owner of her own company and a University of North Caroline graduate, is an expert on business etiquette and a favorite class speaker each year. Because the majority of class members are approaching graduation and anticipating entry into their careers, the lessons she teaches have a significant impact. She gives tips that not only aid in the interview process but that also can produce career success.

In business, projecting a professional, confident image and practicing the nuances of business etiquette are essential components of career success, she writes. Business etiquette is the art of appearing gracious and pointed, while at the same time making others feel comfortable. Dale Carnegie states that 85 percent of one's success will depend on interpersonal skills, including the ability to handle others with tact and style, and 15 percent will depend on technical skills. A courteous demeanor will advance your career and facilitate your interviewing process.

Etiquette is defined as respecting oneself and others, doing what is appropriate and acceptable, showing kindness and consideration, and behaving consistently with the Golden Rule. That rule, of course, is "Treat others as you would like to be treated." Good manners directly affect the bottom line in any economy and may be the deciding factor in whether a person is hired and retained in a job.

The following are some important areas of business etiquette to observe:

- Monitor conversation for business—avoid jokes, slang,

acronyms, profanity, and gossip. Avoid personal topics, such as health, misfortunes, and sensitive subjects.

- Pay attention to introductions, greetings, and names.

- Use good listening skills and show interest in others.

- Practice the art of dining and entertaining. Be a good host and guest.

- Politely use cell phones, voice mail, email, phones, or pagers.

- Make a practice to write notes, send out only professional letters, and observe RSVPs to invitations.

- Practice punctuality in meetings, returning phone calls, and sending information.

- Be careful about alcoholic beverages in business situations.

In today's competitive business environment, paying attention to the details of business etiquette will enhance your ability to obtain job positions and to attract and retain customers in any job capacity, advises Luesing.

~

Students from the course interviewed Bud Shaw, a frequent guest speaker, regarding his concepts of positive leadership. Shaw and his brother Bob are the founders of Shaw Industries, the world's largest producer of carpets. With Shaw Industries, Bud was able to accomplish his personal goal to run a $40-million business by the age of forty. Shaw Industries relied on the strengths of its people, guided by the two brothers.

Bud Shaw feels that there are two types of people in business: the do-it-yourselfers and the delegators. The do-it-yourselfers are able to do only what their own two hands will allow them to do. The delegators are able to extend themselves through others to increase productivity. Success for a delegator depends on a relationship of trust. The leader must take the blame if a delegated job is not completed correctly and pass any received praise to his constituents for a job well done. The skill of finding those in whom you have confidence takes years of practice, and it is a trait that has been one of Bud Shaw's greatest strengths.

For example, in one division of his business, Shaw hired an individual with outstanding credentials and experience. However, upon closer inspection, that person's values and attitude were not suited to the situation, and the venture was unsuccessful. That experience taught Bud that attitude and values are more important than credentials. Shaw is a delegator by nature. He has a philosophy of keeping a "clean plate"—meaning, once a task presents itself and all of the facts are at hand, don't procrastinate: "Do it now."

Bud Shaw believes that every individual defines success differently. In his words, "My concept of success is defined in five parts: professional accomplishment so that my work has improved a chosen industry; community service that has added to others' quality of life; a healthy and happy family; fulfillment of personal goals; and a spiritual life that embraces both understanding and belief."

Following are several additional strategies and techniques Shaw has used in striving for success:

- "Procrastination is the greatest defeater of enthusiasm."

- "Eliminate your mistakes early; don't allow them to compound over time."

- "Admitting your mistakes forces integrity upon yourself."

- "Listen. It is the most important part of communication. Don't think instead about what you're going to say next."

- "I encourage every person to try to be in business for themselves. The backbone of America is people in business for themselves."

- "A financial background is essential for anyone in business."

- "Dare to compete, dare to fail. Athletics teaches you to put yourself on the line."

~

Martha Lanier, president of her own company called "Igniting Unlimited Potential," in her message to the class presented a point-by-point plan for successful, positive leadership:

- Live by choice as opposed to chance.
- Have a plan.
- Be specific.
- Break goals down into small segments.
- Put it in writing.
- Look at it everyday.
- Make it measurable.
- Have a time frame attached.
- Share your goals.
- Take time to review your progress.

- Utilize your strengths—mediocrity is useless.
- Strengthen strengths and delegate weaknesses.
- Have 3 Support Groups:
    1) Masterminds—like minded groups
    2) Advisory Board—support system
    3) Advocates—strengthen professionally
- Develop expertise and focus on solutions.
- Create your own belief system.

~

Hubert L. "Herky" Harris, Jr., chairman and Chief Executive Officer of INVESCO Retirement, Inc., served our country during the administration of President Jimmy Carter and spoke to the class on building success traits to become a positive leader.

His points:

- Luck—Sometimes, being in the right place affects our future.

- Integrity is something that can be easily lost and is very hard to regain.

- Aggressiveness—Figure out what your goal is and strive for it.

- Taking calculated risks—One must understand all of the consequences first.

- Having a keen sense of awareness—Know what is going on around you. Know the circumstances and understand human dynamics.
- Must have flexibility—Change is a fact of life.

- Must do your homework—The more you show you know about a certain person and their company, the more respect you will receive.

These seven principles were important elements in the success Herky Harris has achieved to this day.

~

John Williams founded Post Properties, Inc., and continues as chairman *emeritus* for that prestigious enterprise. He developed one of the most successful apartment-living communities in the United States by living his simple business philosophy. He describes it as "based on the concept of being more than fair—more than fair to customers, more than fair to associates, and more than fair to investors. And, finally, have fun. The work environment should be exciting, stimulating, and especially lots of fun."

~

6

Henry F. "Hank" McCamish, Jr., has been a close friend for many years. In the early 1970s, I put together a leadership seminar at the Pine Needles Golf and Country Club in Pinehurst, NC, at the request of Warren and Peggy Kirk Bell.

At the time, I was Director of Athletics at the University of North Carolina and had just co-authored *Leadership in Athletics* with my good friend, Paul Meyer. The purpose of the conference was to explore the "Total Person—Total Success" concept. Fortunately, I was successful in bringing in experts to lecture and discuss these topics—Paul Meyer, Dr. Ken Cooper, Carl Stevens, Jack Kinder, and Hank McCamish.

Hank and I remained close for years. We met again in 1980 when I moved to Georgia Tech. As we pursued the Total Person

Program for student-athletes, Hank was instrumental in getting the program, and later a separate building, off the ground. He insisted on naming the new facility in my honor. I resisted, but in the end Hank won by saying, "No name, no check!" Hank has been ultra successful as a positive leader. The 50 points he stressed to the class in his lecture are worth whatever space is required to include them in *Leadership Fitness*. They appear in full in Appendix G.

~

Jim Lientz, former President of the Mid-South Bank of America, co-founder of the Triveritas Group, and now the state's first chief operating officer for Georgia Governor Sonny Perdue, made key points to the class about becoming a positive leader:

6

- Everybody is a leader of some kind: quiet, noisy, data driven, emotional/impulsive.

- Emulate the "Think 'Team' Orientation" of positive leaders—there is a reason we have two ears and one mouth.

- Trust your instincts.

- Genuinely care about people.

- Do what you say you are going to do.

- Leaders must be candid and specific.

- Be optimistic and take big chances. (Hugh McCall)

- Be a servant leader. (Governor Sonny Perdue)

- Spend time developing those around you.

- Leaders understand that there is plenty of success to go around.

- Leaders are typically happy and positive people.

- Be an intense competitor, but realize that no one wins 100 percent.

- Leaders don't have time for superficiality or surface people.

- Listen more than you talk.

- Leadership rights are extremely fragile.

~

6

Bill Curry, former gridiron leader and now an ESPN TV football analyst, spoke to the class about goal setting. Bill knew firsthand about our course. When I became director of athletics at Georgia Tech in 1980, Bill was our head football coach. To build our program, I taught this course to our staff and coaches. I might add that Bill was a prize student. His remarks reinforced to the class the lesson on goal setting (Lesson 8). He emphasized how self-motivation is the key to becoming a successful, positive leader, and he made a real impression on the class with his comments.

~

Jack Kinder of Kinder Brothers International Group, Inc., in Dallas, TX, is a sales management consultant to several hundred corporations. He is an expert on positive leadership. His years in management have taught him many things, but none more important than, "Managers manage things; leaders lead people."

The leader's challenge is to achieve both success and significance. This is accomplished when the leader makes a commitment to excellence, defines and steadfastly pursues an organizational vision, builds self-discipline, and lives his or her life in balance.

The leader consistently teaches lessons that stay taught. "Leadership," Kinder noted, "is a succession of lessons that must be lived to be understood."

~

The stories of all great leaders remind us that success is seldom accidental, according to Carl Stevens from Houston, TX, known as the "Creator of a College Education in Professional Selling."

As we all become "chronologically enhanced," it is interesting to reflect on what makes one individual more successful than another. What is your definition of success?

We can agree that the successful person is an individual who does what he or she has predetermined that they want to do and optimizes his or her innate abilities. In the process, everybody involved wins.

"You win with people," according to football coach Woody Hayes. What makes a super-successful winner or leader?

The successful, positive leaders Stevens has known and studied have unique qualities but common denominators. Positive leaders seem to understand these things:

1. The potential for communication magic with words. Some of us think of the late Dr. Norman Vincent Peale as a pioneer in the field of positive leadership. A personal letter Dr.Peale penned to Stevens about a manuscript reflects his elegance in writing. "It

communicates most effectively and is devoid of pedantic phrase-ology that might bewilder the reader," he wrote.

Successful positive leaders don't bewilder their listeners. They inspire them.

2. In a recent survey, 72 percent of leaders said they did not have time to think or plan. A client and friend who sold the business he started immediately after high school for $4 million advised that, "A man needs time to ponder and plan."

3. If you had an IQ four points higher than Einstein, what advice would you give a would-be successful leader? Here's his counsel re-garding decision-making. Evaluate each decision with this ques-tion: Will this choice help me reach my ultimate goal and objective?

4. Napolean Hill said that 98 percent of people fail because they have no chief aim or goal. Many leaders are ineffective. Peter Drucker said, "Being efficient is doing things well; being effec-tive is doing the right things." A professional goal is a prerequi-site to becoming an effective leader.

5. A wise author wrote, "Take time to think. It is the source of power. Take time to pray. It is the greatest power on earth."

In a survey of more than 500 business presidents and vice presidents, poor prioritizing was common. The survey reported that despite keeping long hours, only 47 percent of leaders' working time was taken up with leadership duties. They filled most of the remaining time with hands-on work, "doing" as op-posed to "leading."

6. President Ronald Reagan was referred to as "The Great Delegator." He had a sign in his office that read, "It is amazing what you can accomplish if you don't care who gets credit for

6

it." President Reagan told a *Time* magazine reporter that, "The highest grade I made in college was a C+." So you C+ students— maybe you, too, can become the leader of the free world.

The most successful, positive leaders I have known and studied seem to keep strict scores on themselves. They use benchmarks and keep a close watch on their continuing progress. Talk to yourself every hour, on the hour, to stay focused.

If we are not going to learn from history, why should we value it? Study and learn from the super leaders. A positive leader is a perpetual learner.

7. Critique yourself. At the end of each project and each day, do this: Invest five to ten minutes reconstructing the day, reviewing the key activities, and evaluating your strong and weak points. Ponder and enlist your subconscious to help you twenty-four hours a day!

Follow the lead of our nation's first great leader, General George Washington. Take time to pray. It is the greatest power on earth.

LESSON SEVEN

FINANCIAL INDEPENDENCE

TITHING, AND PROSPERITY

FINANCIAL INDEPENDENCE

Positive, successful leaders strive to be successful in all areas of their lives. They often begin with a spiritual commitment to following God's commandments. They build a positive self-image, seek optimal health, and achieve career success by means of self-motivation. And, finally, they reach financial independence. Some people seek only financial success, and material things become their benchmarks. However, true successful, positive leaders will always include all four areas of the total person-total success plan in their pursuit of real happiness.

It is important to plan to become financially independent by a certain age. We should plan so that our families will have all the things they need whether we live or die. We can do this through life insurance and careful investing. I suggest locating a good life insurance agent and looking into term-life insurance.

After that, build a portfolio through the years that consists of savings, investments, and real estate. I believe the larger part of the portfolio should be in fixed income, such as high-quality corporate bonds, municipal bonds, and U.S. treasury bonds with a broad range of maturity dates. In equities, look for stocks that pay dividends, have had high credit ratings for a long period of time, and represent goods or services that will be in demand and needed into the future. In investments, I believe in real estate. You have your home, a cottage at the beach or lake, and other properties. Then maintain these properties, upgrading periodically to increase the value. Wasn't it Will Rodgers who said of land, "They're not making any more of it"?

TITHING

One area that should never be neglected is tithing. A positive, successful leader should always give first to God's plan. Somewhere along my career route, I began taking 10 percent or more off the top of my gross income each month in order to tithe to my church and other charitable organizations. This is my seventh book. The first three dealt with football coaching and player techniques. The sales from those three books helped finance our three daughters through college.

The next three books were about leadership—particularly my Attitude Technique philosophy (total person-total success concept). The proceeds from those books were disbursed to charity, in addition to my planned tithing, and in most cases to causes that benefited young people. Being a giver brings much happiness and satisfaction. Amazingly, being a giver also has its rewards. I always receive much more than I ever expect from sources of which I never dreamed.

PROSPERITY

Prosperity came to me in various forms and through many people, but I always realized God was the source of all. While financial security may help us feel at ease, however, peace of mind can be found only through a relationship with God. Ezekiel 34:29-30: "I will provide for them so they shall no more be consumed with hunger in the land—they shall know that I, the Lord their God, am with them."

As I write this section, we are in the midst of a volatile market. We have experienced the tragedy of September 11, 2001, and the corporate scandals of 2002—Enron, World-com, Global Crossing, and Arthur Anderson. The long war with terrorism, coupled with these scandals, affects how we respond and the adjustments we must make in future years. Therefore, making a positive plan must be a high priority.

During my early years as a young coach-teacher on the high school level, I struggled sometimes to make ends meet and to provide for my family. To compensate, I looked for other jobs during the off-season. Luck came my way when Ed Cassada, my former baseball manager, connected me with a part-time life insurance sales job. It was a blessing in many ways. I became a million-dollar salesman in six months and at the same time learned how to plan my finances for the future and set goals to become financially independent. This positive approach led me to read and study many books and programs on this subject.

7

SUGGESTED TITLES TO READ

Wealth and Poverty by George Gilder
The Power and Money Dynamics by Venita Vancaspel
Keep Your Wealth in the Family by Phillips Publishing, Inc.

How Much Am I Really Worth? By James P. Poole

The Prosperity Solution by Jonathan Parker

Building Financial Success by Paul Meyer's Success Motivation®
     International, Inc.

U.S. News and World Report—Money Management Library

Financial Genius by Mark Oliver Haroldsen

Free to Choose by Milton & Rose Friedman

The Complete Book of Personal Finance by Boardroom Classics

Personal Finance for Dummies by Eric Tyson

Charles Schwab's Guide to Financial Independence

The Millionaire Next Door by Tom Stanley and William Danko

Beyond your salary, commission fees, bonuses, etc., there are other ways to earn income for your family and special needs as long as they do not interfere with your position of leadership. They may even complement what you do. I recommend speaking engagements, clinic lectures, writing, TV-radio shows, and other related area. Do not overlook any possibilities.

Be certain to have a last will and testament, a letter of instructions, family budget, power of attorney, and all your investment and business transactions in a portfolio in the event of your incapacity to act or death. Seek the advice and help of a good friend who has a background in economics and law to assist with your planning. I was fortunate to meet such people who have helped me significantly through the years. Rick Worsham, a friend with an honors undergraduate degree from Georgia Tech in chemical engineering and a law degree from the University of Virginia, has helped me tremendously.

After being admitted to the State of Georgia Bar and receiving his CPA certificate, Rick co-founded an Atlanta firm. He became my personal financial advisor many years ago. With his advice and counseling, I reached my planned, written goal to become financially independent by a certain age. Rick has been a frequent guest at my Leadership Fitness class at Georgia Tech. His lectures and materials have helped many of my students to embark upon their careers in the real world on a positive note. Following his steps will also aid you in becoming financially successful.

Rick says that during 30 years of working with hundreds of clients in the area of personal financial planning, he has found six key principles that, if adhered to, will vastly improve your overall quality of life and specifically ensure financial security and comfort:

1. Never incur "bad" debt.
2. Never compromise your values for the sake of money or things.
3. Create and revise, as needed, a long-term money plan.
4. If married, remember that your goals must reflect the interests both of you and your spouse.
5. Spending habits are the key to reaching financial goals.
6. Money does not bring happiness.

Here he expands on that advice, giving valuable pointers to us all.

7

1. Never incur "bad" debt. I'm not saying that one should never borrow money or that all debt is bad. Good debt, such as that used to buy a home or to fund a small business, is generally available at lower interest rates than "so-called" bad debt, such as credit cards, and it is usually tax-deductible. If properly and smartly managed, "good debt" purchases should also increase in value. Borrowing to pay for educational expenses can also make sense. Education is generally a good long-term investment, which should increase one's earnings potential.

Bad debt, on the other hand, is usually incurred for consumption. Striving for the "good life" always has been an integral part of the American Dream. But in recent years our lust for material possessions has spiraled out of control. Corporations have convinced us that what once were luxuries—large homes, SUVs and wide-screen TVs, for example—are now necessities. In previous generations, we looked to our neighbors and those with similar incomes and lifestyle aspirations for cues as to where we stood in the social hierarchy. These days, we often look to new reference groups for cues—athletes, overpaid celebrities, top executives, and "regular folks" in our TV shows—whose incomes may be many times our own. Advertisers, retailers, and even the "Joneses" next door exploit this new consumerism. They promote the illusion that all of us should live like wealthy people. Hence, we are encouraged to incur "bad debt"—the exorbitant, non-mortgage debt on credit cards or debt for luxury automobiles.

Every time you buy something, you have a choice whether to pay for it now or to charge it. The ease of charging an item is tempting, and you can rack up big bills without blinking an eye. Responsible use allows you to finance a purchase when cash is temporarily unavailable. But effective use of credit cards means paying off debt each month. Otherwise, you'll be paying interest at very high rates, in effect adding a significant amount to the price of each item you buy.

The "Rule of 72," which can be used to determine the number of years it will take for your investment to double in value or your debt to double in size, is a good tool to illustrate this point. It works this way: divide the number 72 by the percentage rate you are paying on your debt or earning on your investment. Here is an example. You borrow $1,000 at an 18 percent credit card interest rate. Divide 72 by 18, and you get four. That means that in four years your debt will double to $2,000 if you do not have any principal reduction. Remember: 72 divided by the interest percentage equals the number of years the initial investment or debt takes to double. (You can also use 115 to determine how long the amount takes to triple.)

If you have a problem with credit cards, cut them up or put them away. If you have built up credit card debts, establish goals to pay them off as fast as possible. Think analytically regarding automobile purchases. If you must have a new car, take advantage of zero-percent financing. Otherwise, interest paid on the car loan results in raising the effective price of the automobile to much more than the original purchase price (on an asset that will incur considerable loss in value once you drive it off the dealer's lot). The purchase of a used vehicle (or keeping a new vehicle for a longer period of time) is financially prudent. Holding each car you buy for 10 years can result in savings of as much as $400,000 over your lifetime.

Good debt is debt incurred for the purchase of your home. Real estate investments should be part of your total investment portfolio. A sound formula for mortgage loans is that the total annual debt should be less than or equal to 38 percent of household income, and that home mortgage annual debt, plus property taxes and home insurance, should be less than or equal to 28 percent of income.

2. Never compromise your values for the sake of money or things. Despite overwhelming evidence to the contrary, most people still believe that money brings happiness, and some will do almost anything to attain more money, which allows them to get more things. To quote the Apostle Paul in his first letter to Timothy in the New Testament, "Godliness with contentment is great gain, ... but people who want to get rich fall into temptation and a trap and into many foolish and harmful desires that plunge people into ruin and destruction. For the love of money is the root of all kinds of evil. Some people, eager for money, have wandered from faith and pierced themselves with many griefs." (I Timothy 6:6-10) The happiness that money and things bring is short lived and fleeting. Additionally, compromised values have a huge range of effects—anything from feeling down (because a value system is innate to the human psyche) to criminal charges, if laws are broken to attain more dollars (consider all of the recent corporate scandals).

3. Create and revise, as needed, a long-term money plan. Make sure to take time to write your goals. A study done at a Yale University 20-year class reunion found that only three percent of the class had written goals. Interestingly, the combined net worth of those who had written goals was greater than that of the remaining 97 percent who didn't. Writing expenditures allows you to see how much money is spent on discretionary items, such as new clothes, new cars, unnecessary travel, or expensive and destructive habits such as smoking and drinking. If you cut spending on nonessentials and invest that money making eight percent, you can save surprising amounts. Saving $1.50 a day on junk food, alcohol, or tobacco from age 18 to age 67 results in an extra $290,373. Also, a written plan will allow you to see how much you are paying in credit card interest, if you do not pay off your credit cards on a monthly basis. Maintaining credit card debt is one of the most destructive and sure-fire ways to derail your monetary and personal goals. As you develop your financial plan, keep in mind that it's important to be realistic—unrealistic goals will lead to only frustration (remember the Rule of 72). You must recognize that your goals may change and that you'll need to review them regularly to keep your financial plan on course in the face of shifting economic, political, and personal winds.

4. If married, remember that your goals must reflect the interests of both you and your spouse. A written plan will allow you to identify the differences in attitudes between you and your spouse. Alignment of your goals with the goals of your spouse is a major key to personal success. For example, if one spouse wants to put extra money each month towards the purchase of a second home and the other towards funding the children's college education, tension will result. Plans and objectives must be discussed and agreements then reached for effective financial planning and goal attainment. Once you've set your goals, the next step in the personal financial planning process is to figure out how to accomplish these goals, given your income level and net worth. It's at this stage that most people can benefit from the help of a professional financial manager to develop financial strategies for the long term to meet their goals. But it's important to be aware of the pieces that make up any sound financial plan: cash flow analysis; savings; retirement plans and funding; investment strategy (with a rule of thumb being 100 minus your age as the percentage of your investment portfolio that should be invested in stocks); insurance (a rule of thumb is that a married couple should have life insurance coverage in the amount of 10 times the amount of annual income); and estate planning. A financial planner (CFP or CPA/PFS) is equipped to address each of these issues.

5. Spending habits are key to reaching financial goals. I mentioned this earlier when talking about credit cards and discretionary spending, but it is so important in achieving financial goals that it must be highlighted as a key principle. If you are currently in a position where your spending is out of control and/or debts are unmanageable, you need to seek counseling or attend Debtors Anonymous (www.debtorsanonymous.org), if necessary, to align your spending habits and your goals.

As part of the written plan, you need to analyze your cash flow. Find out how much you actually spend each month. It's easy to keep track of the large expenses such as mortgage, tuition, and insurance payments. On the other hand, the more variable items such as food, clothing, and entertainment cause the most surprises. If you are at a loss as to where your money is going, keep track of what you spend for several months or longer, if necessary. Personal budgeting software such as Quicken or Managing Your Money can make this process easier. Compare this cash-outflow figure with your monthly income. If you find that your cash in-flow matches or exceeds your out-flow, it's time to start living below your means. Determine which part of your spending is discretionary and start reining it in.

Living below your means is the only way to save for the future. Saving is one of those things that almost everyone thinks is a good idea but that few people actually commit to. You know the excuses—not enough income, too many bills, too many investing options, and on and on. An easy way to get started is to pay yourself first from each income check. Decide on a percentage of your income (10 percent is a good rule of thumb) to put into a savings account or into an employer-sponsored account. If you put money into a savings account, you can then move the money in larger chunks from the savings account into other investment options on a regular basis. The laws of compounding interest are truly amazing. Using the "Rule of 72" or "115," you can quickly calculate how fast your money will double or triple. Divide 72 or 115 by the expected annual rate of return to determine how many years it will take to double and triple your money. Another rule of thumb is that you should have three to six months worth of living expenses saved as a personal safety net for emergencies. If you are self-employed, you should set up a business contingency fund, as well as a personal savings net.

6. Money does not bring happiness. Of course, neither does poverty. But unmanageable debt can bring great pain! After working with hundreds of clients on money issues over the last thirty years, I've concluded that some of the unhappiest people are wealthy ones who have isolated themselves from friends and family in order to attain wealth. The role of money in happiness is somewhat mystical, in that the amount of money required for happiness differs greatly from person to person. The one constant fact I have learned is that money must be blended with the proper amount of family, friends, personal goals, charity, and spirituality to produce happiness. All must be present, but the amount and nature of the blend differs with each person.

Thanks to Rick Worsham for sharing this information that will benefit each of us!

7

LESSON EIGHT

THE GOALS PROGRAM

8

Throughout this book, my message has been *write it down*—there is magic in writing your thoughts. Doing so will help you to change negatives to positives, defeats to victories, and bad or wrong thoughts to good and wholesome thoughts.

We may struggle with our thoughts—doing the right or wrong thing—but it's a simple matter of choice. By controlling our thoughts, and with God's help, we can strengthen the good side by planting the right seeds within the human computer.

Remember: Your thoughts are being processed inside your human computer, and whatever is received will determine your actions and the type of person you will eventually become. Therefore, to succeed in any undertaking, it's imperative to set a goal, and that process must start with a written commitment clearly defined. Don't be concerned with minute details in the beginning—should changes be necessary, you can make them later. Just starting is the most important step. Follow the plan and you will receive whatever you are seeking, as long as it is realistic and within your capabilities. However, shoot for the top—do not settle for an easy goal that can be reached without a tremendous effort.

GOAL ORIENTED FOR GOOD THINGS IN LIFE!

Some people can picture what they want and go get it without writing their desires—they simply keep their mind's eye on the object and continually push toward their goal until it is completed. Unfortunately, most people are like me. If they want to reach a goal, they must systematically write it, read it aloud each day, and keep written score of their progress until the goal is reached. Written motivation forces us to persevere until we get there.

Regardless of which type you are, once the goal is reached you cannot rest and wallow in victory—you must set another goal to keep from sliding backward. Amazingly, only about five percent of our world's population attempts either approach. And sadly, some people use the technique for evil ends. Positive, worthwhile, ethical, and meaningful values of life must regain center stage for the good of all people. Since only about five percent are really trying to reach worthwhile goals, it's apparent that the field is wide open for anyone to step up and succeed. Ninety-five percent of people are not even attempting to become successful and fulfill a higher purpose in life to benefit others and themselves.

The seven steps in acquiring your goal are:
- Commitment
- Target Date
- Ingredients
- Giving
- Visualization
- Belief and Expectancy
- Positive Prayer

Goals can be categories for the short term, long term or any length of time. Once you have a goal clearly defined and written, it becomes your commitment. This does not mean that you cannot change the phrasing from time to time. But remember that once the goal is set, the action begins. This is your first step. Don't wait. The sooner you write your goal, the faster it will become a reality. Should you think or say, "I can't do this," you are probably right; your human computer picks up your thoughts and agrees with you. It will perform whatever action you give it. Be bold. Change that negative attitude to positive thoughts, and your human computer will perform as you have ordered.

After completing step one, set a deadline—a target date by which you intend to reach your goal. If the goal is to be accomplished in five, 10, or 20 years, that's a long-term goal. If it is something you want in a year or less, it is a short-term goal. I am often asked, "What do I do if the goal is not reached within the time period I set?" My reply is always the same: "Re-set the target date and move on." As you work through the seven-step process and look at your written goal on a daily basis, it may change as new and better ideas develop. Creatively will always come into play.

Once your commitment and target date are recorded, move to step three—ingredients: "What will it take to reach my goal?" Again, write the procedures. You may need to discuss your goal with others, or go to the library and research the subject or any procedures necessary to attain the goal. Remember to record these "ingredients" and look at them daily; then erase, add, or subtract necessary information that will lead you to the action. This step becomes a motivational force toward your commitment. Another friend and frequent speaker to the students of Leadership Fitness is Russ Chandler. His success in life stems from his strong commitment. In Appendix H, he explains the

8

philosophy that has sustained him.

Step four is giving—What are you willing to give in return for what you will receive? We must give before we receive. As I mentioned before, there are two classes of people—the "grabbers" and the "givers." Scientists have discovered that a person of generous spirit generally enjoys a longer life span than a person focused on "taking and grabbing." Helping others reach their goals will increase your capacity to have what you are seeking.

The fifth step is visualization. You must visualize your goal as being already completed. Mentally, you must have in your possession what you are seeking. Remember: Your human computer will accept whatever you imagine. It does not distinguish between what is real and what is imagined. It accepts what you think and feel; it allows information to pass from the conscious to the subconscious.

The builder visualizes the type of building he wants. He sees the structure as he desires it to be completed. His imagination and thought processes become a mold from which the building will emerge. His mental imagery is projected as it is drawn on paper. Eventually, the contractor and his workers gather the essential materials and the building progresses until finished, conforming perfectly to the mental patterns of the architect. A mental picture held in the mind, backed by faith, will come to pass.

Repeating an affirmation—knowing what you are saying and why you are saying it—leads the mind to that state of consciousness where it accepts the statement as truth.

This procedure will help you reach your goal because you can actually see it happening. Here's a wonderful story about never losing sight of your goal:

Florence Chadwick wanted to be the first woman ever to swim the English Channel. For years she trained to reach her goal, disciplining herself to keep going long after her body cried out for relief. Finally the big day arrived. She set after her goal, full of hope, surrounded by the press and well-wishers. Things went well, but as she neared the coast of England, a heavy fog settled in and the waters became increasingly cold and choppy. "Come on, Florence," her mother encouraged her from a nearby boat as she handed her food. "You can make it! It's only a few more miles!"

Then, not realizing she was within a few hundred yards of her goal, Chadwick became completely exhausted and asked to be pulled into the boat. She was defeated and heartbroken, especially when she discovered how close she had been to reaching her goal. She told reporters, "I'm not offering excuses, but I think I could have made it if I had been able to see my goal."

Later, like a true winner, she bounced back from her temporary failure and tried again. This time she concentrated on developing a mental image of the English coastline. She memorized every feature of the distant coast and held it clearly in mind. When the big day arrived, she again encountered the fog and the cold, choppy waters. This time, however, she reached her goal. She became the first woman in history to swim the English Channel. She accomplished what she had set out to do because she could visualize her goal. Even when she could not see anything, her goal was always in focus in her human computer.

8

The sixth step is belief and expectancy. If we do not truly believe and have absolute faith, our goal may not be reached. Our progress will stop right there, and we will be at a dead end. We must keep saying, "I believe, I believe," all the while keeping positive thoughts flowing into the human computer. By writing out positive thoughts or beliefs, we make our subconscious respond positively. Refuse to let negative thoughts of doubt enter the human computer. Change them, and you will become self-confident and the goal will be secured. Once a goal becomes a reality, you will then start expecting success time and time again. We can control our thoughts and, in turn, control our actions to acquire whatever it is we seek.

The seventh and last step is positive prayer, which constantly should be a major part of your thoughts. God allows us to seek and select whatever we want in life. If it benefits others, such as family, friends, or those in need, God will smile on the project and bless us. We should ask in prayer for God's guidance and blessings for what we are seeking. This should be a daily exercise. As we study the bible of God's lessons and teachings, we learn to find the strength to tackle any obstacle. I would even recommend that you write out your prayers. In this way, your written thoughts provide a path to follow. "You will succeed in all you do, and light will shine on your path." (Job 22-28)

More than 90 percent of your mental life is subconscious, so people who fail to control their subconscious minds also fail to control their lives. Your human computer is the builder of your body and maintains all of its vital functions. It is on the job twenty-four hours a day. It is always trying to help you and to protect you from harm.

The highest aspirations, inspirations, and visions for a nobler life spring from this inner power. Your most profound convictions are those you cannot argue about rationally because they do not come from the conscious mind. They come from the subconscious.

Your human computer speaks to you in impulses, hunches, urges, and ideas. It is always telling you to rise, grow, advance, seek adventure, and move forward to greater heights. Great artists, musicians, speakers, writers, and coaches tune in with their subconscious power, become animated, and experience inspiration. Mark Twain confided to the world on many occasions that he never worked in his life. All his humor and great writings were due to the fact that he tapped the inexhaustible reservoir of his subconscious mind.

The interaction of your conscious and subconscious minds requires a similar interplay between the corresponding systems of nerves. The cerebrospinal system is the organ of the subconscious mind. It is the channel. "As you sow, so shall you reap."

Now it is time to begin organizing your written goals. The following charts will aid you in this very significant and exciting undertaking. Make extra copies of these. Keep each goal in a notebook that you can work on daily. Spending just a few minutes each day will charge you positively and energize you for the day. Unbelievable results will occur. Just think—what you are beginning today will actually become your reality.

To enhance this process, follow a step-by-step approach. After writing on the goal sheet, make sure to read your goal aloud. This will connect the work you have done to your human computer. Behind each goal page is a worksheet that will aid you in making progress toward the finished project. You will undoubtedly encounter obstacles and roadblocks along the way. Note these encounters on the appropriate worksheet. This process will help you to understand clearly what problems (opportunities) exist. By understanding these, you can find a solution and turn the negative problem into a positive opportunity.

The written enlightens the clear path to a successful conclusion. Keep score on your daily actions, activities, and progress. And do not overlook noting the benefits you will enjoy. Your visualization and affirmations will sustain your high motivation.

8

MY SHORT-RANGE GOAL

1. I want _____

2. I want this goal fulfilled by _____

3. Necessary ingredients to obtain my goal:

_____
_____
_____
_____
_____
_____
_____

4. I will give in return:

_____
_____
_____
_____
_____
_____
_____

5. I can visualize myself:

_____
_____
_____
_____
_____
_____
_____

6. I believe and expect:

_____

_____

_____

_____

_____

_____

_____

_____

_____

7. My Positive Prayer today is:

_____

_____

_____

_____

_____

_____

_____

_____

_____

Read this Short-Range Goal aloud each day.

8

GOALS PLANNING FORM WORKSHEET

GOAL

TARGET DATE

OBSTACLES & ROADBLOCKS I MAY ENCOUNTER	SOLUTIONS TO OVERCOMING OBSTACLES	DATE I WILL TAKE ACTION	KEEPING SCORE ON MY ACTIVITIES

8

DATE AND PROGRESS MADE	BENEFITS I WILL ENJOY	VISUALIZATIONS	AFFIRMATIONS

8

MY LONG-RANGE GOAL

1. I want _____

2. I want this goal fulfilled by _____

3. Necessary ingredients to obtain my goal:

_____

_____

_____

_____

_____

_____

_____

4. I will give in return:

_____

_____

_____

_____

_____

_____

5. I can visualize myself:

_____

_____

_____

_____

_____

_____

6. I believe and expect:

_____

_____

_____

_____

_____

_____

_____

_____

7. My Positive Prayer today is:

_____

_____

_____

_____

_____

_____

_____

_____

8

Read this Long-Range Goal aloud each day.

GOALS PLANNING FORM WORKSHEET

GOAL _____

TARGET DATE _____

OBSTACLES & ROADBLOCKS I MAY ENCOUNTER	SOLUTIONS TO OVERCOMING OBSTACLES	DATE I WILL TAKE ACTION	KEEPING SCORE ON MY ACTIVITIES

8

DATE AND PROGRESS MADE	BENEFITS I WILL ENJOY	VISUALIZATIONS	AFFIRMATIONS

8

LESSON NINE

YOUR HIGH PURPOSE IN LIFE
AND KEEPING SCORE

We have talked about how to achieve short-term goals and long-term goals. Now let's talk about how to achieve the ultimate goal—finding our high purpose in life.

This may not be anything tangible. It may be something that can never be completely achieved but will bring peace of mind as we work on it for the rest of our lives. It may even be something that will carry on after your death. It's purpose—our purpose—is to make a difference in the world we live in.

Sound simple? Maybe, but it becomes complex because of circumstances we face each day. The first step is becoming a giver, not a grabber. (I recommend that you read and study Rick Warren's book, *The Purpose Driven Life ... What on Earth Am I Here For?*)

Your high purpose should be something that will influence others in a positive, wholesome way. My high purpose is sharing the Attitude Technique philosophy through the classes I teach, lectures, seminars, workshops, articles, manuscripts, coaching,

9

and administration as a positive leader. Amazingly, many people write to me about this philosophy that has helped them to become positive leaders. As successful leaders, they now share the program with others. In mathematics, we call this multiplying!

That positive feedback keeps me going. I am compelled to continue this work. In fact, I want it to continue forever. With my close friend Bud Parker, I am considering creation of a foundation that will continue educating people about the Attitude Technique Philosophy even after my death. I have seen the remarkable results. It is worth every ounce of effort to press onward.

After Lesson One, you were asked to rate yourself on the Keeping Score chart. Let's repeat the exercise. On that chart, you should now be able to change many of the liabilities (weaknesses) into assets (strengths). Make extra copies of the chart and repeat this exercise often. The process will help you grow into the positive leader you desire, day by day.

Once you have completed and updated the Keeping Score chart, begin to discern your ultimate goal using the My High Purpose form. Make extra copies so that you can alter and update it from time to time.

This course is your guide to becoming a successful, positive leader. It can be your personal blueprint for a life of success, happiness, maturity, and growth. You will become a leader who emphasizes trust over cynicism, generosity over selfishness, and making people light up rather than being turned off. As time passes, you will be able to rearrange and adjust this program to your ongoing circumstances. You will be able to control your destiny with a highly organized mind, self-motivation, goal planning, and, above all, your communication with God through positive prayer. The Attitude Technique is a survival kit packaged and ready for action.

This program is real. Your goals can be achieved. You will develop positive leadership. Both you and others will be the beneficiaries. Above all, you will be fit to lead.

9

KEEPING SCORE

Rate: Superior, Excellent, Good, Fair, or Poor.
Then Go Back and Write in Your Remarks.

Subject	Assets (Strengths)	Liabilities (Weaknesses)
Spiritual Values		
Family Relations		
How I Perceive Myself		
How I Think Others Perceive Me		
Social Life		
How I Get Along With Others		
Health Status		
Aerobic Fitness		

9

Subject	Assets (Strengths)	Liabilities (Weaknesses)
Relaxation		
Recreational		
Rest		
Mental Stimulation		
Self-Discipline		
Self-Motivation		
Self-Confidence		
Controlled Visualization		
Goal Setting		
Career		
Financial Planning		

9

MY HIGH PURPOSE

I have these unique talents and abilities that I can use to contribute something worthwhile to the world:

_____

_____

_____

_____

_____

_____

I will influence others:

1. To realize their full potential.
2. To set worthwhile and high goals in life.
3. To develop a positive mental attitude.
4. To practice the total person concept

This purpose is a great human need. I have found the answer to fill that need, and I will render a service to those who need it.

This high purpose will be good for my family and will give me personal satisfaction.

I will fulfill my commitment to this high purpose by accomplishing these goals:

_____

_____

_____

_____

9

MY ULTIMATE GOAL

1. I want _____

2. I want this goal fulfilled by _____

3. Necessary ingredients to obtain my goal:

_____
_____
_____
_____
_____
_____
_____

4. I will give in return:

_____
_____
_____
_____
_____
_____
_____

5. I can visualize myself:

_____
_____
_____
_____
_____
_____
_____

9

6. I believe and expect:

_____
_____
_____
_____
_____
_____
_____
_____
_____

7. My Positive Prayer today is:

_____
_____
_____
_____
_____
_____
_____
_____
_____

Read this Ultimate Goal aloud each day.

9

AFTERWORD

Great leaders are not born; they make their way. They may stumble at times, but they are able to adjust, start again, and continue until they develop a plan of action to lead. They may not be "perfect," but they will always strive toward positiveness by understanding and exercising the *right thing to do*!

Successful positive leaders have a vision, a mission, that can be explained clearly and concisely to their associates. They knit their group into a team, instilling trust in those who follow and forming a "family" that functions together. If we get the player right, the team will be right. The team does it!

At some time almost everyone has the opportunity or is put into a position to lead others. What a great challenge we have to emphasize the positive approach. This one word—*positive*—can make our group, our team, our country, and even the world a better place to live, work, and play.

From our class speakers and others, we have had the opportunity to listen and observe the characteristics that shape their positive leadership. Successful, positive leaders come from all walks of life. From the boating industry came Eddie Smith, owner of the Grady-White Boat Company in Greenville, North Carolina. In the late 1960s, I accepted a position as director of athletics at the University of North Carolina. One of my first assignments involved speaking to a UNC alumni group in Greenville. Eddie Smith, an alumnus of UNC, and his lovely wife, Jo, invited me to spend the night in their home. The next morning, Eddie drove me to an old building that was once a tobacco barn and explained that was the site where Grady-White boats were manufactured. As we drove along, Eddie explained that his desire to design a vehicle for customer comfort had prompted him to purchase the company. The customer came first!

Thirty years later, Eddie Smith was inducted into the Hall of Fame of the National Marine Manufacturers Association. His company is recognized and ranked highest in customer satisfaction by J.D. Powers and Associates. The Grady-White Boat Company became the most respected and admired boat company in the boating industry.

Eddie Smith succeeded to such a high level because he possesses the good qualities of a positive leader: integrity, dedication, and self-motivation. He is a true giver to others —to his "family of employees," but most of all to his customers. Regard for employees and especially for customers has led Eddie down the path of successful leadership.

~

During my early years as Director of Athletics at Georgia Tech, I met Bill Moore, founder and chairman of the board of Kelly-Moore Paint Company in San Carlos, California. Bill grew up the son of a barber in a small community in Arkansas. As a lad, he shined shoes at his father's barbershop to save money to attend college. His mother encouraged him to play tennis. The two activities paved the way to college when Georgia Tech offered him a partial scholarship. The scholarship was only a small portion of the cost, but Bill held down several other jobs to make it through the tough years following the Great Depression in our country.

In 1938, Bill graduated with a degree in Chemical and Industrial Engineering. He also led Georgia Tech to a Southeastern Conference tennis championship, never losing a match. After the All-American served in the Pacific Theater during World War II, he married his lovely wife Desiree and opened a paint company out of their garage. With Desiree at his side, he managed the privately-owned company that, in time, became the largest and most successful paint firm in the nation. His commitment to excellence and fairness paved the way for the company to be recognized throughout the United States. He was known as a man of high character in America's business community—a man of trust and integrity, and one who always did the right thing. His concern for the customer, his many innovations, continual growth and concern for excellence in every detail made his company flourish.

Bill Moore, a "giver," contributed the funds to build the Student Success Center at Georgia Institute of Technology, a facility dedicated to the students. In a talk to my class, he told the students, "May each find the foundation for a successful life: a positive balance of mind, body, and spirit."

In 1988, Bill purchased the Broken O Ranch in Augusta, Montana. At the time, the ranch consisted of almost 62,000 acres. By 1995, Bill Moore had grown the venture to 160,000 acres, making it the largest irrigated ranch in the state, comprising 200 square miles located in three counties.

As a frequent guest to fly fish the beautiful Sun River and Lowry Lake on that ranch's land, I became aware of another positive leader. Bill Moore hired Dan Freeman as president and general manager of the Broken O Ranch. I observed this man and his characteristics in developing the ranch to Moore's high expectations.

Being a leader of a vast area that contains thousands of cattle and buffalo and a farm division consisting of principle crops of wheat, malt barley, alfalfa, canola oil, and oats, required a man highly skilled and respected by the workmen. Knowledge and wisdom were also required to manage such an operation. Some days I traveled with Dan to get a firsthand view of the operation. It was immense—the cattle division, farm division, feed lot, cattle sale, harvesting, grain storage, irrigation systems, and crop rotation. Workers operated equipment from combines to bi-directional tractors, kept up with the many miles of fencing and, with the gravel on the premises, maintained 70 miles of roadway for connecting all of these operations.

A constant battle for water rights exists in Montana, where it is said that "whiskey is for drinking, water is for fighting." The seasons determine what work must be accomplished. Fall: shipping cattle, harvesting grain, draining the 69 pivots, and taking inventory of the crops scheduled. Winter: transporting grains to market, preparing equipment for spring, and the ongoing chore of feeding cattle and buffalo. Spring: calving, seeding crops, assembling pivots for irrigation. Summer: working crops, moving cattle to grassy fields and buffalo to fields with high fences, and developing a financial plan to turn a profit for the coming year.

Dan Freeman managed all of this. He also demonstrated the attributes of a positive leader with his family, workers, ranch hands, community, and church. Undoubtedly, he is a successful positive leader.

~

Whether on a ranch or at a major research university, just who is leading becomes quickly clear. Georgia Tech's President G. Wayne Clough is always a big hit with the class each year when he visits. His guidance of a major university is a real-life example to the students of what it takes to be a successful, positive leader. He set goals to guide Georgia Tech into the 21st Century as a world-class institution.

In his recent lecture to the class, he emphasized the importance of building a strong staff. The people on his teams measured up to the characteristics he looked for when assembling the teams. Those attributes include passion, diligence, expertise, loyalty, integrity, diversity, and optimism. It can be said that President Clough advanced Georgia Tech from the ranks of "good" to "great." His concern for long-run sustainability was evident. His expertise as a problem solver was clear, and he never failed to give credit to the team and its ability to achieve several goals—first, being proactive, reactive and decisive; second, being self-aware of strengths and weaknesses; and third, being complimentary to one another. A positive plan for the future, maintaining a team to carry out the goals set forth, and being proactive for change when change is needed—in addition to unbelievable fund raising ability—reflect his success and positive leadership.

GREAT SUCCESSFUL POSITIVE LEADERS OF

- Nations
- Militaries
- Corporations
- Teams
- Groups
- Religions
- Medicine
- Education
- Inventions

POSSESS CERTAIN QUALITIES AND SKILLS!

- Vision
- Tough decision-making abilities
- Communication, relating to others, being a good listener
- Surrounded by "positive" people who have been hired or appointed.
- Character, integrity, and respect

- High moral standards; a master of persuasion
- Self-motivation
- Effectiveness

After you leave or step down from a position, your positive results will be remembered!

~

Leadership fitness is the base of successful, positive leadership. Whatever field you are engaged in or about to enter will require study and skills to accomplish your goals. However, it is absolutely essential that you shape your life first.

In *Tech Topics*, Georgia Tech's news publication for alumni and friends, Maria M. Lameiras reported how Andrés Núñez followed the example of the Total Person program in creating his business:

> Andrés "Andy" E. Núñez, Jr., knows what it is like to work for a company that doesn't see its employees as key to its success. That is why Núñez, principal and co-founder of TEI Engineers & Planners, took a page from former Georgia Tech athletics director Homer Rice's playbook in running his own company.
> "Happy employees are more likely to stay. We invest a lot of time, effort and money into developing our employees and helping them to have a meaningful career," Núñez said. "We've pursued things that we would have liked some of our employers to do for us. Not to steal from Homer Rice, but we admire the companies who are doing that because it gives you a 'total person' experience."
> Núñez, who earned his bachelor's and master's degrees in civil engineering at Georgia Tech, founded TEI Engineers

& Planners in 1991. Since then, the company has won major awards, including TEI's designation as one of the "Top 100 Companies for Working Families" by the *Orlando Sentinel*.

TEI provides engineering consulting services including traffic engineering, transportation planning, traffic signal system design and implementation. It also specializes in roadway and highway design. The company has a strong community service component that Núñez said is largely directed by employees.

"We've set up a committee of employees who work independently and discuss the charities and activities they are interested in supporting, and we have usually gone with their recommendations," Núñez said. "We are not just dictating, 'Thou shalt do this or that.' We want them to be involved in what they are interested in. We are very active in those activities to show leadership—not just saying things, but doing them."

The company's Philanthropic Committee's mission is to make a positive difference in the lives of individuals and families by improving the environmental, economic, social, education and cultural prosperity of the communities in which they live and work. Those communities value the company's contributions, as evidenced by the many awards the firm has received.

TEI was named Central Florida's 2001 "Organization of the Year" in the large firm category and was ranked 15th among the nation's "Top 50 Best Engineering Firms to Work for" by *Civil Engineering News* magazine. The Seminole County/Lake Mary Regional Chamber of Commerce ranked the company, which has Florida offices in Lake Mary, Tampa, Tallahassee, Fort Lauderdale and Sarasota as well as in Atlanta, Georgia, among the

"Top 25 Companies in Seminole County."

"You have to be forward thinking to get something off the ground—starting with nothing and creating what we have today," Núñez said. "The awards we have won for excellence and employee satisfaction have validated that we must be doing something right."

~

As this manuscript was being prepared for publication late in December 2003, the Leadership Fitness Class at Georgia Tech completed the fall semester. Each member of the class completed the coursework and an individual term project in order to become part of this manuscript for *Leadership Fitness*. Their research, interviews of contributors to the book, notes from guest speakers, and suggested changes, additions, and phrasing enriched this text on its way to publication.

I encourage you to do as my students have done—change words or phrasing to fit the particulars to your situation. Do so until the plan reflects *your* thoughts and *your* principles. Working through this manuscript until it becomes your personal blueprint for your life will create results.

Through the study of leadership fitness, guest speakers, interviews, informational research to obtain facts, and other friends of mine, the class of 2003 had the opportunity to express their personal reflections. As the class members wrapped up their reflections on the speakers, content, and their personal plans for the future, Lauren Weatherly, my effective teaching assistant and a graduating senior, compiled highlights of the class members' findings.

"Each fall, Coach Homer Rice gives his time and effort to a Leadership Fitness class for Georgia Tech students," wrote Lauren. "The students work through the concepts in this book, become inspired by incredible speakers each week, dine together, and learn an unbelievable amount from Coach Rice and the other students in these intimate settings. The students gain appreciation for the leadership techniques of Coach Rice, the history of Georgia Tech, and the importance of giving back as Coach Rice has done. Members of the class offered to share the following lessons they learned from the course:"

I believe the material covered in this course is more valuable than any other course I will take as an undergraduate student at Georgia Tech. Developing and reinforcing leadership skills is invaluable to me. I will be able to use these skills through all aspects of life: in school, business, family, etc. The concepts taught in this class set a foundation for leading a successful life.
— Andrea Inguanti

The Leadership Fitness class that I participated in this fall has been one of the best experiences of my life. Through the use of Dr. Rice's soon-to-be-published book, Leadership Fitness, *I was able to learn more about leadership and living a positive life. I think the class has made me look more at the big picture for after graduation and the amazing possibilities I could be a part of after college.*
— Jeff Rosenfeld

In my third year of college, I am starting to feel that I am gaining more direction in what I would like to pursue in a career and how I am going to get there. I grew up in a Buddhist family, and one main principal of this faith is to live in the present moment. Having this class was a great opportunity to have time to reflect and set

goals in the midst of a busy college schedule. I feel that I am able to accomplish this more now than ever before, and I hope to continue to do so.
— Paul Supawanich

The content of this class was phenomenal. The information presented through the chapters of Leadership Fitness *was truly inspirational and motivational. It really helped to put my life in the right perspective. I always left class realizing that the little things that frustrate and bother me are not really important. What is important is people and being able to make a difference in the lives of others.*
— Jennifer Thornton

I can honestly say that this class was overwhelming. Typically when I say that about a class, I am talking about workload or overbearing professors. This class was a different type of overwhelming—the type where at times you feel an overabundance of joy. I cannot thank Coach Rice enough for his dedication to impressing upon our souls the qualities necessary to be a positive force in others' lives. I will take away more from this class than all of my previous courses combined.
— Ellen Neidlinger

I want to thank Coach Rice for sharing his experiences with me through the class. I viewed his class as "free inspiration" and would always come up with my best ideas directly following class. The class made me think and helped motivate me. This program gives a unique chance for undergraduates at Tech to think outside the box as they take a break from their vigorous

classes to think about more important items. This class provides the chance for students to ponder as well as to learn the importance of balance and leadership.
— Monique Gupta

I was extremely pleased with my experience in the Leadership Fitness class this fall. I always left the class excited and energized, and I definitely feel that I have grown as a leader and as a person by working through the notebook and interacting with such dynamic leaders. This class has been a fantastic experience, an opportunity to learn and explore ourselves under Coach Rice's guidance.
— Ben Lawder

This class has been the experience of a lifetime. I have thoroughly enjoyed getting to meet some of the most amazing Georgia Tech alumni that have graced the campus, as well as the amazing friends and colleagues of one of the most important figures in Georgia Tech history. I have been profoundly changed by this course. It gives me encouragement that when I sit down and plan and make the commitment to study Coach Rice's techniques, I'll be so much more focused, ready to take on the world, and happier because of it.
— Angela Dobson

The total person program has and will continue to be extremely beneficial during the remainder of my college years and beyond. At the beginning of the course, Coach Rice said that these lessons were the kind that you can take with you for life. Having gone through the program and used the book, I can definitely affirm this.

The content of the program was an excellent combination of important life skills and topics. This will be something that I take with me for years to come, and I hope to pass it along to others. I am a definite believer and proponent of the attitude technique and total person program. I have seen the effect that it has had on me in just three months, and I am so excited to see what the long-term results will be.
— Ryan McFerrin

Wow! What can I say about such an incredible class? Leadership Fitness is the one class that I have looked forward to every week. Throughout the course, I learned about setting goals, being a positive leader, the attitude technique, financial planning, encouraging and motivating others, and the list goes on and on. I cannot wait to go through my notebook and all other materials over the holidays and organize them so I can quickly reference all of the valuable information I have received over the past several months.
— Catherine Covington

There were so many beneficial aspects of this class, but there are three lessons that have had a particularly strong impact on me: the importance of planning and writing down life goals and objectives, the impact of a positive attitude, and the best ways to interact and lead others in a beneficial way. As a result of this class, I feel truly empowered to shape my future and achieve whatever I set out to do. Also, I recently had a friend compliment me on how positive I have been acting lately and how impressed she was by my upbeat attitude. It means a lot to me to see that other people are noticing

my outlook. In my positions on campus, I have been much more conscious of the type of leader that I am, and I really think that I have been a more effective and encouraging leader.
— Suzannah Gill

After taking Coach Rice's Leadership Fitness class last year and serving as his teaching assistant this year, I have witnessed the true impact of the Leadership Fitness techniques over time. When these techniques are followed, people can positively change their own lives and the lives of those around them. Coach Rice is a true friend of Georgia Tech, and through his efforts to spread the Leadership Fitness techniques, his gifts will continue to impact our society forever.
— Lauren Weatherly

I can think of no greater testament to the power of this program to change your life than what these students have written. I hope this has been, or will be, your experience too.

— Homer Rice, 2004

~

In 2009 I decided to get the Leadership Fitness classes together. I called on Lauren Weatherly McDow (as I had on numerous occasions) to help me with this undertaking. During Homecoming weekend we met for lunch at the Downtown Capital City Club for a fun luncheon. Georgia Tech president Bud Peterson and his wife, Val, joined us. I was so proud of this group. Each student had become positively successful with the help of the Leadership Fitness class. The 2009 luncheon was such a success that we met again in 2010, and we plan to continue our reunions each year.

The Leadership Fitness Class at Georgia Tech from fall semester 2003

APPENDIX A

LEADERS FOR FREEDOM:

THE SACRIFICES OTHERS MAKE FOR US

Thoughts by Monique Gupta

Monique Gupta, a member of the Leadership Fitness class, also expressed her thoughts about patriotism. When first asked about the subject, she did not know how to respond. She is proud to be an American citizen, but she had not given much thought to the fact. The right to live in America was something she appreciated but often took for granted, she said. Her parents had had the foresight to move from India to the United States to allow her to have freedoms not possible elsewhere. They voluntarily left their families and moved across oceans to provide the best for their children. They chose a magnificent nation, one filled with opportunities, hope, and freedom.

Freedom does not always come cheaply. The documentary "D-Day: Down to Earth" reminded her of the millions of people who sacrificed so that she could feel safe and experience independence. Because of other people, today she enjoys the freedom to voice her opinions, the freedom to gain an education, and the freedom to truly live. She is thankful for the independence that no others in the world share.

"The willingness of Americans to help others always amazes me," said Monique. Americans are willing to stand up to evil and at times to sacrifice themselves for a cause greater than the individual. It is because of this unselfishness that many people across the world enjoy some rights as simple as shelter and food. America's generosity has no borders and is experienced around the world.

"I wonder how I am as lucky as I am to have earned the good fortune of being an American. The answer is, of course, that I didn't earn it. America's soldiers, their heroes, earned this for me," she wrote. "I may never be able to repay America's heroes. However, I mean to live a good life and to never forget that I was given an opportunity that so many others have not been given. I will probably never be a soldier, never sleep in a trench, never be truly afraid or alone—all of the things that others have been. But I will remembers the ones who did those things for me."

APPENDIX B

LEADERSHIP DEVELOPMENT— THE ODK® WAY

By John D. Morgan
Executive Director of the Omicron Delta Kappa Society, Inc.

Omicron Delta Kappa was established in 1914 at Washington and Lee University in Lexington, Virginia. Beginning as a means to recognize leaders from all phases of the campus, including faculty and administrators as well as students, the organization provides an opportunity for these individuals to collaborate for the improvement of the campus and community. Begun at a men's college, it became fully coeducational in 1974. ODK® was the first collegiate honor society of a national scope to accord recognition and honor for meritorious leadership and service in extracurricular activities and to encourage the development of general campus citizenship. It has become abundantly clear that ODK® has proved to be beneficial to many colleges and universities. Growing to more than 285 chapters is testament to the value that colleges and universities have placed and are placing on the development of citizen leaders.

A number of college curriculums have stressed the study and the development of leaders for many years. In more recent years, the specific focus of a curriculum on leadership has occurred. One of the earliest and arguably the best examples of this attention to leadership was the establishment of the Jepson School of Leadership Studies at the University of Richmond. Other schools have followed with the opportunity to complete a major or minor in leadership studies.

Leadership itself is a worthy subject of study. As has been demonstrated with the proliferation of chapters of ODK®, student leadership is worth recognizing in a special way. How does Omicron Delta Kappa define "leadership"? Does ODK® attempt to describe a particular type of leader? The answer is "yes." Those chosen to become members of this society have exhibited leadership, not only by achieving positions of leadership but also, and importantly, by behaving as leaders. This special kind of leadership occurs as leaders collaborate with others—both other students from different parts of the campus as well as faculty—with the aim of continually working together to improve their campus and community. It has its roots in ethically sound character recognition and enhancement.

While not all are selected, the honor of becoming a member of this prestigious organization is a reflection of one's integrity and perspective. Members are students of honor as well as honor students. Perhaps one of the most integral parts of this kind of leadership development is the understanding that one can always learn more, grow more, and become more.

The Omicron Delta Kappa Society, Inc., *The National Leadership Honor Society* for college students, recognizes and encourages superior scholarship, leadership and exemplary character. Membership in Omicron Delta Kappa is a mark of highest distinction and honor.

APPENDIX C

SPIRITUAL IMPACT/GROWTH AND DIFFERENCE THAT THE FELLOWSHIP OF CHRISTIAN ATHLETES MAKES IN LIFE

By Dal Shealy
President, Fellowship of Christian Athletes

Dr. Billy Graham once said, "A coach will impact more people in one year than the average person will in an entire lifetime."

A major corporation did a study and found that 97 percent of all the people in the world are influenced in some manner by sports. In our sports-minded world today, athletes and coaches have greater influence (along with entertainers) than most parents and teachers. They are role models, good or bad, whether they realize it—or want to be—or not.

FCA was founded in 1954 to train, equip, and encourage Christian athletes and coaches to use their platform of sports as a vehicle to share their faith. In 1956, the first FCA Camp was held at the YMCA of the Rockies in Estes Park, Colorado, with 256 athletes and coaches attending. Dr. Louis Evans, Sr., (Chaplain of the U.S. Senate) was the chaplain for the week; Branch Rickey (General Manager, Pittsburgh Pirates) spoke about signing Jackie Robinson as the first black athlete in the modern era of major league baseball (1947 with the Brooklyn Dodgers).

Outstanding professional and college athletes and coaches were fed spiritually, mentally and physically for a week. Thus, FCA was launched full-speed with its mission: "To present to athletes and coaches, and all whom they influence, the challenge and adventure of receiving Jesus Christ as Savior and Lord, serving Him in their relationships and in the fellowships of the church."

Does FCA make a difference in life? Does FCA have a spiritual, physical and/or mental impact? Does it help growth in performance, inspiration or motivation, as it demonstrates a whole-life transformation through Christ in sports?

During 2003, we experienced too many tragic situations with high-profile coaches and athletes. Improper conduct, drinking, and fraternizing, murder of a player, attempted cover-ups, misuse of school credit cards, stealing, gaming, etc. So, how successful is FCA in making a difference on and off the field or arena of competition?

On nearly 10,000 campuses across the country, around 300,000 students are being led in Bible studies and small group discussions, learning how to live their lives for Christ. As a sports-based ministry, FCA is teaching them how to compete for an "audience of One."

Let's look at the reasons behind the success.

TEAM FCA: TEAM FCA is made up of athletes and coaches (and everyone they influence) who seek to compete for Christ. Beginning in the fall of 2003, competitors officially can become part of TEAM FCA by signing the Competitor's Creed:

THE COMPETITOR'S CREED

I am a Christian first and last.
I am created in the likeness of God Almighty to bring Him glory.
I am a member of Team Jesus Christ.
I wear the colors of the cross.

I am a Competitor now and forever.
I am made to strive, to strain, to stretch and to succeed in the
    arena of competition.
I am a Christian Competitor and as such, I face my challenger
    with the face of Christ.

I do not trust in myself.
I do not boast in my abilities or believe in my own strength.
I rely solely on the power of God.
I compete for the pleasure of my Heavenly Father, the honor of
    Christ and the reputation of the Holy Spirit.

My attitude on and off the field is above reproach—my conduct
    beyond criticism.
Whether I am preparing, practicing or playing;
I submit to God's authority and those He has put over me.
I respect my coaches, officials, teammates and competitors out
    of respect for the Lord.

My body is the temple of Jesus Christ.
I protect it from within and without.
Nothing enters my body that does not honor the Living God.
My sweat is an offering to my Master. My soreness is a sacrifice
    to my Savior.

I give my all—all of the time.

I do not give up. I do not give in. I do not give out.

I am the Lord's warrior—a competitor by conviction and a disciple
   of determination.

I am confident beyond reason because my confidence lies in Christ. `

The result of my efforts must result in His glory.

Let the competition begin.

Let the glory be God's

FCA seeks to develop competitors for Christ through leadership training with the values of Integrity, Serving, Teamwork
and Excellence:

Integrity. . . We will demonstrate Christ-like wholeness, privately
   and publicly.

Serving. . . We will model Jesus' example of serving.

Teamwork. . . We will express our unity in Christ.

Excellence. . . We will honor and glorify God in all we do.

Many times a person will read the sports page or a sport
magazine, but they will not read the Bible. They will go to an
athletic contest before they go to church. Our desired goal is to
produce and mentor athletes and coaches to join TEAM FCA
and live and play by The Competitor's Creed.

Christian coaches must understand that they may be the only
Bible their athletes read, and their game may be the only church
folks attend. Their influence in and outside the arena can and
will have a very positive impact on FCA's vision: "To see the
world impacted for Jesus Christ through the influence of athletes
and coaches."

FCA is broken down into the 4C's of ministry:

Coaches Ministry—At the heart of FCA are coaches. Our role is to minister to them by encouraging and equipping them to know and serve Christ. FCA ministers to coaches through Bible studies, staff contacts, prayer support, discipleship and mentoring, resources, outreach events, national and local conventions, conferences, and retreats.

Campus Ministries—The Campus Ministry is initiated and led by student-athletes and coaches on junior high, high school and college campuses. The programs of the Campus ministry include Huddles, Team Bible Studies, Chapel Program, Team FCA Membership, *One Way 2 Play—Drug Free!** and Special Events.

Camps Ministry—Camps are a time of "inspiration and perspiration" for athletes and coaches to reach their potential by offering comprehensive athletic, spiritual and leadership training. The types of Camps are Sports Camp, Leadership Camp, Coaches Camp, Youth Sports Camp and Partnership Camp.

Community Ministry—The non-school based FCA ministries reach the community through partnerships with the local churches, businesses, parents and volunteers. These ministries not only reach out to the community but also allow the community to invest in athletes and coaches. Community Ministries include Stewardship Ministries, Adult Ministries, Sport-Specific Ministries, Membership, Urban Initiatives, Global Sports Development, Clinics, Product and Resource Development, and Professional Athlete Ministries.

---

*The *One Way 2 Play—Drug Free!* Program is the only one of its kind. It is based on Faith, Commitment (signed card) and Accountability, where an individual meets with another person on a weekly basis to give account of his/her actions during the past week.

In a survey of the FCA OW2P! program, written by the George Gallup organization and executed by Public and Private Venture, the effort was found to be 81percent successful. The athletes and coaches who signed abstained from drugs, alcohol, steroids, and tobacco.

Another section of the survey asked the following question: Who or what influenced you to sign the OW2P! commitment card?

28 percent said that it was their coach.
22 percent said it was an FCA teammate.
19 percent said it was their belief in God.
12 percent said it was fear of becoming addicted.
10 percent said it was a speaker at a FCA event.
Only 7 percent said it was (a) parent(s).

Another way to look at it is that nearly 70 percent said it was either something with their relationship with the Lord and/or their sport—the two things that define FCA.

TEAM FCA members also are taught:
  • use of weapons and acts of violence are not the way to solve personal problems;
  • to promote healing of relationships and reconciliation among peers;
  • to honor all life, born and unborn; and
  • to treat each other with respect and dignity.

When athletes and coaches make a faith commitment to be all God created and gifted them to be, and to be a disciple (follower) of Jesus Christ, they strive to take out of their lives the things that cause them to stumble and fall. Many of those who are failing get noticed publicity and give the 95 percent who are striving to be their best a difficult task in the public eye.

APPENDIX D

NUTRITION

By Chris Rosenbloom, Ph.D., R.D.
Associate Dean, College of Health and Human Sciences
Associate Professor, Department of Nutrition
Georgia State University, Atlanta, Georgia

The Atlanta Journal-Constitution publishes a column called "The Vent," where people write or call the paper and "vent." My favorite vent was, "If you are what you eat, then I'm fast, cheap, and easy." Too many Americans fall into the fast, cheap, and easy category. In fact, most Americans probably give more thought to choosing gas for their cars or food for their pets than they do for themselves.

What does nutrition have to do with leadership? As you read the pages of this book, you learned that leaders need to attend to their physical, mental, and spiritual well-being. Good nutrition is a big part of physical and mental well-being. Without proper fuel, in the form of food and fluids, the brain is not as effective or efficient and the body will lack energy. People are always saying they need more energy; the best way to get more energy is to start with your food habits.

My five tips for a healthy body are:

1. Eat breakfast every day. Breakfast does what it says—it breaks the fast. People who eat breakfast get more nutrients during the day than breakfast skippers. Breakfast eaters have more energy to get through their morning activities and are less hungry when lunchtime rolls around. And, for those of you still in school, breakfast eaters score better on exams. Breakfast supplies your body with needed glucose and your brain prefers glucose as a fuel. What is a "good" breakfast?

Any combination of whole grain carbohydrates and protein makes a healthy breakfast. Some examples are:

- Pumpernickel bagel with peanut butter

- Whole grain toast with a slice of cheddar cheese

- High fiber breakfast cereal with low fat milk

- Fruit-flavored yogurt topped with chopped nuts

- Scrambled egg rolled in a whole-wheat tortilla

2. Choose a colorful diet. Nature provided foods with a rainbow of colors for a reason. The colorful pigments in foods help protect foods against diseases, and when we eat plants we are afforded some of that protection. Choose a diet with a wide variety of colors, as these foods have been shown to be protective against the two most prevalent diseases of Americans: heart disease and cancer. When choosing foods, go for the most colorful ones you can find. For example:

• Select pink grapefruit.

• Toss blueberries on your cereal.

• Snack on frozen red grapes.

• Bake a sweet potato instead of a white potato.

• Make trail mix with whole-grain cereal and dried cranberries.

• Eat dried apricots and peaches instead of cookies after a meal.

• Sprinkle low-fat frozen yogurt with fresh or frozen raspberries.

• Choose dark green leafy salad greens over iceberg lettuce.

• Top your salad with bell peppers, cucumber slices, and tomatoes.

• Try spinach, mushrooms, and green peppers on pizza.

3. Be savvy about healthful fats. Fats are an important part of the diet, but not all fats are created equal. Solid fats, such as butter, stick margarine, hydrogenated fats, and animal fats found in whole milk, cream, cheese, and meat, are high in saturated fat and can raise blood cholesterol levels. Softer or liquid fats are better choices. The best choices are olive oil, canola oil, safflower oil, or soft-tub margarines. All fats have the same amount of calories, even though their effects on blood cholesterol differ, so even the "good" fats should be kept to moderate portions. Suggestions for eating more healthy fats are:

- Read labels to uncover hidden hydrogenated fats.

- Use olive oil and flavored vinegar to toss your salad.

- Switch to light or non-fat versions of cream cheese, mayonnaise, and sour cream.

- Learn to enjoy grilled, baked, or broiled meats instead of fried meats.

- Say no to fried appetizers like mozzarella sticks, jalapeno peppers, and fried vegetables.

- Sautee vegetables in olive oil and add to cooked pasta.

- Put a slice of avocado on your sandwich instead of a high fat spread like mayonnaise.

4. Eat whole grains, fruits, and vegetables for quality carbohydrates. People perceive that carbohydrates are "bad" and protein is "good." The truth is that both nutrients are important for good health and to fuel an active lifestyle. Make the switch to quality carbohydrates—those carbohydrate-rich foods that provide fibers, vitamins, and minerals. Whole-grain breads, cereals, pasta, rice, fresh or frozen vegetables and whole fruits all contain quality carbs.

- Choose breads that contain whole-wheat flour as the first ingredient.

- Don't be fooled by the word "wheat" bread—only whole wheat has fiber.

- Try brown rice instead of white rice.

- Choose whole grain pastas over refined white pasta.

- Select whole fruit more often than fruit juice.

- Pick fresh fruits in season; when out of season, try frozen fruit without added sugar.

- Check out the wide variety of washed and sliced fresh vegetables and fruits in the grocery store produce section.

- Pumpernickel bagels are a good alternative to wheat bagels.

5. Work activity into your life to prevent weight creep. Growing old and gaining weight don't have to go hand-in-hand, but you have to work hard to prevent it. People who are active not only keep their weight in check, but they decrease their risk for high blood pressure, heart disease, colon cancer, and osteoporosis. Active people have positive mental outlooks and suffer form less depression than sedentary people. As we age, we lose muscle and gain fat. Try to work as much activity into your daily life as possible to help avoid weight creep.

- Start a weight-training program to preserve muscle mass – use free weights or weight machines to keep and build muscle.

- Run with your dog; play touch football with your kids, or go for family bicycle rides.

- Walk around the block after dinner instead of watching television.

- When shopping, make frequent trips to your car with pac ages and walk around the mall a few times before making your first purchase.

- Use the "five and ten" rule for stairs—walk up if it is five flights or fewer and walk down if it is 10 flights of stairs or fewer.

- Buy a pedometer and measure your steps—aim for 10,000 steps a day

By making these small changes in your diet, you can have more energy, reduce your risk or chronic disease and avoid weight gain. And remember: It's never too late to start!

APPENDIX E

THE CASE FOR NUTRITIONAL SUPPLEMENTATION

By J. Alexander Bralley, Ph.D.
CEO—Metametrix Clinical Laboratory

For many years, nutrition scientists have said that Americans can get all their nutritional needs from eating a good diet. Supplementation of vitamins and minerals was not necessary and simply created "expensive urine." More recently, this conventional wisdom is being challenged as evidence accumulates on the benefits of supplementation.

It is really quite difficult, as it turns out, for people to eat a healthy diet with the use of fast foods and/or the highly processed foods common in the standard American diet. It is very easy to eat a lot of calories but these calories are, more often than not, empty calories—high in fat and carbohydrates but very low in essential nutrients like vitamins and minerals.

In an article published in the prestigious *New England Journal of Medicine* in 2001, Dr Walter Willett, chairman of the Nutrition and Epidemiology Department at Harvard's School of Public Health, argued that individuals need to start taking supplemental nutrients to help maintain optimal wellness. He also pointed out that the risk of chronic disease was significantly decreased in those who did. [1] This groundbreaking article set the stage for greater understanding and general acceptance of the great health value that regular supplementation can provide. In the same light, Dr. Bruce Ames, noted cancer researcher at UC Berkeley, has published several articles indicating vitamin, mineral and anti-oxidant supplementation can decrease cancer risk and slow aging of the brain. [2, 3]

What do essential nutrients do? Why are they so vital to the maintenance of good health and prevention of disease? Vitamins and minerals are called essential nutrients because the body cannot make them. They must, therefore, be consumed in the diet. So if one is eating a junk-food diet with low nutrient content or if one has increased demands for certain nutrients, it is relatively easy to develop nutrient deficiencies which can adversely affect health.

Vitamins are also called coenzymes and minerals are called cofactors. They function in the body to assist in the conversion of one compound into another. Special proteins called enzymes perform this task. All the functions of the human body boil down to the ability of these enzymes to work properly. If a cofactor or coenzyme is not present in the appropriate amounts, the enzyme does not work as it should and a dysfunction can occur. About 22 percent of all enzymes in the body require a coenzyme or vitamin to work properly. Many enzymes also require mineral cofactors to work. More than 300 enzymes, for example, use zinc, yet the body needs only about 10 mg. per day of zinc before a deficiency develops.

While the classic deficiency diseases such as pellagra, beri beri, rickets, etc., rarely exist in developed countries like the U.S., the work of researchers like Drs. Willett and Ames is showing the health benefits of essential nutrient adequacy. I refer to this situation as avoiding the development of nutrient deficiencies. That is, one may not be so deficient in a nutrient to cause a classic deficiency disease, but one still might be in a situation where enough of the nutrient is not present to adequately allow the enzyme to function optimally. Dr. Ames recently published a paper illustrating this point using genetic diseases as a model of how nutrients can prevent disease. [4] In this paper he points out that many disease processes may benefit from nutrient supplementation in higher doses than the RDA amounts, particularly the anti-oxidants such as vitamin E, C and lipoic acid.

So if you eat the standard American diet, are over or under weight, under stress, are still growing, pregnant, nursing, sick or have been sick recently, participate in sports, don't get enough sleep, smoke, or any of the above, you would do well to be taking at least a good quality vitamin and mineral formula with additional anti-oxidants. Everyone is different, and what may be adequate for one person may not be sufficient for another. This situation can be caused by either the unique genetics of the person or increased needs for a particular nutrient.

A more recent trend has been to actually test a person for unique nutritional needs. Metametrix has had 20 years of experience in this area. Laboratory testing at Metametrix allows one to design custom nutrient formulations for all types of people, ranging from those with chronic illnesses to high-performance, professional athletes. It has always been interesting for me to see the diversity of nutrient needs in the population. Children in particular are in need for supplementing their diets, which in most cases, in my experience, are of exceedingly poor quality. Good nutrition at this age is important for several reasons. Chronic illnesses of aging really begin when we are young. Prevention pays off early. Also, I feel the dramatic increase in behavioral disorders in children is due to poor nutrition that dramatically affects brain function.

The bottom line is this: Do you and your family a favor and

invest in a quality nutritional supplement program for a happy
and healthy future.

SOURCES:

1. Willett, W.C. and M.J. Stampfer, *Clinical practice. What vitamins should I be taking, doctor?* N Engl J Med, 2001. 345(25): p. 1819-24.

2. Ames, B.N. and P. Wakimoto, *Are vitamin and mineral deficiencies a major cancer risk?* Nat Rev Cancer, 2002. 2(9): p. 694-704.

3. Liu, J., et al., *Delaying brain mitochondrial decay and aging with mitochondrial antioxidants and metabolites.* Ann N Y Acad Sci, 2002. 959: p. 133-66.

4. Ames, B.N., I. Elson-Schwab, and E.A. Silver, *High-dose vitamin therapy stimulates variant enzymes with decreased coenzyme binding affinity (increased K(m)): relevance to genetic disease and polymorphisms.* Am J Clin Nutr, 2002. 75(4): p. 616-58.

APPENDIX F

HOW TO BE A SURVIVOR: GUIDELINES ON LIVING WELL TO AGE 100

By John D. Cantwell, M.D.
Cardiology of Georgia, P.C. Medical Director of the
Homer Rice Medical Clinic, Georgia Tech

Let's begin with the opposite approach. If you wish to shorten your life, or to make your so-called "golden years" more miserable, there are several things you can do. Heading the list is to smoke cigarettes. This can make you a prime candidate for an early heart attack, often fatal. It can appreciably increase your risk of lung cancer, and multiple other types of cancers (mouth, esophagus, stomach, pancreas, uterine, cervix, colon, bladder, and kidney). Cigarettes are also a major cause of chronic disabling lung diseases such as emphysema.

Eating too much and exercising too little leads to diseases such as obesity and diabetes, both in epidemic proportions. These disorders can accelerate cardiovascular disease and contribute to kidney failure, heart failure, blindness, and loss of an extremity.

Don't pay any attention to your blood pressure level, and eat all the salt and fast foods you desire. This can increase your chance of developing a stroke, with the disability that so frequently accompanies it. Over the years uncontrolled hypertension can also damage the kidneys and lead to heart attacks and heart failure.

The same applies to ignoring your blood cholesterol level. This easily treated disorder, if elevated, can facilitate the premature onset of coronary heart disease, peripheral vascular disease, and strokes.

Binge alcohol drinking is another good way to shorten your life, especially if coupled with reckless driving, preferably without a seat belt. Heavy alcohol use (a steady dose of more than two standard-sized drinks daily) can over a period of years damage the liver and the heart muscle. It can also contribute to interpersonal woes and marital discord.

A disregard for feelings of depression can add to the misery of life by creating an "inability to experience pleasure" and can be a risk factor for suicide, the third leading cause of death in young people.

ASSESSING YOUR HEALTH STATUS

As Henry David Thoreau once wrote, "Every man is the building of a temple, called his body.... We are all sculptors and painters, and our material is our own flesh and blood and bones."

What kind of temple are you building? Let's take an inventory of your health status by answering the following 10 questions:

1. Using Figure 1 (on page 197), calculate your body mass index (BMI), based on your height and weight. Your BMI is _____, placing you in the

           normal   overweight   obese

           (circle one) category.

2. List the average number of aerobic-exercise minutes you get each day.

_____ None
_____ 5-10
_____ 10-30
_____30-60
_____over 60

3. Do you smoke? _____ Yes _____ No If yes, _____ packs per day.

4. Get a blood test to learn your total cholesterol _____ and your HDL cholesterol _____ levels.

5. Measure your waist circumference (_____ inches).

6. Fill out the depression questionnaire (Figure 2, on page 198).

7. List your average weekly alcohol intake:
_____beers _____1½ oz. hard liquor _____4oz. glasses of wine

8. Check your own blood pressure at a drug store, grocery store, or fire station: _____ mmHg.

9. Indicate if you almost always wear seatbelts in a car:
_____ Yes _____ No

10. Review your family history.
Any men with heart attacks before age 55?
_____ Yes _____ No
Any women with heart attacks before age 65?
_____ Yes _____ No

Any sudden, unexplained deaths?
_____ Yes _____ No
Any relatives with depression?
_____ Yes _____ No

PUTTING PREVENTIVE MEDICINE INTO PRACTICE

The foundation of a good preventive medicine program is daily exercise and a sound diet. Current guidelines recommend 30-60 minutes of endurance exercise most days (brisk walking, jogging, cycling, rowing, swimming, aerobics, etc.). Weight training at least three times a week is advised, along with regular stretching exercises. Men over age 40 or women 50 or above with certain coronary risk factors (hypertension, elevated cholesterol level, prior cigarettes, family history of heart attacks) should consider an exercise test before beginning a program more strenuous than just walking.

A Mediterranean-type diet seems prudent, emphasizing fish, vegetables, fruit, nuts, and lean meat, reducing the dietary calories enough to achieve a normal body mass index. The Ornish and Pritikin diets work for a few but are too rigid for most. The Atkins diet and other low-carbohydrate programs are somewhat controversial and don't seem the answer to long-term weight management.

Alcohol can be used in moderation—no more than two standard-sized drinks per day for men and one for women (who don't metabolize alcohol as well as men). Those with a family history of alcoholism, or with inability to moderate their own alcohol intake, had best abstain. Red wine is hyped in the media, but most studies suggest equal health benefits from beer, wine, or hard liquor.

The ideal blood pressure is less than or equal to 120/80 mmHg.

Those with readings between 120-139/80-89 are now considered to be "pre-hypertensive". A diagnosis of hypertension is made when readings average 140/90 or above.

Non-drug ways to control blood pressure include exercise, weight loss if overweight, reductions in dietary salt and stress, and increases in dietary potassium. When the blood pressure remains above 140/90 mmHg despite therapeutic lifestyle changes, a variety of very effective medications are now available. For young, athletic people with hypertension, I generally start with a drug that blocks the angiotensin-converting enzyme (ACE), leading to muscle relaxation and dilation in the arteries. Angiotensin-receptor blockers (ARBs) work in a similar fashion. For others, I'll use a low dose of a diuretic, a beta-blocker drug (that reduces the adrenaline effect in the arteries) or, infrequently, several medicines are combined to achieve a normal blood pressure.

Patients with hypertension are encouraged to monitor their own blood pressure, using a simple digital home blood pressure monitor, and to record the results on graph paper.

When the blood LDL (low-density lipoprotein) cholesterol level exceeds 100 mg/dl, dietary cholesterol should be decreased to less than 300 mg daily, and saturated fat to less than 10 grams daily. Take Control and Benecol can be used in place of butter or margarine, as they help reduce cholesterol absorption from the intestine.

For those with LDL cholesterol levels still above 160 mg/dl, despite dietary efforts, effective drugs are available to achieve the desired goal. So-called "statin" drugs (like Lipitor, Zocor, Pravachol, etc.) can be tried in tiny doses, like 5 to 10mg, three times a week. Those drugs block an enzyme in the liver that is involved in the manufacture of cholesterol. Other effective drugs include fibrates (Tricor, Lopid) and the B vitamin, niacin.

TWENTY-FIVE GUIDELINES
ON LIVING WELL TO AGE 100

1. Keep the body mass index well below 25 by eating less and exercising more.

2. Try to do at least 30-60 minutes of endurance exercise (fast walking, jogging, cycling, swimming, aerobics, etc.) most days.

3. Stay mentally active. Keep busy. Learn new things.

4. Avoid hardening of the arteries (atherosclerosis). Keep the total cholesterol under 200 mg/dl, ideally under 180 mg/dl. Strive for a HDL level well above 40 mg/dl, a triglyceride level below 150 mg/dl, an LDL cholesterol level at least under 100 mg/dl and preferably below 80 mg/dl.

5. Take a buffered 81 mg aspirin table at least every other day, beginning at age 25. Also take a multivitamin that contains at least 400 mcg of folic acid.

6. Women should get regular Pap smears beginning at age 30, and yearly mammograms starting at age 40.

7. Prostate cancer screening, with the PSA blood test, should be done at ages 40, 44, 48, and then yearly beginning at age 50.

8. A colonoscopy test to screen for pre-cancerous polyps is advised at least every 10 years for men and women, starting at age 50. Those with polyps may need more frequent follow-up exams.

9. Do bone density tests to screen for osteoporosis, every 10 years beginning at age 60, for men and women.

10. Preserve your hearing by avoiding exposure to loud noises (above 75 decibels).

11. Live close to your children and grandchildren in later years, if possible.

12. Don't smoke, and avoid oral tobacco and second-hand smoke.

13. Avoid trans fatty acids (in fast foods and a lot of baked goods). Read labels on food to assess trans fat and saturated fat content.

14. Wear seat belts in motor vehicles. Drive defensively. Don't drink alcohol and drive.

15. Limit daily alcohol to an average of less than or equal to two standard-sized drinks for men, one for women. Go some days without any. If you have a family history of alcoholism, or have difficulty using alcohol in moderation, avoid it completely.

16. Get regular check ups, especially when you reach age 35, to include at least a brief office visit, rectal exam, stool test for occult blood, and blood cholesterol and HDL measurement.

17. Get adequate sleep.

18. Have your home checked for radon and asbestos.

19. Avoid small airplanes whenever possible.

20. Minimize sun exposure. Use sunscreen and wear hats.

21. Avoid anxiety-producing situations as much as you can. If prone to depression, get medical help early and take suicide precautions.

22. Know your blood fat, blood sugar, and blood pressure numbers. Strive for a blood pressure at least under 130/80 mmHg (under 120/80 mmHg is ideal) and a blood sugar below 110 mg/dl.

23. Try to drink up to eight glasses of water daily.

24. Simplify your life. It is a curious paradox that "finding a way to live the simple life is one of today's most complicated problems."

25. Develop a spiritual base. Do things for others and focus less on your own wants.

REFERENCES

1. Perls, T.T. and Silver, M.H. *Living to 100*. Basic Books, New York, 1999.

2. Yahn, G. "The Impact of Holistic Medicine, Medical Groups and Health Concepts," *JAMA* 1979; 242: 2202-2205.

Figure 1: Body Mass Index (BMI chart).
Figure 2: Zung Self-Rating Depression Scale.

FIGURE 1
WEIGHT YOUR RISK WITH BMI

How to use this chart:

1. Look down the left column to find your height.
2. Look across that row and find the weight nearest your own.
3. Look to the number at the top of the column to identify your BMI.
4. If your number is 27 or greater, you may be at risk.

BODY MASS INDEX CHART

Body Weight (pounds)

Height (inches)	19	20	21	22	23	24	25	26	27	28	29	30	31	32	33	34	35
58	91	96	100	105	110	115	119	124	129	134	138	143	148	153	158	162	167
59	94	99	104	109	114	119	124	128	133	138	143	148	153	158	163	168	173
60	97	102	107	112	118	123	128	133	138	143	148	153	158	163	168	174	179
61	100	106	111	116	122	127	132	137	143	148	153	158	164	169	174	180	185
62	104	109	115	120	126	131	136	142	147	153	158	164	169	175	180	186	191
63	107	113	118	124	130	135	141	146	152	158	163	169	175	180	186	191	197
64	110	116	122	128	134	140	145	151	157	163	169	174	180	186	192	197	204
65	114	120	126	132	138	144	150	156	162	168	174	180	186	192	198	204	210
66	118	124	130	136	142	148	155	161	167	173	179	186	192	198	204	210	216
67	121	127	134	140	146	153	159	166	172	178	185	191	198	204	211	217	223
68	125	131	138	144	151	158	164	171	177	184	190	197	203	210	216	223	230
69	128	135	142	149	155	162	169	176	182	189	196	203	209	216	223	230	236
70	132	139	146	153	160	167	174	181	188	195	202	209	216	222	229	236	243
71	136	143	150	157	165	172	179	186	193	200	208	215	222	229	236	243	250
72	140	147	154	162	169	177	184	191	199	206	213	221	228	235	242	250	258
73	144	151	159	166	174	182	189	197	204	212	219	227	235	242	250	257	265
74	148	155	163	171	179	186	194	202	210	218	225	233	241	249	256	264	272
75	152	160	168	176	184	192	200	208	216	224	232	240	248	256	264	272	279
76	156	164	172	180	189	197	205	213	221	230	238	246	254	263	271	279	287

Source: National Heart, Lung, and Blood Institute.

MEASURING BODY MASS

The new body mass index (BMI) applies to both men and women. To determine BMI, weight in kilograms is divided by height in meters, squared. To calculate your body mass index from the table on page 197, locate your height in inches in the left-hand column, then follow it across until you locate your weight; the number at the very top is your body mass index. A BMI of 25 to 29.9 is considered overweight and one of 30 or above is considered obese.

FIGURE 2
ARE YOU DEPRESSED?

Answer the questions below to find out your potential for depression.

	Yes	No
1. I feel downhearted, blue, and sad.	___	___
2. I don't enjoy the things that I used to.	___	___
3. I feel others would be better off if I were dead.	___	___
4. I feel that I am not useful or needed.	___	___
5. I notice that I am losing weight.	___	___
6. I have trouble sleeping through the night.	___	___
7. I am restless and can't keep still.	___	___
8. My mind isn't as clear as it used to be.	___	___
9. I get tired for no reason.	___	___
10. I feel hopeless about the future.	___	___

If you answered "Yes" to at least five questions, and you answered "Yes" to Question 1 or Question 2, and these symptoms have persisted for at least two weeks, you may be suffering from serious depression. To find out more about how depression may be affecting you, get in touch with a mental health professional or your family physician.

If you answered "Yes" to Question 3—regardless of how you answered the other questions—you should seek help immediately.

If you suspect a loved one is depressed, give this questionnaire to him or her.

Adapted from the Zung Self-Rating Depression Scale© (William W.K. Zung, 1965, 1974, all rights reserved).

APPENDIX G

50 STEPS TO POSITIVE LEADERSHIP

By Hank McCamish
McCamish Group, Inc.

1. Write Your Story
Write, in a paragraph or two, the story of the future you desire. Write what you'll be doing, where you'll be living, and the successes you'll be enjoying. This will be a motivator for you in both the immediate present and the future.

2. Visualize Into the Future
Close your eyes and see yourself doing whatever it is that you wish to be doing. If you want to get in shape, picture a slim, healthy you running or working out. If your dream is to start a small business, see yourself on opening day, greeting customers and employees.

3. Visualize Backwards
When you visualize backwards, you see where you were and how far you have come. If your goal was to get organized and you have made enormous improvement in that area, visualize back to when things weren't going so well. This will keep you heading in the right direction.

4. Dream Big

When you think about your future, don't be afraid to dream big. This will make short-term failures easier to handle. When you hit an obstacle, it won't stop you because your eyes are set on a bigger goal.

5. Educate Yourself

Learn, read, talk about, listen, and experience everything you can about your particular goal or dream. If you wish to be an author, you can take classes, read books, write, talk with other writers, join workshops, etc.

6. Get Organized

A clean, tidy, and well-organized home, office, and life is a must for the motivated mind. Physical clutter can easily lead to mental clutter. Keep your life organized, and you will find more energy and clarity in every day.

7. Place Motivators in Your Home and Office

Place symbols, signs, notes, or objects that remind you of your goals and dreams in your home, office, car, wallet, and write them into your planner or calendar. These reminders will guarantee a constant stream of motivation.

8. Volunteer

Volunteer your time to helping others. When you give of yourself, you will realize how much you have in your own life and how satisfying it is to make others happy.

9. Help Others with Motivation

Only when you teach others do you fully understand the subject at hand. Help your children to get motivated, help your friends to set effective goals, help your husband or wife to achieve personal dreams.

10. Spend Time with Children

Spending time with children will put things in perspective for you. You may be stressed out from work and worried about getting everything done on time, but when you play with your kids, the worries and stress seem to melt away. Children have a simple way of looking at things, and that is something we could all benefit from.

11. Create a Buddy System

Do you have a close friend who is trying to accomplish something? Is your wife or husband setting goals for improvement? If so, join in a buddy system. You will each serve to motivate the other, offering words of encouragement and helpful reminders as you both progress towards your particular goals.

12. Find A Role Model

Choose a role model to learn from. You won't have to reinvent the wheel when you can follow an exemplary person you respect.

13. Take a Walk or Drive

Take a walk around the block or a short drive through the neighborhood to relax, reflect, and enjoy some quiet time. We all need a break now and then, and a quick walk or drive is the perfect solution.

14. Read Success Stories

Read the success stories of those around you. In the daily newspaper alone there are dozens of small success stories that can motivate and inspire you to action. The library is filled with autobiographies and biographies of ordinary men and women who have done extraordinary things.

15. Listen to Music

Music can calm, excite, sadden, and even motivate. Listening to the "Rocky" theme song while running is a great way to use music as a motivator. What's your motivating song?

16. Watch Motivating Movies

One reason people enjoy watching movies is because of the hero's tale. A young, unexpected hero is called to action. After struggling throughout the movie, he learns, grows, and is victorious in the end. This is motivation at its best. Make a list of movies that motivate you and build a small library to use as your motivation station.

17. Read Motivational Quotations

Located on the Internet and in books are thousands of quotations that inspire, motivate, and cause us all to think about our lives in a different way. Search the Internet for quotations, and you will find thousands of pages that match just what you are looking for.

18. Create a Healthy Diet

Energy is very important to living a happy life, but that depends upon healthy eating. Be sure to create a healthy diet that includes all of the necessary nutrients, minerals, and vitamins for your system. Following the basic food table is a good guide, for starters.

19. Get Enough Sleep

Some people can get by on six hours, while others require seven to eight. Regardless of what you need in sleep, make sure you get enough. A few nights in a row of only three or four hours will take its toll on your motivation, energy, and attitude.

20. Use Goals in Your Life

This is the most important tip about goals: use them! Without goals, you will have a difficult time improving any area of your life. Leaving your future up to chance isn't a good way to get what you want. Make use of goals throughout your life and enjoy the success and happiness they bring.

21. Brainstorm

Get out a clean sheet of paper and a pen. Sit in a quiet, well-lit area, and think, think, think. Write any ideas that pop into your head—financial goals, personal goals, relationship goals, health goals, etc. Write every idea, and when you're finished, you'll have more than enough goals to work with.

22. Write Your Goal on Paper

Once you select a goal to work towards, write it on paper. This makes it more tangible and concrete. A goal that is left to float around in your head may be forgotten before you have had a chance to work on it.

23. Make Your Goal Specific

Goals must be specific in order to be effective. Improving your relationship with your children is an important and worthwhile goal, but it may be too broad. Instead, your plan could include a play-day once a week, family dinnertime each night from 6:00 to 7:00, and a game night once a week. Such plans have a greater chance of success.

24. Use Deadlines

Procrastination is deadly to your goals and objectives. A great way to leapfrog that problem is to give your goal a deadline. As with the goal itself, make your deadline specific.

25. Use a Start Date

Deadlines are very important to goal setting, but we can't forget about their counterpart—start dates. Once a goal is created, you may have many reasons for putting it off. Give your goal a start date and stick to it.

26. Make Your Goals Challenging

In order for goals to be effective, they must be challenging. If your goal is too easy to achieve, your motivation and dedication will decrease. Your goals should make you reach and extend your current abilities and skills.

27. Make Your Goals Achievable

Setting a goal that is completely out of your reach will cause frustration, anger, and self-doubt. Be sure to set goals that challenge you but that are also reasonable.

28. Make a Detailed Plan of Action

Create a detailed, step-by-step plan of action for each part of your goal. One of the main reasons many goals are not accomplished is the lack of understanding of what needs to be done. Plan your work, and work your plan.

29. Don't Overdo It

Don't set too many goals at once. One to three is a good number to start with. Spreading yourself too thin will create a situation where no single goal will receive the attention it requires.

30. Measure Your Progress

Measure your progress as you work on your goal. You may wish to write a 300-page novel. Don't set 300 pages as the only goal. Break it up into 25- to 50-page increments and keep a daily tally of the pages you complete. Measuring your progress keeps your motivation peaking during your goal's lifecycle.

31. Wish List
Make a list of 10 things that you want to do in life—start a business, run a marathon, visit Europe, learn French, etc. Put the list in a drawer in your office or home.

32. Quick Reminders
Sticky notes are great tools to help you remember your daily tasks and goals. Just don't overdo it. You don't want so many notes stuck to your computer screen that you can't read what's on it.

33. Reward Yourself
Set a reward for yourself. If you accomplish a small step or your entire goal, celebrate. You've worked hard and you deserve it. Go out to dinner with your family, take a short vacation, or do anything else that makes you happy.

34. WIIFM?
Why are you setting this goal? Write "What's In It For Me?" for each one of your goals. You must be able to state clearly the reasons why you are setting this goal. If you cannot, delete the goal from your list and move to the next one.

35. Use the Right Words
Use statements like, "I have a positive attitude," or, "We'll find a solution," in daily conversation. The words you use on a daily basis have a major impact on your attitude and moods.

36. Strive for Optimism
I have spoken with many people who see being a pessimist or an optimist as a 50/50 chance, believing one is just as good as the other. That is a trap! Having a positive attitude is something you should strive for. It isn't something you are or are not. It is something you can become.

37. What Company Do You Keep?

Do your friends have negative attitudes? Does it rub off on you? Many times the company we keep can affect our attitudes. If your group at work or at home negatively affects your attitude, take the necessary steps to change the situation.

38. When You Know You Need a Change

When you know you aren't happy, admit it to yourself and take action to reverse it. This is a very difficult thing to do, especially if you aren't in the mood to admit things to yourself. It may be hard, but it is worth it. When you are being negative, realize it and change it.

39. Listen to What Others Say

We may like to tell ourselves that we are positive people, but it's not always true. Listen to what your friends and family say about your attitude. They may say things that you don't want to hear, but sometimes the best changes in life come from constructive criticism.

40. Learn What Makes You Tick

When you know what makes you upset, you will be able to avoid those situations and save yourself the tension and frustration they bring. If you cannot avoid the situation, learn how to make the best of it

41. What Makes You Happy?

This is vital to your attitude and mood. Your "happy" buttons will serve to improve your attitude again and again. When I'm not in a good mood, I first ask myself if I have eaten that day. More often than not, after getting food into my system, my attitude does a complete 180-degree turnaround.

42. Give Yourself a Break

Give yourself a quick time-out now and then when you are becoming stressed or upset. Often a short break can help you put things in perspective and return to the situation with a positive demeanor.

43. Think Twice Before You Act Once

Before you act, think about what your action will cause. If an employee does something wrong that negatively affects you, don't attack. Think about the best response. Only after you have done this twice should you take action.

44. React vs. Respond

These two words are the difference between a happy, enthusiastic, positive person and a sad, frustrated, negative person. When anything happens in life that affects you, both directly and indirectly, respond to the situation. This means you think about it, use reason to find a solution, and take appropriate measures. When you react, you skip the reasoning stage and do what comes naturally in the moment. This only causes more problems and frustrations. Respond. Do not react.

45. Appreciate the Things You Have

Look around you and learn to appreciate everything you have in your life—your friends, family, career, home, etc. This is enough to create a positive attitude because no matter how bad things get in life, we still must be thankful for everything we have. Put things into perspective and enjoy the good things in your life.

46. You Don't Always Have To Be Happy

Being in a down mood is OK sometimes. You don't always have to be upbeat, excited, and outgoing. This could lead to burnout or a blowup. There are days when things aren't going right or we just feel a little out of it. These days are OK, and the problems will pass.

47. Think About It
Look at problems logically. When you let emotions take over, you may do things that made sense at the time but in the end weren't the best choices.

48. Don't Join the Gossip
Don't join in on the negative conversations around you. If you see a conversation heading down that road, excuse yourself politely and leave.

49. Start in the Right Direction
Wake up with a smile and with energy. You have a lot to accomplish and enjoy today. Life is short, and you are going to make the most of this day and of every day after it.

50. Never Stop Learning
This is the most important lesson of all. Never stop learning about the world around you. Read, listen, and learn about the things that interest you. Instead of asking a question and being satisfied with an "I don't know" answer, go and find the answer. Be curious. Attitude is everything. These tips will help you create a winning attitude and help others to do the same.

MOTIVATION MYTHS

Many people have goals in mind but don't take the steps to achieve them. Why? Because of the myths they believe in. Following are some of the major myths that people believe, and why you should avoid them.

I can't do it.
Yes, you can! What others have done, you can do. With the same size brain, same two arms and legs, and with the same amount of time during each day, men and women have done extraordinary things. What they did, you can also do.

I can start tomorrow.
Maybe you can't. Never put off things that you can do today. Tomorrow is never a guarantee, and no one can know what the future holds. All you can be sure of is that right now, this moment, you are here and can accomplish your goals.

It may not be right for me.
You'll never be 100 percent sure that what you are striving for is the perfect thing for you. This process takes time, and you will make many turns along the way. Don't wait for the perfect opportunity to knock on your door. You must go after it yourself.

START TODAY

Whatever goal you may have, whatever dream you want to achieve, start today. You can go about your days and weeks like you have been doing for the past few years, or you can set a goal, dedicate yourself to it, and do what it takes to make it come true.

I'll start tomorrow.
I'll start this summer.
I'll start when I graduate.
I'll start when the kids get out of school.
I'll start when the kids go back to school.
I'll start when the weather gets better.
I'll start when I get a new job.
I'll start when the moment is right.

The moment *is* right. Start today.

APPENDIX H

COMMITMENT

By A. Russell Chandler, III
Founder and former owner, Qualicare

In 1983, and for several years after I sold the healthcare company that I had founded 12 years before, I spoke often to college undergraduates and MBAs, listing the 10-12 key elements of success. After all, I, as graduate of Georgia Tech and the Wharton School of Business, possessed significant training and knowledge. Success certainly had to be a complex combination of applying all of that great knowledge with a tremendous work ethic and insight. When I sold the plastics company 10 years later and, being perhaps a bit more insightful, I streamlined this list to five or six key elements of success. Some items on the first list just didn't' seem appropriate anymore, particularly as I was able to analyze not only my own experiences but also those of other entrepreneurs whom I had had the opportunity of observing.

A few years later, after my once-in-a-lifetime Olympic experience, I concluded that success is really determined by two things: one controllable, the other not. As for the former, it was simply one word: commitment. I am convinced that one's degree of success is directly related to one's commitment to succeed. The term "driven" so often is used to describe successful athletes, coaches, businessmen, politicians, even ministers. But is that term ever used to describe unsuccessful people? Certainly not. And the truly committed person sets aside personal impediments to achieving the goals he or she has established. Simply stated, that is what it takes to emerge at the zenith of the competitive world.

Unfortunately, this commitment can have a down side. That is why the connotation of a "driven" person is often negative. Driven people can become so committed to a single objective that other aspects of a fruitful life (such as family, friends, health, integrity, morals, etc.) may become compromised. In the development of my company Qualicare, I would estimate that my typical workweek exceeded 100 hours and that I was on the road, on average, four days a week. I had no vacation for nine years. As distasteful as that sounds to me today, it was wonderful and exciting—not for the financial reward but for the satisfaction of creating and growing a successful and worthwhile enterprise. That essential commitment was possible then only because there was no family to be compromised at that time. With a wife and three daughters today, I could not, and would not, make such compromises. And today, balance is more important to me than any success in business.

Interestingly, however, the most important aspect of our success is uncontrolled by us; rather, it is the gift and plan that God has given us. Yet we often overlook this and claim all victories as if they were totally our own. Lest we forget, the single most important variable in determining our destiny is one thing we have no control over: our conception. We have not one single vote in determining our gene pool, circumstances, or the environment in which we are raised in our critical foundational years. How could I possibly argue that my life would have been no different if I had been raised in Memphis, Egypt, rather than Memphis, Tennessee? Or if I had been born to a family with little work ethic or upward mobility, or had been severely disabled? I couldn't. And my point is only this: all our skills, intelligence, motivation, personality traits, and opportunities are gifts from God. Thus, we must be mindful not to take too much of the credit for our own successes. The Bible reminds us that we will be judged not by the absolute amount of accomplishments we have on earth, but by what we do with that which has been given to us. Of those to whom much has been given, much will be required, so we had better recognize that and, as we are blessed, be prepared to share those blessings.

Not coincidentally, these same concepts apply to the principles essential to successful leadership. Commitment is observable and infectious; it inspires those around us. Once others realize their leader is committed not only to the success of the endeavor but also to them, they too must rise to the occasion—or else they will fall by the wayside. Likewise, as we each humble ourselves in admitting to the influence and value of God throughout their lives, they too can find their own blessings and exceed their own prior expectations. As a result, inspired co-workers create great leaders and sustain successful endeavors.

APPENDIX I

INFLUENCES ON THE MANUSCRIPT FOR *LEADERSHIP FITNESS*

The following people contributed not only inspiration to *Leadership Fitness* but also generously offered to write text to be incorporated into the manuscript for this book. They made this book complete.

Dr. Alexander Bralley, Founder, Metametrix Clinical Laboratory

Dr. John Cantwell, Chief Medical Officer 1996 Olympic Games

Russ Chandler, Founder, Qualicare and United Plastic Film

Dr. G. Wayne Clough, President, Georgia Institute of Technology

Bill Curry, ESPN Football Analyst

Randall W. Engle, Chair, School of Psychology, College of Sciences, Georgia Tech

Dan Freeman, Ranch Foreman, Augusta, MT

Don Harp, Senior Minister, Peachtree Road United Methodist Church

Hubert Harris, Chairman, Invesco Retirement, Inc.

Dr. Bevel Jones, Bishop, United Methodist Church

Jack Kinder, President, Kinder & Associates, Dallas, TX

Martha Lanier, President, "Igniting Unlimited Potential"

Jim Lientz, President, Mid-South Bank of America, and Chief
    Operating Officer for Georgia Governor Sonny Perdue

Carolyn Luesing, President, Luesing & Associates

Jack Markwalter, Head of Atlanta Trust Co., NA

Hank McCamish, Chairman of the Board, McCamish Group

Bill Moore, Founder, Chairman of the Board, Kelly-Moore Paint Co.

John D. Morgan, Executive Director, Omicron Delta Kappa Society, Inc.

Andrés Núñez, Co-founder, TEI Engineers and Planners

Albert Bud Parker, Beck & Gregg Hardware Co.

Dr. Chris Rosenbloom, Associate Professor, Georgia State University

Bud Shaw, Founder, Chairman of the Board, Shaw Industries

Dal Shealy, President, Fellowship of Christian Athletes

Eddie Smith, Grady White Boat Co., Founder and Chairman of the Board

Carl Stevens, President, Carl Stevens & Associates, Inc.

John Williams, Founder, Post Properties, Inc.

Rick Worsham, Founder, Worsham & Sammons, Inc.

It has been a pleasure each year to invite Dave Braine, the highly successful Director of Athletics at Georgia Tech, and members of his staff to address my class. A number of people from his office gave presentations to the 2003 Leadership Fitness class.

Rob Skinner, Director, Homer Rice Center for Sports Performance and
    the Student-Athlete Total Person Program

Mary McElroy, Senior Associate Athletic Director

Allison George, Director of Communications

Kyleen Bell, Staff and former outstanding student-athlete

Larry New, Senior Associate Athletic Director

Over the years, many people have given of their time to share their experience and knowledge with my Georgia Tech classes. The final manuscript owes a debt to their past efforts.

Arthur Blank, Founder, Home Depot

Charles Brady, Executive Chairman, Invesco

Don Chapman, CEO, Tug Manufacturing Corp.

Mark Dash, Partner, Goldman Sachs & Co.

A.D. Frazier, CEO, Invesco

John Imlay, President, Imlay Investments

Dr. Randy Martin, Dean, Emory University Clinical Development

Shirley C. Newborn, V.P., Southern Engineering Co.

Dr. William Osher, Director of Success Programs, Georgia Tech

Pete Petite, Chairman, Healthdyne, Inc.

Dr. Catherine Ross, Former Executive Director, GRTA
    Currently Director of the Center for Quality Growth and Regional
    Development, Georgia Tech

Dr. Gary Schuster, Dean, Georgia Tech College of Science

W. Thomas Smith, V.P., IBM

John Wallace, Senior Partner, King & Spalding

Ambassador Andrew Young, Chairman, Good Works International

PERSONAL NOTES

CHALLENGES

Since *Leadership Fitness* was first published in 2004, the book has been reprinted several times, first as a hardback and now in a paperback format. Thousands of readers have provided highly positive feedback about the book. Rather than writing a new title, I would like to update the book and add more positive information to what has become an excellent format for teaching about leadership fitness. My own experiences in the last few years illustrate how I have used the Attitude Technique Philosophy to overcome a personal family situation.

My life's biggest challenge was not my experience in World War II as part of the U.S. Navy in the South Pacific theater or the malaria I contracted while serving in the Philippine Islands. It was not the two life-threatening cancer surgeries I have survived. The most challenging moment I have faced was receiving the heartbreaking information that four expert physicians gave me about the illness of my dear wife Phyllis. In 2005, she was diagnosed with Alzheimer's disease.

On duty in the U.S. Navy during the liberation of the Philippines.

I was devastated. Immediately, I cut myself off from the outside world to take care of her at home. I withdrew from outside
concerns and devoted my entire attention to her welfare. Was it
possible to heal? To slow down? If not, what could I do to encourage the best care for her for the rest of our lives? I read, researched, and studied every possible report. I discussed with
many people their experiences with this dreaded disease.

Finally, I heard from an old friend and colleague, Frank
Broyles. Frank was one of the most outstanding college football
coaches in America at the University of Arkansas. He was a
National Coach of the Year honoree and had won national championships. As director of athletics, he had been highly successful
in turning his school into one of the most competitive programs in

the history of the National Collegiate Athletic Association. Frank had gone through the same experience I was facing.

Coach Broyles, a successful, positive leader in my own profession, had become a caregiver to his devoted wife, Barbara. His approach was one of positive focus. He brought his family together and set out to celebrate their *todays* and their *memories*, making each day the best possible day. He organized a book for other caregivers, like a coach mapping out a football playbook. As a caregiver coach, his approach was similar to how he would attack an opponent on the football field. He developed a solid game plan and formed a dedicated team. *Coach Broyles' Playbook for Alzheimer's Caregivers* helped me to form my own game plan. (His book was published by the University of Arkansas but is available online from www.alzheimersplaybook.com or by calling Coach Broyles' daughter, Betsy Arnold, at 479-313-5079.)

No medication could reverse the process of this dreadful disease. Realizing this, I tried to learn what I could do to improve the situation.

Phyllis and Homer at their winter home on Marco Island, Florida

After three and a half years at home, our doctors advised me that Phyllis needed care beyond what I was capable of giving. Selfishly, I did not want to give her up to the care of someone else. Finally I relinquished when it became evident that she needed specialized assistance and, as was pointed out to me, my own health was deteriorating as well. If I did not take care of my own health, I would not be able to take care of Phyllis. My dear lovely wife entered the Lenbrook Health Care Medical Unit in Atlanta in December 2008. To this day, I visit her each day unless I am out of town for some purpose, but I am never away for more than one or two nights.

Although Phyllis was receiving professional care, she was not alert, she slept a lot, and she seemed to be lost in thought. She soon had a stroke, which placed her in the hospital for nine days. Miraculously, she recovered and returned to the health care center. As time went on, I kept thinking there had to be something that could be done to improve her situation. Then the light went on: Norman Cousin!

Author Norman Cousin began a laughing campaign to cure his illness in a hospital, as I've discussed. His book *Anatomy of an Illness* triggered my own intense study to understand just how humor healed. One Sunday, I spoke to our Timothy Sunday school class at Peachtree Road United Methodist Church in Atlanta about leadership fitness (my Attitude Technique Philosophy). I explained that I had been working with Phyllis on two subjects: laughter and inspiration.

When you truly laugh, you are not sad, and there is no pain. When you are inspired, you are not depressed. I had found that by bringing the enjoyable aspects of the past back to Phyllis, such as watching old comedy shows like *I Love Lucy*, *Bewitched*, *Candid Camera*, and *The Dick Van Dyke Show*, Phyllis was beginning to laugh again. Afterward, I would read from a devotional titled *Daily Word*, the Holy Bible, and inspirational real-life stories from *Guideposts*. She appeared to be more alert and interested. We would finish our time with her by saying a positive prayer together.

The health care staff began to notice a big difference in her behavior. These moments were priceless and also improved my time with her in our exciting undertaking. After the Sunday school class, my friend Bill Prichard gave me the title of another Norman Cousin book, *Head First*. By now, Cousin had accepted a position as an adjunct professor at the UCLA Medical School and Hospital. His philosophy, in a nutshell, was that if a negative attitude could cause illness or make it worse, then why not work for a positive attitude to heal or improve an illness? This made perfect sense to me. It was the Attitude Technique in action.

His further studies, research, and examinations proved this to be accurate. Laughter and inspiration were the keys to making my dear wife's *moments* extremely positive. Recently, I was reading Laura Hillenbrand's article "Facing the Enemy (The Power of Forgiveness)" in the January 2011 issue of *Guideposts* about veteran Louie Zamperin's story of survival and redemption. Phyllis seemed to be especially interested in his story and asked more questions than usual. Our communication gave me hope that we were moving forward. My *moments* with Phyllis became more rewarding. Although she would not remember *this moment* later, she showed me that it was a special time for her.

Any special occasion such as Thanksgiving, a birthday, an anniversary (and particularly our sixtieth anniversary of marriage in 2010), Christmas, or Easter—whatever the time might be—I arranged a private dining room at Lenbrook for a meal with all the family. Our waitress, Denise Cody. always took special care of Phyllis and the family.

I must thank our primary care physician, Gladstone Sellers, for staying constantly aware of her situation and keeping the family informed of all the details of her illness.

Phyllis Rice

He also encouraged me to get back to my work, to exercise, and to regain the weight I had lost while caring for Phyllis at home.

On November 15, 2013, my dearest Phyllis passed silently away into God's Hands. Our three daughters and I huddled for a prayer to ask God to take care of our dear Mom. She had suffered more than nine years with Alzheimer's disease. We knew that she would be Phyllis again, as we had known her. Phyllis and I were in our sixty-fourth year of marriage, and I loved her so much.

The funeral service was held on November 21 2013, at the Peachtree Road United Methodist Church in Atlanta. Phyllis was the loving mother of our three daughters: Nancy Hetherington, Phyllis Ingle, and Angela Miller. Each daughter and the seven grandchildren participated in admirable style in the service for their mother and grandmother. Ministers Bill Britt and Don Harp led the worship service.

Our dear friend Gregory Colson, a talented pianist, accompanied our granddaughter Leigh Hetherington as she sang Phyllis's favorite hymn, "On Eagle's Wings." Organist Scott Atchison provided special music, and the church was overcrowded with friends and well-wishers. Many said it was the best funeral service they had ever attended.

Prior to the church service, Phyllis was buried at the Arlington Memorial Park Cemetery in Sandy Springs. During Phyllis's convalescence at the Lenbrook Health Care Center, I visited her almost daily. Now I can visit her at the gravesite. We had a great life together, and we had a happy family. I will miss her in life, but I can still talk to her every day. When my time comes, I will be buried next to her.

I decided to get back to my consultant position with Georgia Tech and chairman of the Lee Candler Endowment Fund for the Student/Athlete Total Person Program at the Georgia Tech Athletic Association, as well as work I was doing for other groups. This required some travel on my part, and my daughters stepped in when I was away or out of town for an engagement. My girls had been supportive through the years, and they continued to be ready to jump in when the occasion necessitated their help. I am so fortunate to have three loyal and special daughters: Angela Miller, Phyllis Ingle, and Nancy Hetherington.

My time with Phyllis made me realize that she was not quitting. This gave me added motivation to get back to my program of leadership fitness. Even more help came my way in the form of three books that I read and researched as I restarted my thinking process.

Gene DeFilippo, a good friend and the successful director of athletics at Boston College, sent me the book *What to Say When You Talk to Yourself*, by Shad Helmstetter. Dr. Helmstetter, an author and lecturer in the field of motivational behavior, describes amazingly well what I call the Attitude Technique Philosophy described in Lesson One: Are you fit to become a positive leader? He explains how the brain works with the two minds, with the conscious and subconscious, to give us a human computer. Dr. Helmstetter writes an entire manuscript on how to apply this philosophy through talking to yourself in positive ways to achieve positive success in your life. Reading and studying his book helped me to refresh my theories, and it confirmed that I was on the right track.

In a conversation about my book one day with my friend Keen Reese at our Capital City Club in Atlanta, he mentioned Tim Irwin's *Derailed: Five Lessons Learned from Catastrophic Failures of Leadership*. I had not read the book, and Keen passed his copy on to me. I began reading immediately when I realized he had focused on the failures of leadership. Since my book focuses mainly on positive leaders, I was anxious to learn more about negative leaders from Dr. Irwin, a leading authority on leadership development. His fascinating book went into great detail about the many reasons a person fails as a leader. His book covered some of the top corporate presidents and board chairmen in the country. The two glaring problems I picked up on were arrogance and being a poor listener to the boards, employees, and shareholders. Of course, Tim explained many reasons for failure, but those two stood out to me. When you add greed, untrustworthiness, and corruption to that pair of glaring weaknesses, you get a bright, flashing light that a person needs to step down.

While browsing through some bookstores, as I often do, I spotted *How Successful People Think,* by John C. Maxwell. I had met John through a dear friend, Jack Kinder, several years ago, and I have followed his work since. His success in training today's leaders is a tremendous story. We become what we think about. Dr. Maxwell demonstrated throughout his book many lessons in accomplishing a positive life and a successful career. His book is a must-read if you are serious about being a positive leader.

Throughout each day of the past and the present, I find myself studying people to decide, "Is this person capable of being a positive leader in their field of leadership?" A person does not have to be the president of a large company, coach of a championship football team, or minister of a large congregation. Anyone can assume responsibility for making something better.

It was not long until things began to happen. The first opportunity resulted in a call from Grant Teaff, executive director of the American Football Coaches Association and former National Coach of the Year. Grant has accomplished unbelievable results as executive director of our professional organization. He is definitely a positive leader. He called and asked if I would consider speaking to the President's Breakfast at the annual convention in Orlando, Florida. They would have six

Coach Yosh Yoshida

thousand coaches in attendance. Wherever I spoke, I always gave my book *Leadership Fitness* to every attendee. I joked with a friend that someday I might have to file bankruptcy for giving away so many books, but continuing this custom was what some people labeled my silent ministry. The book was not advertised or marketed except through word of mouth.

I supplied people with a free book in the hope that they would glean something from it to help them in their personal lives or careers. As the number of books given out approached thirty-five thousand copies, the feedback was so positive that it brought happiness to me of the sort that happens when we help others without expecting anything in return. My interest continues and motivates me to carry on. In other words, it keeps me studying, researching, and writing.

Just before I spoke to the group, a young coach from Japan presented a book to me, written in his country's language. Inscribed on the inside cover was "To Coach Homer Rice, Thank you! Yosh Yoshida." A memory came front and center in my mind. I had met Yosh several years earlier at one of our conventions, corresponded with him, and sent him materials from the Life Skills–Total Person Program with which I had worked for so many years. In presenting his book to me, he said, "This is your book in our language." What a surprise! They do play American football in the universities in Japan, and Yosh is a football coach and teacher. He also promotes the life skill program throughout his country. In my opinion, Yosh is a positive leader in promoting important life skills to the young people of Japan.

ROOTS (AND STORIES)

Have you ever wondered how and why you became what you are today?

In shaping our careers we just have to look back on our early years, as insignificant as they may seem, to find the answers. Our beginnings were the roots that later directed our lives. My thoughts each and every moment led to what I have eventually become. When I learned that I could control my thoughts, I then could control my actions. This was the result of my human computer.

I would like to share how my early years later shaped my life and career. These are my *roots* (and *stories*!).

Our dear friends John and Vivian Landrum, of Harrodsburg, Kentucky, contacted me and asked whether I would be interested in returning to my hometown of Pineville, Kentucky. Vivian and I had been classmates during the six years I spent in Pineville growing up, from the first through the sixth grade.

The Kentucky Mountain Laurel Festival takes place each year in the beautiful Pine Mountains of southeastern Kentucky, and they invited me to witness it with them. John and Vivian were board members of this spectacular event, and their invitation interested me very much. The festival is a gala event with queen candidates from the colleges and universities throughout the state of Kentucky. I decided to attend with my son-in-law Jeff Miller (joking that Jeff would be my personal chauffeur), and we had a great time. It brought back memories from long ago and made me realize that Pineville was where I had decided to become a football coach.

My older brother was a star athlete at the school, and during the football season I would show up for every practice. Finally, Coach Walter Grabruck decided to make me the team's mascot. After finding a uniform that fit, I led the team onto the field for every home game (although I must not have made the traveling squad because I don't remember any away games). Coach Grabruck was such a positive influence on my life at that time that I made a commitment to become a football coach.

The Mountain Laurel Festival also brought back old memories. As ten- and eleven-year-olds in 1937 and 1938, Ben Fuson and I played trumpet for the winning queen to march down and accept the honor of being crowned by the Commonwealth's governor. We were decked out in white silk uniforms (which of course we did not approve of) as we performed our duties.

We became so famous locally with our trumpet playing that we were called on to play taps for graveside services. At one funeral, Ben and I decided that he would climb up the mountainside and be the echo. I was to play the first few notes, with him playing the same notes to give an echo effect. However, we got mixed up and he got ahead of me, so I became the echo. Somehow we got through it without anyone detecting the mistake. Ben went on to become a prominent dentist, and I entered the coaching-and-education profession.

At age ten, Homer Rice performed as the herald (trumpeter)
for the Mountain Laurel Festival in 1937.

While in Pineville, I met several former classmates and
friends making their own trips back, stirring more recollections
for me. One incident I recalled was when I was eight or nine
years old at the famous Chain Rock on the side of Pine
Mountain, high atop Pineville. The chain from the rock support
crossed a chasm some hundred feet deep. A young friend dared
me to "hand walk" the chain, which of course is a very danger-
ous undertaking. I accepted the challenge and, fortunately, made
it across. I then threatened my friend so he would not tell my
mother. What I remember most after my feat was breaking the

bottle of Lime Rickey that I had in my knapsack with my meal for the evening. I watched the bottle as it slid out of my hand and fell the hundred feet and crashed on the large rocks below. My friend told me to be thankful that it wasn't me falling from the chain, but I really wanted my Lime Rickey for dinner.

When I returned as an adult and attended the festival board dinner, held at the state's oldest park lodge restaurant, I was introduced as the trumpet player from the 1938 affair. I met Governor Steven L. Beshear, who told me that he had run for the state office so he could serve as governor at the Kentucky Mountain Laurel Festival. Months later, I was invited to be the grand marshal for the city of Fort Thomas, Kentucky, at the Fourth of July parade and given three certificates: one each from Governor Steven L. Beshear, Mayor Mary H. Brown of Fort Thomas, and Katie Kratz Stine, president pro tempore of the Commonwealth of Kentucky Senate. The trip to Pineville elevated my standing in the Commonwealth. It also helped me to realize how much we owe the people who help us along the way of our life's career through their positive influence.

Coach Walter Grabruck was that person in my early years. Before we left Pineville, I was able to visit with the first college quarterback that I coached in a long and storied career. Dr. Jerry Woolum had gone into general surgery and primary care at the Pineville Community Hospital. Jerry not only was a great football player, but he also moved forward with his skills to become a positive leader in the medical profession. As a young offensive coordinator at the University of Kentucky in 1962, I was fortunate to have a senior quarterback to work with and guide me through my first collegiate coaching year. Jerry was an outstanding student, leader, and person. Seeing and hearing former players who have succeeded in their lives makes all the effort and hard work worth every moment of my formative years. I was certainly blessed in many ways as I experienced my profession.

My father, a Methodist minister, served as the district superintendent of the Kentucky Southeastern District while we lived in Pineville. He was a fine athlete himself in the 1920s, competing in rugby, baseball, and tennis. He also was an avid outdoorsman and enjoyed fishing and hunting. One sport he did not approve of for his two sons was boxing. Of course, I got involved in Golden Glove Boxing, fighting in the lightweight division.

Through boxing, I learned a lot about myself. I had quickness and toughness, as our trainer would point out. This discovery gave me added confidence. The matches were only three rounds, with one minute for each round. After winning the championship, I quickly retired from the ring to devote my time to sports that were in season, like football, basketball, track, and baseball. My father never mentioned my boxing to me, but I did find out later that he had asked how I was doing—and smiled after someone told him about my victories. We never discussed my boxing, so somehow I had dodged a lecture.

We lived next to the Methodist church, but because my father was gone each weekend to other churches in his district, a minister from nearby Union College Seminary in Barbourville preached. I always sat next to my mother and brother. As the service began, I could slump down in the pew, slide underneath, and crawl out under the rows of seats without being detected. Once out in the churchyard behind our house, I could play imaginary football, baseball, or other sports by myself. I knew the cue when to go back inside and slide back into my seat. I do not believe my mother ever noticed my absence. My brother did, but he never told on me. In this way, Pineville was my "roots" and started my focus on what I would become. I had many more positive opportunities to attach to the list, however.

In 2012 I was inducted to the Kentucky Athletic Hall of Fame. Later that year the Pineville Schools brought me back to be honored as a member of the charter class of their Hall of

Fifteen-year-old Homer with his parents, Grace and Dr. Sam Rice.
(Inset): Homer's brother, Robert Cecil Rice.

Fame. The induction class also included Dr. Jerry Woolum, my dear friend and former University of Kentucky quarterback. That honor made me recall even more strongly how Pineville shaped me in my early years.

In 1939, my father was appointed to a church in Middlesborough, Kentucky, situated in the national park area of Cumberland Gap in Kentucky, Tennessee, and Virginia. Atop the pinnacle in this beautiful area in the mountains, one could see seven states on a clear day, as the saying went. (I do not remember a clear day where I saw that far, but I am sure it's true.) The city name was shortened to Middlesboro, and the area thrived on the iron ore and coal in the mountains. A wealthy group of immigrants from Middlesborough, England, built a city of wide streets and large Victorian homes, and they brought English culture from their homeland. My first day in school was both pleasant and rewarding.

I noticed a very pretty girl in my class and quickly ran home after school to tell my mother that I had found the girl I was going to marry. Her name was Phyllis Callison Wardrup. My mother remarked, "But, Homer, you are only twelve years old." I responded that I wanted to settle that now, because I would not have time to look around if I was going to play football. If you fast-forward my life, you will note that Phyllis Callison Wardrup and I were married on August 12, 1950.

The second day of school was interesting, but . . . well, here's what happened. On my way home, a gang of boys followed me, yelling, "Preacher's kid, preacher's kid," taunting and bullying me with a lot of pushing and shoving. I walked as fast as I could without running. When we reached the front of my home, I turned to face them and said, "Okay. I can't take on the whole bunch, but if you want a fight, let one of you step forward." The biggest, toughest, and probably the leader of the gang stepped forward. He laughed at me, and we squared off. What he and the gang did not know about me was that I knew how to fight. A year before, I had won the Golden Gloves Championship. I licked their leader without receiving a blow from him. That quickly changed things, and the gang walked away not knowing quite what had happened. From that day on, there was no more taunting. Word got around quickly.

At Middlesboro, I remember being asked to play in a small dance band with Gregory Colson at the piano and Bobby Rush on the drums, with our singer Fred arranging a contract with the

Silver Slipper, a roadhouse. My father found out about our evening plans, making the event a one-night-only engagement. So much for our dance band! However, moving to Fort Thomas, Kentucky, where I attended high school, I was asked to play in a much larger band. That led to an audition to play for Jimmy Dorsey's band at the famous Moonlight Gardens at Coney Island in Cincinnati. Mac McKenna, the popular band director at Highlands High School, advised me not to audition for first trumpet but rather say I was a second trumpet. The band traveled with the first section and picked up seconds on location. Somehow, I made it through the audition and played for three nights with the band. Each member had to solo on one number, and mine on "Stardust" runs through my mind to this day. I don't believe I played much trumpet after that, except an occasional solo at church or some related place, because World War II very soon afterward became my focus, and I left for the navy and the Pacific.

Greg Colson, the piano player, ended up being the music director at Georgia Tech, where I became the director of athletics forty years after we met. Mac McKenna made many contributions to Highlands's school songs. I will never forget the band playing "Oh, Hail Highlands Team" as the football team ran onto the field for each game when I was a player and as a coach. Mac's son Jim McKenna was several years behind me at Highlands, but we became close friends through the years, and Jim became a doctor in San Francisco. He served as team dentist for the San Francisco Forty-Niners professional football team from 1968 to 1980. When the Forty-Niners played in Atlanta, Jim and I would meet for dinner. He became close to Dusty Baker, one of baseball's greats and the manager of the San Francisco Giants. Jim's dad was definitely a positive leader during those good ole days in Fort Thomas.

I was always working odd jobs to pick up some income for a junior high schooler's lifestyle. I had a paper route, cut grass, and did anything I could that did not interfere with school and sandlot football games. During the summer, it was baseball that I saved my time for. We entered a team in the local league, but before we could play a game, we had to find a sponsor to pay our entrance fee, buy uniforms, and supply equipment. I knocked on the door of my neighbor, Mr. Cawood, and asked for his help. Mr. Cawood was delighted to be our sponsor. He was looking for a marketing tool, and we seemed to be able to provide it, because the local newspaper covered all the games, and fans came to see us play. It happened that our neighbor owned a funeral home, so we were the Cawood Funeral Home baseball team. Our sponsor wanted to put a picture of a casket on our uniforms for good publicity, but the team voted against it since we already were being called the Dead Team.

The teasing in the league stopped as soon as we started to play, because we always won and ended up taking the championship. Mr. Cawood treated us to a milkshake at the local dairy each time we won—which was every game. He also had a beautiful golden Persian cat that he presented to me after we won the championship. The cat was named Jim Farley, after the U.S. postmaster general in 1937. I never understood why she was named Jim Farley, but that cat became a treasure to me. She was also tough, chasing off any dog that came around and often following me on my bike rides around the community. After the baseball season ended one summer, a teammate's father, Buddy Holbrook, who managed Cudjo's Cave in Cumberland Gap National Park, gave us jobs as guides in the historical cave. A lot of stories developed from our experiences of taking groups through the cave.

One formation I remember from the cave resembled the American flag, minus the stars. You could only see the flag by bending down and looking straight up. A wise guy in the group would always comment, "Where's the stars?" To which we would respond that if he stood up quickly enough, he would see the stars. Like clockwork, he would get up, bang his head on the low spot in the cave's ceiling, and we would get the chance to remark, "Do you see the stars now?" We might have thought it funnier than our guests, but this did keep the perpetual loudmouths quiet for the rest of the tours. The cave itself was named for Cujo, an African American slave who lived in the passage and ran messages back and forth for the Union army during the Civil War.

Famous travelers passed through the Cumberland Gap into Kentucky. Daniel Boone himself walked through the gap into Kentucky to hunt and explore new land in 1769 from his home in North Carolina. Stories of the earlier settlers coming west made Cumberland Gap and Cujo's Cave interesting reading, and Buddy and I passed many of our off-hours hiking through parts of the cave that were closed to the public. We tied a heavy cord around our waists, crawling through cramped spaces and wearing miner's helmets with a gaslight on the front helping us to explore. It was scary business, but at the time we were too young to realize we should be concerned. It was breathtaking when we found large rooms and shone our flashlights to see the stalactites forming from the ceiling and stalagmites from the floor. We discovered what we thought was a bottomless lake, with fish that had no eyes. At that point, we knew it was time to head back. The cords we wore on our waists tied us to where we had begun, and we followed the lines back to where we had started, leaving adventures in the cave for another day.

In 1942 my father was assigned as district superintendent of the Northern Kentucky District. It was time to move again. This time we would moved to Fort Thomas, where I would enter my sophomore year at Highlands High School. My career and more *roots and stories* would shape my future to this day.

FORT THOMAS STORY

Fort Thomas, Kentucky, is in the greater Cincinnati area, atop a hill overlooking the Ohio River and downtown Cincinnati. Fort Thomas is in a beautiful setting with a population of fifteen thousand people. It is a friendly, family-oriented community that is proud of its school system and churches. Highlands High School is the center of a community that embraces strong academics, athletics, music, and other cultural activities. Highlands is considered one of the top schools in the United States. The school was named a National Blue Ribbon School by the No Child Left Behind program and recognized by *Newsweek* and *U.S. News and World Report* as one of the country's best. It consistently leads the Commonwealth of Kentucky in Standardized Achievement Test scores, National Merit finalists, and Commended Students.

The school's pride extends to its football program, which leads the state in the number of championships won ever since the Kentucky High School Association began the state playoff system in 1959. Bill Thomas captured this history in *Fort Thomas Highlands Football*, a book about the many years of the Highlands football program.

Ewell "Judge" Waddell's first year at Highlands High School as head football coach and teacher was 1942. I was fortunate to enter Highlands at just that time. As a fifteen-year-old, I had no inkling that in the future I would be asked to become the coach of this program, much less that of the University of Cincinnati Bearcats and the NFL Cincinnati Bengals. As it turned out later, I served as a head football coach at the high school, college, and professional level in the Cincinnati area, and I was the first and only person to do so. But that is getting ahead of the story.

As a sophomore at Highlands High School in the fall of 1942, I looked for Coach Waddell's office so I could sign up for the football team. I had never played an organized school team sport before. I met Coach Waddell, and he encouraged me to try out for the team. I was a transfer student, but he informed me that while I could practice during that semester, I would be required to sit out the season due to a state ruling at that time. I decided to accept his proposal, which would prepare me for playing in my junior and senior years. When Coach Waddell inquired what position I wanted to try out for, I informed him that I was a quarterback. I was not actually sure what that meant, but in sandlot football (without pads) I had been the runner and passer for our neighborhood team. I figured quarterback would be a good place for me to start. In practice that year, I was considered a "scrub," which meant I would scrimmage against the varsity team.

On defense the first day of practice, I lined up as a defensive halfback. I had no idea what to expect because I had never played organized football before. Soon after the scrimmage began, one of the big varsity fullbacks raced around the end and headed for my territory. I don't remember what I was thinking at the time, but I knew from my sandlot games that I had to tackle him. I ducked my head, ran forward and hit that big fellow with an instinctive reaction that surprised even me. That collision started my football playing career.

We both landed out of bounds on the cinder track surrounding the playing field. The impact knocked him out, but I landed on top of him, probably saving me from losing consciousness too. I had been playing with a boil on my right thigh, and the force of our crash punctured my sore, spurting blood in every direction, over both of us. By habit I jumped up as quickly as possible and said, "I'm okay, let's move on." I trotted back to my defensive halfback position, through the players and coaches who had gathered around us. As they dispersed and we got ready to continue scrimmage, I overheard one of the coaches say, "We have a football player in that young lad." I still have cinders under my skin at the place where my thigh was injured. That instant turned out to be highly productive. Coaches started paying attention to me, and some of the players were very kind from then on.

Before the next practice day, our backfield coach, Bernie Sadosky, took me into the equipment room. What I had worn the day before was stained with blood. My old shoes were two sizes too big, and the headgear had been gleaned from team discards. Coach Sadosky just shook his head, threw the old uniform into the trash bin, and gave me a new uniform. I now had clean, safe equipment.

The varsity quarterback was "Bo" Carothers. Bo took me under his wing and helped me gain entry into that position. Dick Kruer, our captain Jack Pogue, and Morris Cecil were also mentors to me, even though I was just a youngster who had only recently come from out of town. Our next year's team in 1943 claimed the state title, defeating a strong Ashland High School team at the University of Kentucky Stoll Field on Thanksgiving Day.

In my senior season in 1944, lineman Roger Neff and I were elected captains. We captured our conference championship, and as the season ended I was headed to the Great Lakes for naval training boot camp. Our group soon was sent overseas to the South Pacific for duty during World War II. After the war years, I returned briefly to Fort Thomas before I began my college playing years. Although Fort Thomas and my time as a Highlands High School student-athlete were behind me, Fort Thomas remained important in other ways, forming the *roots* that projected me into a very interesting career.

I attended Centre College in Danville, Kentucky, also playing quarterback, and was named captain my last year. A college quarterback in the fall, I was a professional baseball player by the summer. In the spring school term, I left school and was a catcher with the Brooklyn Dodgers. The year was an important milestone for baseball as well, because during 1947 Jackie Robinson became the first African American to play in Major League Baseball. Another player entered the scene soon after, a catcher named Roy Campanella, who was a future hall of famer. I told my friends that competing with Campanella perhaps helped me make the decision to be a football coach rather than a Major League Baseball player.

I started my first football coaching season in 1951 at Wartburg Central High School in Wartburg, Tennessee. Wartburg is a small community in the hills of east Tennessee. We used to joke that Wartburg was so small that it had a welcome sign with the town's name on both sides. As I began the program at Wartburg, I realized that I faced an acute shortage of equipment. We were short of shoulder pads, headgear, and pants to outfit the players that began the season. Fortunately, the father of one of my players was the warden at the nearby state prison. I visited the warden and explained my dilemma, asking whether he had any old football equipment from the teams that the prison occasionally had. The warden agreed to let me borrow the equipment—in exchange for coaching the prison team.

Looking back, the prison job turned out to be one of the best jobs in all of coaching. We had all home games and no problems with the alumni. In fact, when the alums returned, I simply put them back into the lineup. I was friends with the area sheriff, and when I heard his siren, I hoped that he was picking up a tight end or fast running back.

Both teams finished their seasons undefeated. After coaching all sports at the school, I accepted the coaching position at Spring City, Tennessee. After two more successful seasons, I received a call from my former coach at Highlands High School, informing me that he planned to accept the position of superintendent of the Fort Thomas School System. As I carefully listened, he went on to ask me whether I would consider coming back home as the head football coach of Highlands. I later told a friend that I was practically there before he finished that sentence. Returning to Fort Thomas was my highest goal. I would be going back to serve under the man who had made a tremendous impact upon my career direction.

Below is a statement of Coach Waddell's influence on many young players like me. A capstone at the Plaza of Influence at the American Football Coaches Association Foundation at their headquarters in Waco, Texas, honors our coach:

COACH "JUDGE" WADDELL
HIGHLANDS HIGH SCHOOL
FORT THOMAS, KENTUCKY 1942–1953
A MAN OF INTEGRITY: TAUGHT HIS PLAYERS
TO BE CHAMPIONS IN FOOTBALL AND LIFE.

This Plaza of Legends represents the high school and college football coaches of America who have profoundly influenced the lives of thousands of young players throughout America. I thought it was time to honor our coach for all that he had contributed to our school. As a superintendent after his coaching years, he became an outstanding educator of students in the Fort Thomas school system.

I contacted his three sons—Don, Bill, and Phillip—and they agreed to help. We formed a committee to seek and manage contributions for an endowed scholarship in his memory. We reached our goal, enabling us to provide scholarships to Highlands graduates planning to major in education and serve in American school systems. When we began the project, I right away contacted my dear friends Boonie and Gloria Fennell. Our families have been friends for many years, and Phyllis and I always stay at the "Fennell Hilton" when we visit my hometown. Our favorite bedroom is always ready, because Boonie and Glo approve wholeheartedly of the effort to raise funds for the Ewell "Judge" Waddell Endowed Scholarship, which supports young boys and girls graduating from Highlands.

I started with Coach Waddell's first team at Highlands in 1942 as I sought to build the fund. I called on the players who had been generous to me on the football team, asking their families to contribute. Dick and Shirley Kruer, Jack and Jean Pogue, and Bo and Sue Carothers all responded positively. They gave the project a great kickoff and propelled our efforts so that we soon reached our goal. Many other contributors also signed up and continued to meet the challenge, even today.

Going back to Fort Thomas landed me in the environment that produced all of these fine people. In 1960 my team won the first official state championship. Backed up by number-one rankings in the media polls, Highlands had claimed state titles in 1930, 1943, and 1957, before the Kentucky High School Playoffs began in 1959. We made it to the final game that year, and in 1960 and 1961 we were the state champions.

In August 2010 the team and all the cheerleaders were invited back to Highlands to celebrate the fiftieth anniversary of that first championship. It was a grand occasion to see all those players again. The captains of the 1960 team were John Burt, Alan Berry, Jim Burt, and Bob Steinhauser (now deceased). My assistant coaches, Owen Hauck and Bill Hermann, also were present. Both later became head coach at Highlands, adding several more state titles. Our quarterback, Roger Walz, became the head coach in later years, also producing state championships. With Owen Hauck, my first and only assistant in 1954, we built the foundation and building process that propelled the program into a highly successful achievement. Owen Hauck and I became partners, and many experts at that time said that we were ahead of our time in producing winning football.

In 1962, I accepted the offensive coordinator position at the University of Kentucky. Coach Hauck eventually moved to a new school in Boone County High School in Florence, Kentucky. He immediately developed some winning ways for his new team, developing all-state running back Shaun Alexander, who later became an all-American at the University of Alabama and an all-pro selection with the NFL Seattle Seahawks. He brought the school many championship years. Hauck became so famous that they named their new stadium in his honor. I reminded Owen that most states require an honoree be dead before naming an educational building or stadium after him. He joked back that he had been declared legally dead for the dedication.

Owen Hauck could have been successful at any place on the football spectrum. He is a true positive leader and a legend of high school football in the area around Cincinnati. His record of wins ranks at the top of the list. Hauck's decision to stay in high school coaching and administration showed his sense of honor and an awareness of how his continued work at that level could benefit many young people. Shaun Alexander was his prize student-athlete. In Cecil Murphey's book *Touchdown Alexander*, Shaun thanks Coach Owen

Hauck for his leadership and friendship, as well as for producing great memories and showing Shaun the value of a good team. Shaun Alexander himself must be counted in the list of great positive leaders. He excelled at Boone County High School, at the University of Alabama, and with the Seattle Seahawks, where he was named an NFL Most Valuable Player. Shaun puts God first in his life and family. When the football playing and the roar of the crowd stops, Shaun has his true *faith* to live on throughout his lifetime.

One reason I began the Total-Person Life Skills program for student-athletes is because I know how important it is to have a solid, balanced life after the last game in college has been played. There has to be something more than wins and losses. Playing on a team with competent and inspiring coaches provides lessons that will carry us on through life, but to that we need to add becoming a positive leader and bettering the society in which we live. The Total Person Life Skills program for student-athletes is an answer.

In 1993, a new era of Highlands football erupted when a young coach named Dale Mueller, a former Highlands outstanding player, took over the program's reins and elevated it to an even higher level. In 2009, Coach Mueller's team was ranked number two nationally. He also was honored as National Coach of the Year. His nine state championships brought the school's count to twenty. In the 2010 state playoffs, his team captured the twentieth state title, defeating a favored opponent, 50–0. I have never witnessed more precise, synchronized coaching than what Coach Mueller demonstrated in that game. At halftime, the 1960 team was recognized as Highlands' first state champion. Coach Mueller supplied fifty points in his win to match the 1960 team's fifty years. What a tribute to the Fort Thomas legacy!

As I look back sixty-nine years later, *my roots* in Fort Thomas and Highlands High School certainly are the years that

I cherish most. I will always be thankful to everyone who made those memories possible. It has been a privilege to return, whether to speak for a class reunion, accept the Alumni of the Year Award, serve as grand marshall of the Fourth of July Parade, or to pay tribute to the Junior Football League made distinctively great by Boonie Fennell and George Ratterman, a former Cleveland Browns quarterback .

Now it's time to turn the page to some special football highlights of my coaching career. My wife Phyllis and three lovely daughters were always a big part of all the action.

Homer Rice is known as the legendary coach
of Highlands High School football.

COACHING HIGHLIGHTS
OF
PARTICULAR GAMES

During my coaching years, I learned lessons from each practice, game, and preparation for competitiveness. To become a positive leader, it is extremely important to follow the principles stated in this book. In the climb to achieve positive leadership that produces success in a game when the pressure is on, we find out if we can make it to the top of the ladder. There are so many examples of doing this, and I have thoroughly enjoyed every moment of mine. I also had temporary defeats. The highlights of your experiences are the ones you should retain in your human computer.

The highlights from a coaching career of twenty-seven years covering high school, college, and pro football would take multiple volumes. It would take just as many volumes to describe the heartbreaks and tough losses of the same career. As I have said before, we must always concentrate on our successes. We learn from our temporary defeats, but we must not carry them into the future, lest a negative cloud hang over us.

As I think back through my coaching years, so many players deserve recognition and many spectacular performances come to mind. As my publisher has preached to me, however, we only have so much space. I will share some of the most outstanding memories that I keep in my own human computer.

I returned home to begin my college playing career at Centre College after two years in the navy during World War II, which had begun just after high school for me. When I graduated from college, I wanted to be a head coach. I received only one offer for head coaching. Phyllis and I headed for my first football coaching position at Wartburg, Tennessee. When we arrived at the town's "Welcome" sign, Phyllis asked, "Well, where is it?" As I have often said, if there were a hall of fame for coaches' wives, Phyllis would qualify. We did not find many people moving about in our new town, but after a few days of practice with my first football team, what I did find was group of young boys eager to learn and compete.

The high school's quarterback, Ray Bardill, became not only the first quarterback in my coaching career but also the first quarterback in the history of the game of football to execute the triple option.

~

The triple option play had its origins during the summer I was playing baseball for the Brooklyn Dodgers organization in Columbia, Missouri. Columbia also is the home of the University of Missouri, whose program at the time was led by innovative Head Football Coach Don Farout. He coached the navy program called the Iowa Pre-Flight Seahawks during World War II. He filled his staff during the war with people who later became famous coaches themselves, including Jim Tatum of Maryland and Bud Wilkinson of Oklahoma. During their time with the Iowa Seahawks, they developed the split-T option offense.

While in Columbia for the summer, I spent all my time away from baseball learning this new football offense. When I returned to Centre College for the fall football season, I suggested to my coach that we use the option play in our offense, which at the time was the single wing, double wing, box, and some tight-T formations. We worked it into a series called the buck lateral. In the process, we somehow deployed an unorthodox three-way option.

During my first coaching job at Wartburg Central High School, I employed the split-T formation and the option play. I called this play the "Triple." The 1951 Wartburg Central High School players took part in this innovation and became the first and only undefeated team in the school's history. In 2011, I will reflect on the sixty-year reunion of that championship team.

In just a short time, many coaches began using the three-way option play in various formations. Darrel Royal, the famous coach at the University of Texas, invited me to come to Austin to discuss the play. I spent three days with Coach Royal going over the details of the option. He put the three-way option play into a formation that he called the wishbone offense, later beating Notre Dame in the Cotton Bowl for the national championship. When members of the media asked Coach Royal what play he was running, he remarked, "That is Homer's triple." As soon as he made that statement, I began fielding calls from sports magazine reporters for articles. I soon made trip after trip throughout the country, speaking on the now-famous play called the triple option.

Phyllis, our first daughter Nancy, and I spent only one year at Wartburg, but the way that those players responded to my first year of coaching is unforgettable. We accepted the next job offer, moving down Highway 27 to Spring City, Tennessee, on Watts Bar Lake.

A particular game in my early career while at Spring City High School was unforgettable. At the end of the season, our team was invited to meet Greenville in the Tobacco Bowl. Sportswriters predicted that the winner would surface as the best team in East Tennessee. We played on a cold and rainy evening, and even saw light snow at game time. The field was somewhat muddy. As the game drew to a close, we found ourselves still behind, 19–14. We had moved the ball to the five-yard line, with one last play to either win or lose the game. I called time-out to give quarterback George Perry the last play. I told him to sprint out and either pass the ball into the end zone or tuck the football under his arm and drive for the goal line. He went back onto the field, but after a long time in the huddle he called a time-out and came to the sidelines.

"Coach, Leroy wants the ball," he said. Leroy Thurman was our strongest running back. He had been strong all season. He wanted to score the winning touchdown and claim, for his team, they were the best in East Tennessee. I could not deny Leroy this opportunity, even though a running play on the five-yard line would be a risky call. I told my quarterback to give the ball to Leroy. One way or another, we would get out of the cold weather, get back on the bus, and go home.

The football was snapped to our quarterback, and as he handed the ball to Leroy, our offensive line looked like it was moving in slow motion. Inch by slow inch, the line moved forward. It seemed like an eternity until I witnessed the miracle. The official raised his arms, signaling a *touchdown*. We won the game 20–19.

As the exuberant players were coming off the field, Leroy Thurman ran with them and collapsed when he got to the sideline. He had almost turned purple. This young man had given every ounce of his body and energy to cross the double stripe to achieve the winning score. What a tremendous effort! That scene will stay with me forever. Leroy Thurman went on to become a positive leader in his home community.

From Spring City, we moved to Fort Thomas to coach the Highlands Bluebirds. With all-state quarterback Roger Walz providing the positive leadership, we won back-to-back state championships in 1960 and 1961. At the end of that 1961 season came another decision regarding the future. The University of Kentucky offered me the position of offensive coordinator. Leaving my hometown would be difficult, but it was an opportunity to coach on the college level in the tough Southeastern Conference.

The game between the University of Kentucky and the University of Mississippi, ranked number one in the nation, stands out as a highlight. We played the game in Lexington. With only minutes to play, we led the country's best team with a score of 10–9. Our all-American quarterback Rick Norton took huge losses on each play in an attempt to run out the clock and seal a stunning victory. Ole Miss called a time-out after each play to stop the clock, forcing us into a punting situation. Punter Larry Seiple stood on our ten-yard line ready to punt us out of danger.

I had taught Larry a technique to stutter-step after receiving the snap from center so that our players would have more time to race downfield and cover the punt. If an all-out rush came, he punted right away, but he could delay the kick if the defense had their return ready. We had noticed during games that when a team had a return on, only one player was responsible for the punter. Our film study of Ole Miss before the game led us to agree that their one rusher did not do a very good job.

I had instructed Larry that if the lone rusher crossed his face while he still had the ball, he should just tuck the ball under his arm and run for the first down. Our situation was fourth down and forty yards to go due to our attempts to run off as much time as possible. Should we not get a first down, our opponent would have the ball already in field-goal range. And their placekicker just happened to be the best field-goal kicker in the country.

As offensive coordinator, I called the plays from the press box. We broke the huddle to line up in punt formation, with Larry standing on the ten-yard line. The ball was on the twenty-five-yard line, and our punter was fifteen yards from the center. That meant that Larry would have to run fifty-five yards to get a first down.

I looked down on the field and realized the confluence of events and training clashing at that moment. Surely he would not try to run if they did not rush him. I held my breath, praying for Mississippi to put an all-out rush on to block the punt. As the ball was snapped, our opponent showed they had their return on, with only one player responsible for the punter. Larry started his stutter-step as I witnessed the defender cross his face. And then we watched Larry *run with the ball*. My college coaching career was at stake with this one play.

Larry ran ninety yards untouched for a touchdown, and we won the game 17–9. That would have been the end of the story except that a few years later Larry was punting for the Miami Dolphins. He pulled out a victory over the Pittsburgh Steelers with his stutter-step technique, propelling Miami into the Super Bowl. Don Shula later told me that Larry had pulled that trick on his own—that he had learned it during his days at Kentucky. Larry Seiple built on his experience and became responsible for Miami's opportunity to become world champions.

After four years at Kentucky, I was approached by several colleges for head coaching positions. Oklahoma, one of the top football programs in the nation, was among those schools. When Bud Wilkinson retired from coaching, his top aide, Gomer Jones, became director of athletics. The head job was accepted by Jim McKenzie, the top assistant at Arkansas, who came from the highly successful program of Frank Broyles. Coach McKenzie played collegiate football at the University of Kentucky under Coach Bear Bryant, and Jim was considered the top defensive coach in America.

Jim called and asked me to join him in Norman as offensive coordinator. I accepted his offer and came on staff.

Darrell Royal, the astute head coach at the University of Texas, remarked at the time that our staff was "the strongest in major college football." Jim put together a group that included Pat James, another Bear Bryant protégé, to head up the defense; as defensive secondary coach, Chuck Fairbanks, who later became head coach at the University of Oklahoma, of the New England Patriots, and at the University of Colorado; and Swede Lee, a former linebacker coached by Darrell Royal, as linebacker coach. Jim's offensive line coach, Barry Switzer, became head coach at Oklahoma before moving on to lead the Dallas Cowboys. Galen Hall, Jim's receiver coach, later became head coach at the University of Florida before joining Joe Paterno at Penn State University.

1966 University of Oklahoma Football Staff
Left to right: Galen Hall, Barry Switzer, Homer Rice, Jim Mackenzie,
Pat James, Chuck Fairbanks, and Swede Lee

The one game I will never forget was our nationally-televised Thanksgiving Day game against Nebraska, then coached by Bob Devany. The undefeated Cornhuskers were looking forward to a national championship. They were the defending Big Eight champions and had set their sights on playing the University of Alabama in the Sugar Bowl. During the week of the game, I met with Bud Wilkinson, who would be supplying the color commentary for ABC's broadcast. I spent several hours with him, explaining our strategy for the game. Bud was a legend as the former football coach at Oklahoma and for winning several national championships. He was a top coach, and I always had a lot of respect for Bud as a person, as well. When I coached the Cincinnati Bengals in coming years and Bud served as head coach of the Kansas City Chiefs, he and I would meet at midfield before game time. Recently, writer Wann Smith was putting together a book on Oklahoma football and contacted me to ask how our Sooners pulled out a victory with less than a minute to play. Our conversation brought back all the details of that memorable game.

The game with Nebraska turned out to be very close throughout and to the very end. The Cornhuskers took a slim lead down the stretch and were ahead 9–7 with only minutes to play. After receiving the kickoff, quarterback Bobby Warmack moved our team quickly into Nebraska's territory. On third down and facing a long-yardage situation, I prepared to call the play. We were out of field-goal range and needed a first down to have an opportunity to kick for the winning points. We had the ball on Nebraska's forty-five-yard line. Down by two points and facing a third-and-long situation, everyone realized the call from my perch in the press box would be crucial.

Earlier in the game, whenever we were on defense, I had spent the time reviewing our opponent's tendencies during specific situations. In each of the third-and-long situations, Nebraska lined up in an even defense, with the defensive guards over our offensive guards and rushing from the outside. This left the area over our center vacant.

I had not called a draw play the entire game. Doing so now would be a high-risk call. Should we not get a first down, we would remain out of range for a field goal attempt. Nevertheless, I sent the play to the sideline, where Coach Barry Switzer would signal the play to quarterback Bobby Warmack. Coach MacKenzie heard my call, grabbed the headset and yelled at me, "What in the—are you calling, Homer? We need to throw the—football to get into field-goal range!"

All I could say was, "Coach, trust me." Just as I had done during the Kentucky and Ole Miss moment, I put myself into a situation where my football coaching career was riding on one play. My own game plan was that if the play didn't work, I was going to walk out of the stadium, get on a bus, and go home.

The ball was snapped. Warmach handed the ball to fullback Mike Harper, who broke through the vacant spot as the defense was rushing outside on the assumption that we would pass. Mike made it all the way to the two-yard line. We quickly lined up and kicked the field goal for a 10–9 victory. After the game, I met Nebraska's young offensive coordinator, Tom Osborne, who congratulated me on the call. Tom later became Nebraska's head coach and won back-to-back national championships. One week later, our own head coach, Jim Mackenzie, was named Coach of the Year.

More head coaching job opportunities beckoned after that season. Phyllis and I discussed each one, but we decided not to move again so quickly. Going into spring practice, friends from Cincinnati called us to urge us to come home and coach the University of Cincinnati Bearcats. After going through some sleepless nights, we finally decided to return to our home area. We would again live in our hometown of Fort Thomas, Kentucky, across the Ohio River. Jim Mackenzie came to visit us to speak at a clinic we had for the area's high school coaches. When he boarded the plane back to Norman, Oklahoma, I did not realize that I would never see him again. One month later, Jim died of a massive heart attack at the young age of thirty-seven. What a tragic loss that was. In my opinion, Coach Jim MacKenzie could have been one of the nation's top coaches of all time in football. He was a proven positive leader.

At the University of Cincinnati, our staff put together a very exciting team going into our second season. Our offense operated out of a spread formation running the triple-option play. We also demonstrated a backup passing attack that would lead the nation in offense. Quarterback Greg Cook later became an all-America selection. Cook and wide receiver Jim O'Brien teamed up to become the nation's scoring leaders. We went into the last game of our season facing our most important rival, Miami (Ohio) University, coached by Bo Schembechler. Miami was the best defensive team in the nation, and our Bearcats were the leading offensive team. The media built up the game as a national-level showdown between offense and defense. As the game progressed, it was a typical Miami-controlled game with that team scoring in each quarter but keeping its opponent off the scoreboard. Going into the fourth and final quarter, Miami led 21–0. Given our team's strength in offense, this was an unusual position for us to be in during a game. We had previously scored in each quarter throughout the season.

We were still behind 21–0 with four minutes to play. Then our team exploded with a score, making it 21–7. An on-side kick recovery gave us an opportunity to score again, and we were at 21–14. We scored again, making it 21–20, but we failed to convert on a two-point play and did not take the lead. Resorting again to an on-side kick, we were not successful in maintaining possession. Our effort gave Miami the ball at midfield, with less than two minutes to play. With our defense holding them, we called time-out after each down to bring the situation to a fourth down, forcing Miami to punt. Their punter kicked the ball into the end zone.

We now had the ball on our twenty-yard line with only twenty seconds remaining. With no time-outs left, our quarterback completed two passes with the receivers stepping out of bounds to stop the clock. We were in Miami territory with three seconds left on the clock. We lined up for Jim O'Brien to attempt a forty-seven-yard field goal with a strong cross wind. I remember instinctively yelling to Jim, "Kick into the wind!"

The ball was snapped to our holder, Greg Cook, and he placed

The University of Cincinnati's Jim O'Brien kicks the winning field goal to defeat Miami with three seconds to play. All-American Greg Cook took the snap for the famous comeback win in 1968.

the ball down as Jim O'Brien kicked the football in a high, swirling arc through the goalposts. We clinched a 23–21 victory— and one that is impossible to ever forget. Afterward, Coach Schembechler left to become the head coach at the University of Michigan. He became one of our most successful coaches, serving as president of the American Football Coaches Association.

I later coached at Rice University and had the opportunity to develop another all-America quarterback, Tommy Kramer. Our offensive statistics topped the nation, and Tommy was the unanimous choice for quarterback of the all-America squad in 1976.

I saw Tommy as my fourth quarterback, with potential to be an All American and drafted in the NFL's first round. He accomplished those distinctions by setting several SWC season passing and rushing records, and finishing in the top category of balloting for the Heisman Trophy. He was the first player in the Southwest Conference to register 3,000 yards total offense in one season. Tommy led the nation in both passing and total offense in 1976.

In December 2013 I traveled to New York City for the National Football Foundation's College Football Hall of Fame induction ceremony. Tommy had been selected for this prestigious award. In his remarks, Tommy generously gave me credit for his rise to fame as an outstanding quarterback. Tommy went on to be a superior quarterback for the Minnesota Vikings for several years.

From Rice, Phyllis and I accepted Paul Brown's invitation to coach the Cincinnati Bengals. That position completed my football coaching career, and one game will always belong in my memory.

The Cincinnati Bengals played the World Champion Pittsburgh Steelers on October 14, 1979. The matchup pitted us against Steelers' Coach Chuck Noll and a team that would go on to win a fourth Super Bowl championship. "Mean Joe" Greene anchored a defense known as the Iron Curtain, and

Tommy Kramer

quarterback Terry Bradshaw directed a scoring machine that featured wide receiver Lynn Swan. The team ranked as one of the best offensive units in the NFL. In preparation for this big game in Cincinnati, our quarterback, Ken Anderson, studied the Iron Curtain blitz patterns. He developed an automatic play that would get us out of a bad situation and, hopefully, become a big gainer for us. Our game the year before with the Steelers in Pittsburgh had been very close, and we believed we had a chance in the game at Cincinnati.

In Pittsburgh the previous year, I had been at one end of the bench during a play when the Steelers punted to us. As all the players jumped up to watch our safety receive the punt, I moved

Homer with legendary coach Paul Brown
at the Cincinnati Bengals preseason camp.

slightly onto the field to get a view of our return. One of the
Steelers' players hit me from behind as he covered the kick return.
The collision knocked me completely off my feet. I went flying on
the wet turf and actually slid under our bench. It all happened so
fast that none of the players or coaches following the play at the
other end of the field saw any of the action at my end of the
bench. Only when one of our equipment men moved back toward the bench to pick up some headgear for a player did anyone
realize that I was under the bench.

"Coach, what are you doing down there?" he asked me. I responded that one of the Steelers had hit me. As Bengals players
turned back toward the bench, they began to talk among themselves, especially at the end of the game after our close loss to
Pittsburgh. They determined to remember this incident when the

Steelers came to Cincinnati the next fall. To this day, I do not know whether I was hit by accident or on purpose.

When that game approached, I remembered the last year's encounter and wondered whether any of the players remembered. The kickoff took my attention to the field as the game started. Ken Anderson picked up six flaws in the Steelers blitz in that game, allowing us to score four touchdowns and two field goals, pummeling our opponents, 34–3. They finally scored a touchdown on the last play of the game, making the final score 34–10. During Pittsburgh's Super Bowl championship years, that game with the Cincinnati Bengals ranks as one of the Steelers' worst defeats. That win closed out my coaching career. Isaac Curtis, all the Bengals, and I could put that win in our memory banks.

Archie Griffin was one player who had a big game on that day. I have always been a strong admirer of Archie, who is the only two-time Heisman Trophy winner in the history of college football. He is much more than a great football player for the Ohio State University and the Cincinnati Bengals. He is a positive leader in all of life's undertakings. He was outstanding in the business world, but he chose to come back to Ohio State as the senior associate athletic director of all sports. He now serves that great institution as the head of the Ohio State Alumni Association, and his leadership role keeps him in touch with alumni and friends of Ohio State. What better person to represent his university? Wherever Archie speaks he shares his faith. He is an inspiration to young people who aspire to become leaders in their own careers and lives.

From coaching at three levels (high school, college, and pro) for twenty-seven years I certainly had highlights to look back on, but I became interested in the entire program on the collegiate level. I became director of athletics at the University of North Carolina, at Rice University, and at the Georgia Institute of Technology (Georgia Tech). At the latter, the title of executive assistant to the

Ohio State University's Archie Griffin is the only two-time
Heisman Trophy winner in history, and Homer's favorite running
back with the Cincinnati Bengals.

president was added. My seventeen years at Georgia Tech did not
end with my retirement in 1997. At the age of seventy, I became an
adjunct professor, teaching a course titled "Leadership Fitness" to
an outstanding group of young people. This actually kept me
young, too, and inspired me to continue my work. During the
1996 Summer Olympic Games, I served as the senior administrator. My work with student-athletes in the Total Person Program
continues to be enough to keep me busy for as long as I am capable. My book *Lessons for Leaders* speaks more about the college
athletic administrative side of my work. Overall, this has been a
very interesting career for my family and me. I can't wait for the
next day to arrive so I can get up early and keep on keeping on.

TRACKING
POSITIVE LEADERS

TRACKING
POSITIVE LEADERS

In everyday life I come across more *positive leaders* than *negative leaders*. It is amazing how many more people are positive rather than negative leaders. Of course we hear more about the latter, but I look for the positives! I am often asked, "What is the difference between the two types of leaders?" Leadership has many styles, but *negative* refers to specific traits. A person may be arrogant or not listen to employees, the board, or any supportive group. He or she can be dishonest, greedy, a poor communicator, or any number of negatives. This type of person might have success, but in time he or she will fail. In some cases, that person may take the company, team, or any group down.

On the other side is the positive leader. This person has integrity and is honest, is a good listener and communicator, is moral, and exhibits a host of positives. He or she will always succeed because of doing the right thing time and again. Real integrity is doing what is right without knowing that anyone will know whether or not you did. Despite any temporary setbacks, a positive leader takes his or her company, team, or organization to the top.

Each of these two types of leaders possesses the knowledge necessary to know how to lead, but those who lean toward the negative will always fail and in most cases bring failure to the entire group they pull in their direction. In *Leadership Fitness*, I have emphasized and brought forth the positive. Although we recognize the negative, we simply must not dwell on this type. Applying positive principles to our lives will give us the best chance to succeed and influence others for the better. However, we must always remember that we cannot do this alone. We need a strong relationship with God as a foundation to carry on.

My extended network has allowed me to come across many people and organizations that provide examples of positive leadership. Each of the following twenty-two cases merits entry into the Hall of Positive Leadership.

JOHN TONER

If I were called upon to name the one person in intercollegiate athletics who has made the most impact and is most respected in this profession, I would not hesitate to name John Toner. He excelled as a player, a coach, and an administrator at each level. Most important, he did it with the highest principles, integrity, and purpose.

I first met John in 1957 when he was a football coach at Columbia University. He came to my high school, Highlands High School in Fort Thomas, Kentucky, seeking outstanding football players in the greater Cincinnati area with academic achievement equal to Columbia's tough admissions policies. Highlands High School, where I was head football coach, was one of those schools.

We immediately became friends. I realized upon our meeting that Coach Toner was ahead of his time. He gave me important pointers in weight lifting and other fitness exercises. I applied these to my high school program. By the next fall, Highlands High School had the highest ranked team in our state, enabling us to claim the title of state champion. Weight lifting and off-season training were new features for football programs at that time, and very few teams added such activities to their regimens. This training gave us an edge over our opponents.

In early September 2010, I received a call from my good friend Dutch Baughman, executive director of the Division 1A Athletic Directors Association and another noted positive leader. Dutch informed me that John Toner had been selected as the recipient of the Homer Rice Athletic Director of the Year Award. I was the first president of the 1A Athletic Directors organization, which attached my name to the award given each year at the association's annual meeting in Dallas, Texas. After receiving the call from Dutch, I called Jack Lengyel to inform him that John Toner would be receiving the award. We both made arrangements to attend the ceremony because of our three-way friendship. Someone once called us the three musketeers.

At the moment John received the large plaque, I realized again what a great career this man had achieved. His mother was responsible for starting his career as he grew up on the island of Nantucket in the 1930s. She realized that the only way to keep her eight children (and particularly her two sons) out of trouble involved sports. When a sports-minded Congregationalist minister named Fred Bennett moved to the island and built a gymnasium, Helen Toner became Nantucket's unofficial sports commissioner. She organized youth leagues for both boys and girls and encouraged the high school to start sports programs. By the time John reached his midteens, Nantucket's high school teams were among the best in New England.

John was involved in every aspect of those sports. Each season, his father's drugstore became the hangout for all sports enthusiasts. John's interest in attending college grew as he realized he could continue his education and also become an even more talented football player. He had the support of his parents and all the sports fans who patronized his dad's drugstore.

John planned to attend Boston University and play football following his high school graduation in 1941. But events changed his plan: first, his father becoming ill that summer, and then the Japanese bombed Pearl Harbor in December. John enlisted in the army and put his athletic aspirations on hold while he served in the Signal Corps. In the months leading up to the D-Day invasion, that role led him to his first experience as a true athletic administrator. One of the challenges the army faced during the war was how to keep tens of thousands of restless troops occupied in southern England. John organized sports activities on the bases, and then he was charged with developing recreation fields and activities behind the front lines for troops as they rotated from combat. He gained abilities as a sports administrator from this experience and made a contribution to the physical and mental effectiveness of soldiers.

After World War II, John resumed working toward his original aspiration of becoming an outstanding football player for Boston University. His success on the team presented him with an opportunity to enter the coaching field as an assistant football coach at Boston University. In 1954, he became head coach at Connecticut's New Britain High School. That team won state championships and was invited to play Miami Senior High School in Miami, Florida, creating what many considered to be the matchup that determined the high school national champions in the United States. The governors from Connecticut and Florida both got involved because of the stature of the game. The two coaches facing each other in that game also became distinguished. John faced Coach Charlie Tate, who later coached under Bobby Dodd at George Tech and was head coach at Miami University during the time that John was head coach at the University of Connecticut.

From New Britain High School, John accepted the position of backfield coach at Columbia University. He next became head football coach at the University of Connecticut. Soon after, he accepted the added responsibility of being director of athletics, and John's work played a key role in saving the football program at that school. After five years as head coach, he turned the coaching duties over to Bob Casciola, his top assistant. Bob Casciola is another positive leader in our Hall of Positive Leaders group, and he eventually was named president of the National Football Foundation and College Hall of Fame.

John Toner's leadership skills provided Connecticut with many successes. The Huskies' soccer teams were national powers. John hired men's basketball coach Jim Calhoun, who became a national championship coach. Geno Auriemma, the famous women's basketball coach, headed up another national championship program. John set the tone for Connecticut to move into Division 1A football, and he put his school on the map in NCAA competition. His development of connections with ESPN and the NCAA broke ground for the exceptional cable television coverage of the college sports scene that we enjoy today.

John Toner's leadership talents led him to become president of the National Collegiate Athletic Association (NCAA). Serving for two terms, he led our organization to its highest level, benefiting all colleges and universities in America.

His influence will be felt for years to come. In his honor, the National Football Foundation and College Hall of Fame present each year the John Toner Award to a deserving director of athletics. However, a single award cannot pay sufficient tribute to this distinguished man in our association who exhibits the highest of integrity.

John and I served on various national committees together, and our friendship continues. John has retired to Savannah, Georgia, but he still plays a big role as a national leader in collegiate sports programs. It has been a privilege in the past several years to invite John and his lovely wife, Claire, to meet us in Atlanta for a Georgia Tech football weekend. Being a friend of the Toners is a special treasure I will always cherish.

JOE K. McCUTCHEN

Recently I traveled to Ellijay, Georgia, in the foothills of the beautiful Blue Ridge Mountains at the request of my good friend Joe K. McCutchen Jr. to appear on his television show, *Focus on Excellence*. Joe publishes a newsletter each month titled *McCutchen Reports* regarding issues in our country affecting taxpayers. His work is thorough, entertaining, and thought provoking. He is on top of all the news that produces information important to every American. I have benefitted from his newsletter each month, increasing my understanding of what is going on in our government and where our country is headed. Joe "fights" for what is right. I believe in his approach and respect his hard work to obtain information. His "grading" of congressmen helps me to keep track of congressional votes and to know whether what is going on is in the long-term best interests of our nation. Joe McCutchen is a positive leader. He gave up a lucrative carpet business to spend each day looking out for us, and I asked him why he did that. Here is his reply.

"In 1985, my wife, Betty, and I took our three children on a trip to Europe and decided to visit Czechoslovakia, which was still a communist country at that time. It was quite an intimidating experience to go behind the Iron Curtain and see it firsthand. When we entered the country to visit the city of Bratislava, the guards and guard dogs thoroughly checked our car. There were lots of papers to be filled out, and all of the personnel gave us unwelcoming and hostile looks. After passing the inspection point, we traveled into Bratislava and have never seen such gloomy buildings and subdued and unhappy-looking people on the streets.

"We had a prolonged search for a restaurant, and when we found one, the food was terrible and the people very unfriendly. At the border you had to exchange a certain amount of currency per person to enter, and you were not permitted to take it out of the country when you left. The downtown was filled with many four-story buildings, but we could not find a store of any kind in which to spend our money. After driving around for quite a while, we at last found a shop which had souvenir items, and we succeeded in getting rid of our money.

"After the day's visit, we arrived back at the border crossing and had to go through two checkpoints, where the guards and guard dogs inspected our car again. While there we heard a gunshot ring out. The next day in Vienna we found out that a man had been shot trying to escape to freedom—and that was the shot we had heard.

"This experience made me so aware of what communism can do to a country and its people that my parents and I closed down our carpet mill, and I decided to spend the rest of my life doing everything in my power to protect our precious freedoms and to prevent our country from moving toward socialism. Since 1985, with my newsletter and television and radio show, I have done my best to communicate to the American people that we must keep our budgets balanced and taxes low so that we will not lose our freedoms to too much government. People like Ronald Regan, Pat Buchanan, Larry McDonald, and Margaret Thatcher inspired me to spend my time working for less government and more freedom. I have appreciated so much the people who have supported my efforts and encouraged me with my newsletter.

They have inspired me to do a better job of fighting for capitalism and the great free enterprise system that has given us such a
high standard of living in our country."

It is a privilege to add Joe McCutchen to my list of *positive
leaders*. No one in America has worked longer and harder than
Joe to keep us informed of the right path to pursue in our government. Congressmen and congresswomen had better do what
is right or they will be singled out, and Joe McCutchen will let
us know quickly. We are fortunate to have positive leaders in our
nation fighting for freedom.

JACK LENGYEL

On November 14, 1970, Southern Airways Charter Flight
932 took off from Stallings Field at Kingston, North Carolina,
en route to the Tri-State Airport at Huntington, West Virginia.
The Marshall University football team, coaches, and boosters
were on board after playing the East Carolina Pirates at Ficklen
Stadium in Greenville, North Carolina. On the plane's final approach, the aircraft crashed into a hill just short of the Tri-State
Airport, killing all seventy-five people on board. The tragedy
was the worst in the history of collegiate football.

On the same afternoon, the young head coach of the College
of Wooster (Ohio) football team was playing for the Ohio
Conference championship. Thirty-four-year-old Coach Jack
Lengyel went home after the game to enjoy dinner with his wife
Sandy and their two young sons. As Coach Lengyel watched television to pick up game scores around the country, a news flash
on the screen told about the terrible crash of the Marshall football team. The tragedy had killed everyone on board: players,
coaches, many boosters, and several prominent citizens, including four physicians, state legislators, and city councilmen. As it

Jack Lengyel

turned out, seventy children lost at least one parent in the crash, with eighteen of them left orphaned. After a few days went by, Marshall University made the announcement that the school was considering discontinuation of the football program.

Jack Lengyel pondered this announcement and in a few days, after discussing it with his family, Jack wrote to Marshall University's president about his interest in taking the position as their new coach to restore the program and aid in the community's recovery. Coach Lengyel was hired as the head coach only thirty-one days before spring practice, but he produced a miracle. He put together a team that became competitive, and he spent endless hours helping community members work through the healing process.

Jack Lengyel had an attractive coaching record serving Akron University; Fort Bragg, North Carolina; Barberton (Ohio) High School; Heidelberg College; and Cornell University. At the College of Wooster, he was the youngest head coach in the NCAA. He always approached life as a highly positive leader. Jack laid the foundation for Marshall University's most winning seasons of football in the 1990s.

Recently, we all have seen the movie *We Are Marshall*. Jack commented on the movie, in light of his deep knowledge about what the university community went through during the tragedy and in coming back from it. He said, "The *We Are Marshall* movie is not a football movie, rather it's a story about a community, university, and a football team facing adversity." This related to the greatest lessons in life and football. "To face adversity, get back up off the ground and go on to recovery and success." Jack Lengyel displayed positive leadership in leading a community back.

Jack went on to become one of the top collegiate athletic directors in history at Fresno State, Missouri, and the U.S. Naval Academy. In March 2008, he received a phone call from the Canadian Public Television station director. She had seen *We Are Marshall*, and she told Coach Lengyel news about a recent tragedy in Brahurst, New Brunswick, Canada.

On January 16, 2008, a basketball coach was returning home after a game with his team when his van skidded across the road and hit a semitractor trailer, killing his wife and seven players. Coach Lengyel called the principal of Bathurst High School and offered to fly to the school at his own expense to help them understand what they needed to be prepared to do after the tragedy. He met with the students, teachers, coaches, administration, and parents of players lost in the tragic accident sharing his experiences from the Marshall tragedy. At the press conference upon his arrival, Jack advised that the Province of New Brunswick should eliminate the use of fifteen-passenger vans to transport students and athletics teams. "We should not be putting our most prized possessions, our children, in unsafe vehicles," he said.

One of the mothers accepted his suggestion that she take up the issue of banning the vans as a way to honor her son and the other players who had lost their lives. Subsequently, three of the mothers led an effort to get legislation passed regarding use of the large transport vans. Those three women won, and the legislation was passed. Jack Lengyel's inspirational message had been well received and was tremendously appreciated. Jack Lengyel will always qualify as a true positive leader in my book.

MIKE LUDE

In putting together a list of positive leaders with whom I have been associated in intercollegiate athletics, it is impossible to leave one name off the list: Mike Lude. Mike and Rena Lude have been our dear friends for more than forty years. If I had a goal in college sports that needed to be accomplished, I would call Mike. He is number one for getting a job done with perfect success. He also would handle the job with integrity at the highest level. Mike has an unbelievably successful career. He is a graduate of the famous Hillsdale College, where he was an outstanding football player and the captain under legendary football coach David Nelson.

After college, Mike joined Coach Nelson at Hillsdale College and the University of Maine before going to the University of Delaware, where the famous winged-T offense was developed. Mike continued on to become head coach at Colorado State University. From coaching, Mike became an ultrasuccessful director of athletics. His superb job as head of the University of Washington's program produced success after success, culminating in a national championship. Lieutenant Mike Lude served his country in World War II as a platoon leader, 5th Battalion, First Amphibian Group, Fleet Marine Force Pacific, in the U.S. Marine Corps. Mike will always be in my Hall of Positive Leaders.

JOHN ROUSH

In August 2009, *Forbes* magazine named Centre College in Danville, Kentucky, the best university or college in the South. This topped Duke, North Carolina, Virginia, Georgia Tech, and other great institutions. Back in the late 1940s after World War II, all of us who attended Centre at the time knew this—and now we are glad that finally everyone else does too. At our reunion in 2010, we felt extremely proud of the ranking.

Centre College gave me a college education at the best school in the South after I had attended one of the best high schools in the nation and served in the U.S. Navy during World War II. With small classes, we were able to interact directly with our professors. My memory, thinking back, is that they cared for us. My undergraduate education gave me special training before I accepted my first job.

The president of Centre College is John Roush. When I go to Centre for a visit, I always spend time with President Roush and his lovely wife, Susie. The Roushes are real winners. John as president and Susie as first lady serve the students, faculty, and alumni as family.

John is a highly productive individual. As an outstanding student-athlete and former football coach at Miami (Ohio) University, he became one of the top administrators and educators in collegiate circles. He has brought many positive aspects to the Centre campus throughout his term as president. His leadership is greatly appreciated by all of us who attended this excellent institution on one of the most beautiful campuses in the nation. President Roush also teaches a leadership class on campus, and I am looking forward to accepting his request that I interact with his class and perhaps teach some of the principles from *Leadership Fitness*. John Roush is definitely a positive leader in our society.

MIKE CLEARY

Mike Cleary is one of my favorite friends. I first met Mike over forty years ago, when I was entering the sports profession as director of athletics at the University of North Carolina. At the time, Mike was the executive director of the National Association of Collegiate Directors of Athletics (NACDA). In January 2010, Mike stepped down as the leader of NACDA, the largest professional organization for athletic administrators in America. Mike was the first leader for this group when it formed. The group's growth from 1966 to today is a story in itself.

Mike's positive leadership has provided every person in an athletic administrative role the opportunity to excel and achieve successful results. It wasn't long after I first met Mike that I became involved in several opportunities to serve the organization. In the early 1970s we instituted a program to train young administrators in the varied operations of a sound and successful intercollegiate system. My role was in the first level, which brought out leaders of major institutions to teach aspects vital to running university programs. And Mike did not leave out the smaller schools. He always included everyone in the progress of learning. Those seminars worked. Many of the top leaders look back on those sessions as contributors to their own successes.

At the time, not one book was available for training a person in the role of director of athletics. I got busy and authored a program with my good friend Paul J. Meyer titled *Leadership in Athletics*. I added a slide presentation to teach this book in a class setting. Mike Cleary had the vision to identify those who needed such a program, how to grow people as professionals, and how to keep up with the changing training needs for administrators. During those years we had only one graduate degree program in the United States in athletics administration: Ohio University in Athens, Ohio. Today we have hundreds.

We must give Mike credit for being at the forefront of preparing all of us who have gone on to direct outstanding departments in educational institutions throughout the United States, Canada, and other locations. As Mike retires, we are fortunate to have Bob Vecchione, former deputy executive director, to move into the top leadership role of NACDA. A marketing expert, Bob is ready to assume this responsibility and to provide the leadership necessary to continue the organization's many successes. Associate Executive Pat Manak, another positive leader at NACDA, will continue to serve the organization.

It is only fitting that at our annual convention Mike is being honored with the association's Merit of Honor Award. On top of that, that award will in future years be called the Michael J. Cleary Merit of Honor Award. Mike always stood on the sidelines and allowed others to receive credit and awards, but this time he will just have to accept a truly prestigious honor. Mike Cleary will add another plus to the Hall of Positive Leaders.

JOHN SWOFFORD

John Swofford, commissioner of the Atlantic Coast Conference, is the 2011 winner of the National Association of Collegiate Directors of Athletics (NACDA) James J. Corbett Memorial Award, the highest honor given by NACDA. John Swofford will always be a member of my Hall of Positive Leaders.

I shall never forget in the early 1970s when John visited my office in Chapel Hill during my directorship at the University of

North Carolina. He inquired, "What would it take to become a director of athletics?" On a Saturday afternoon in beautiful Kenan Stadium that same week, John would quarterback Coach Bill Dooley's Tarheels to victory over the Vanderbilt Commodores, with four touchdown passes. The next evening, Phyllis and I were tuned in to watch *The Ed Sullivan Show* on Sunday. Ed Sullivan pointed out John Swofford in the audience as the quarterback who had thrown four touchdowns to beat Vanderbilt. I wondered what John was doing in New York City attending *The Ed Sullivan Show*. Mr. Sullivan went on to introduce John's older brother Oliver, the famous singer who performed that night with his popular rendition of "Good Morning Starshine."

John Swofford graduated from the University of North Carolina as a Morehead Scholar and embarked upon his career by attending the master's degree program in sports administration at Ohio University in Athens. His first position was with another Hall of Positive Leaders person, Gene Corrigan at the University of Virginia. John then came back to his school at UNC and in time became the youngest director of athletics in the nation. He spent seventeen years heading the program at UNC. His remarkable leadership landed him the commissioner of the Atlanta Coast Conference position. His stellar performance and outstanding positive leadership earned John the coveted NACDA Corbett award.

His professional and friendly approach earns unbelievable respect from his peers and athletic programs throughout the United States. It is always a pleasure for Phyllis and our daughters to see John and his lovely wife, Nora, when they pay a visit to our box at football games in the Bobby Dodd Stadium at Georgia Tech so we can spend special moments with these two wonderful friends. John Swofford is the ultimate leader of positive leadership.

BEN RICE

My wife, Phyllis, graduated from Middlesboro High School in 1945 before attending the University of North Carolina Women's College. Although I moved from Middlesboro in 1942 to Fort Thomas, I was a member of that class while living in Middlesboro from 1939 to 1942. I was always invited to the class reunions along with Phyllis. One person who always impressed me was Ben Rice.

Ben was the leader of the 1945 class, and his personality has kept class members coming back year after year. After earning his undergraduate degree at Lincoln Memorial University, Ben attended Richmond Technological Seminary and became a pastor. He enlisted in the navy in 1945, returned to earn his degree and then went back in the navy to become a chaplain. Lieutenant Rice spent twenty-five years serving in the military and retired as Captain Ben Rice. Not long into retirement, he began serving many people through church work and goodwill leadership.

One task he undertook was contacting every member of his Middlesboro High School class. He not only contacted them but also kept up with their activities and whereabouts. He publishes a newsletter each quarter for the class members, keeping everyone connected with up-to-date class news, and arranges the annual reunion each year. I do not believe another person anywhere spends the time and effort serving his classmates that Ben Rice does. As of this writing, the class will next celebrate sixty-six years since graduation. Ben Rice is a positive leader who has dedicated his life to helping and serving others as a pastor, chaplain, and classmate.

THE KNOWLEDGE IS POWER PROGRAM

My friend Bill Pritchard picked me up early one morning with his son, Tom Pritchard, volunteer chairman of the Knowledge Is Power Program (KIPP) board of directors. The metro Atlanta board for KIPP is comprised of business and community leaders, and Tom is president of E2 Capital Group. We shuttled off to one of the KIPP schools in southeast Atlanta, a low-income section of the city. I had no idea what I was getting into. I knew very little about the program.

I was prepared to see a typical school, with kids running in the halls, loud voices, and maybe some unclean restrooms and a cafeteria. In my days as a college football coach, I had recruited players from schools throughout the country, including from many rundown school environments. However, this was different. At the KIPP school, disciplined students worked hard at their studies. I saw teachers with happy faces, working close to students, and a clean school in every section. I was excited when I learned what this school was all about.

After touring the school, I was given Jay Mathews's book, *Work Hard, Be Nice.* Mathews told the story of Mike Feinberg and Dave Levin, who had founded KIPP, and I just had to add them to my list of positive leaders. As I mentioned, I did not know a lot about their program when I went to the school. I did know about Teach for America, because some of my students from the leadership fitness class at Georgia Tech had volunteered for this two-year program. Kendra Christensen, one of my former students and a class student assistant, entered the Teach for America program and kept me informed.

Mike Feinberg and Dave Levin had started in that program. They realized the change they could make by taking a group of kids from low-income situations, beginning in the fifth grade, and continuing teaching them through the eighth grade. If they could do that, Mike and Dave knew they could dispel the belief that inner-city kids and rural children raised by parents who themselves struggled in school were largely doomed to low grades, low test scores that led to menial jobs, and difficult lives.

Mike and Dave did exactly as they had planned. When I went back to the charter school that I had visited, I saw that these KIPPsters excelled academically, above their peers across the state of Georgia. The school I saw was named Georgia's top performing nonselective middle school serving a majority of low-income students. Those students have proven that they are capable of achieving exceptional results, with the help of the KIPP school. I suggest that you support this program for building a better tomorrow, making our country a better place to live and work. Mike Feinberg and Dave Levin are most certainly positive leaders.

POWELL/KAISER

Through the years, I have been fortunate to meet many wonderful and positive people. A book on just these exceptional people in our midst would be fascinating and worthwhile, but I must stick to the space limits of a publisher for now. A pair of couples whom I have enjoyed being around are Josh and Karen Powell and Roger and Beverly Kaiser.

Josh and Roger were basketball teammates at Georgia Tech, and they were on the school's first team to reach the NCAA playoffs. Roger was an all-American and one of the most outstanding athletes in Georgia Tech's history. He went on to become one of the nation's winningest basketball coaches, capturing four national championships. Josh is from Stanford, Kentucky, just a few miles from Centre College, where I was an undergraduate, and that connection gives us a lot to talk about when we get together. Karen and Josh operate a boys camp each summer, and Beverly and Roger drop by often to help out. Josh is an outstanding baritone and sings professionally. As he has promised to sing at my funeral, I often joke that his health is a constant concern for me so that he is around when my time comes. These two couples are included in my Hall of Positive Leaders. Their influence for good has been a blessing to many over the years.

During the writing of *Tracking Positive Leaders*, my dear friend Josh Powell passed away. I can't remember how many times his positive e-mails were so fun to read that they added instant pep and energy for me. Josh was loved by many people, and he will be dearly missed.

As I look back on how our friendship took on increasing importance for me, I can visualize the moment my Phyllis lost her favorite dragonfly pin. When Phyllis fished with me on the Sun River at the Broken O Ranch in Montana, she was fascinated with the dragonflies hovering around the river. I explained that the trout feed on the dragonflies that fly about or land on the water. Phyllis was so interested in the flies that I decided to find her a dragonfly pin. She loved that pin dearly.

On one occasion she wore the pin to dinner at a restaurant on Marco Island. After we got in the car to go back to our condo, she noticed that the pin was missing from the sweater she had been wearing that evening. We went back into the restaurant and looked around our table, with no success. The proprietors also joined in the search, but could not locate the pin, so we left our name and telephone number. After we arrived home, the telephone rang. Someone had found Phyllis's pin!

We rushed back to the restaurant. Karen Powell and her sister, Elaine Freeman, had sat at the same table and Karen found the pin. She presented it to us as soon as we arrived at the restaurant. Phyllis gave Karen a big hug and loved her dearly from that point on. Our friendship with the Powells grew even stronger.

The Kaisers were close friends with the Powells, and they also visited Marco Island. The six of us became the best of friends. Sadly, misfortune hit both Josh and my Phyllis. They became extremely ill and now both are gone. The Powell, Kaiser and Rice families remain close friends, our lives brought together by a dragonfly pin and Phyllis's appreciation for one of God's smallest creatures.

KAREN SUE POWELL

As I look for positive leaders for this section, I cannot overlook Karen Sue Powell. Karen's husband, Josh Powell, captain of the 1961-62 Georgia Tech basketball team, graduated from Tech and the Emory Law School. Then in 1972, with a dream of creating a camp for boys and girls, he bought a piece of land north of Atlanta. Then he bought an old bulldozer and an old sawmill and began clearing the land, sawing lumber, and building a camp. The Josh Powell Summer Camp became a reality.

Josh passed away in May 2011 after a three-year battle with multiple myeloma. By that time the camp had become ultra-successful, with so many children visiting every summer.

Karen had lost her first husband at age forty-four to Lou Gehrig's disease (ALS). She reared their children, and several years later she met and married Josh. She stepped in and for ten years assisted Josh with the camp. Josh died fourteen days before children would be arriving for the 2011 camp season, and Karen knew she had to jump in and keep the camp alive for those thousands of youngsters.

After four years of operation, Karen keeps the Josh Powell name alive by her hands-on approach to developing expert counselors and with a loving touch for the children, offering tender care to each camper and being there every moment.

I think of presidents of large corporations, bankers, ministers, educators, and any leader of large numbers of people. Karen is in that league of leaders. Because of her positive attitude, she stands out.

On pages 286, I mentioned how the Powells and Rices became close friends. The story of the dragonfly pin that my dear wife Phyllis had lost and Karen found. After observing her expertise as a true leader, it is a pleasure to add this outstanding individual to my Hall of Positive Leaders.

G.P. "BUD" PETERSON

In the mid-1960s, I was the offensive coordinator for the University of Oklahoma football team. Several universities approached me for head coaching positions, and one was Kansas State University in Manhattan, Kansas. Had I accepted that offer, I would have coached a young, slim, and tall wide receiver named Bud Peterson. Four decades later, our paths have finally crossed.

On April 1, 2009, G.P. "Bud" Peterson, PhD, was appointed as the eleventh president of Georgia Tech. I am not sure how our relationship would have worked out when he was in college, but I have never been more impressed with an educator in the world of higher learning than this man, a former chancellor of the University of Colorado at Boulder, who is now the leader of Georgia Tech. Although I retired in 1997 as director of athletics and executive assistant to the president for athletics and served for ten years as an adjunct professor, I have continued as chairman of the Lee Candler Fund for the Total Person Program. Bud Peterson serves on that board.

We have laughed over our near-miss as coach and player, but it has been a wonderful experience working with him for the

G.P. "Bud" Peterson and his wife, Val Peterson

Candler Fund. Bud and his lovely wife, First Lady Val Peterson, are a big hit on campus and at each place they travel in the Georgia Tech nation. We are fortunate to have the Petersons leading our school. Through the Foundation for Global Leadership, he aims to take Georgia Tech to the next level as a nationally and globally preeminent institution of higher learning. Although this is a high challenge, I am convinced he will take us there. President "Bud" Peterson is a true positive leader.

TERENCE MOORE

Through the years in my position in the world of sports I have become acquainted with many people and made great friends through those meetings. With one young sportswriter in 1978, I began an instant friendship. His name is Terence Moore. The legendary football coach Paul Brown was introducing me as head coach of the Cincinnati Bengals, and Terence Moore, right out of Miami (Ohio) University, was covering the announcement for the *Cincinnati Enquirer*. Terence was a bright-looking young man, and I predicted to myself he would go far as a sportswriter. Later in my career, I decided to return to the collegiate ranks and accepted a position as director of athletics at Georgia Tech in Atlanta. In a few years, Terence arrived in Atlanta as a sportswriter for the *Journal-Constitution*. He looked strikingly familiar to me when our paths crossed. I asked my good friend Tony Barnhart, at the time college editor of the Atlanta paper, who this new reporter was.

Upon hearing the name Terence Moore, it all came back to me. As we became reacquainted, Terence reminded me of our first meeting in Cincinnati. Terence had left the *Enquirer* in Cincinnati for the *San Francisco Examiner*, becoming a prominent staff writer for five years before being lured to Atlanta. In 2000, the National Association of Black Journalists honored Terence for the distinction of writing a sports column for a major newspaper longer than any African American in history. Terence now is a national sports columnist and an award-winning sports

Terrence Moore

journalist. He also is a member of the Bobby Dodd Coach of the Year Foundation board and serves his community through many charitable organizations. He is a champion working with young people, moving them to their futures. It is an honor to include Terence Moore as a positive leader.

STEVE HATCHELL

One of the top administrators in the collegiate world is Steve Hatchell, president and CEO of the National Football Foundation and College Football Hall of Fame. Throughout the year, his organization sponsors many activities that honor football student-athletes and coaches at various institutions. Every December, New York City's Waldorf Astoria Hotel is host to the foundation's annual awards dinner and associated events. The awards event is a spectacular, noteworthy occasion. Steve Hatchell's superb leadership brings all of these activities into focus, and his ability to do so is a remarkable undertaking. Steve must be included in the Hall of Positive Leaders for his success in these endeavors.

ARCHIE MANNING

The chairman of the National Football Foundation and College Hall of Fame is none other than former National Football League quarterback and league Most Valuable Player Archie Manning. Archie has been a "giver" to many people and programs during his days of positive leadership. An all-American at the University of Mississippi, he has shown excellence in every field he has entered. He also is the father of two other famous quarterbacks: Peyton Manning of the Indianapolis

Colts and Eli Manning of the New York Giants. Archie Manning has been selected for practically every award given in the sports arena and many more in the civic sphere. His distinguished manners and kindness toward others are markers of his outstanding character. It is with great pleasure that I add him to the Hall of Positive Leaders.

GENE CORRIGAN

Although I have praised my good friend Gene Corrigan in the acknowledgments section of *Leadership Fitness*, I feel compelled to mention him again because of his continuing positive leadership during his retirement years. Gene and his lovely wife, Lena, have been close friends of the Rice family for more than forty years.

Recently, I received a call from Gene that he would be in Atlanta and wanted to see me. He would be visiting the city as chairman of the board for the National Football Foundation and College Hall of Fame, which was convening in Atlanta. Gene invited me to dinner and to sit in on their meeting. It was great to see him and to reflect on our association over the years.

Gene is the only person I know who has been a student-athlete, coach, director of athletics, commissioner—and president of the NCAA. I hope that in the near future a complete account will be written of his many accomplishments and the tremendous contributions he has made to intercollegiate athletics. I once called Gene Corrigan a super positive leader, placing him in the highest category, and I can only continue that ranking.

BERNADETTE McGLADE

Bernadette McGlade, one of my former associates, recently

dropped by Atlanta to give me her personal greetings. Bernadette McGlade was an outstanding student-athlete at the University of North Carolina in Chapel Hill, and she still holds the rebounding record in both women's and men's basketball at UNC. She came to Georgia Tech in 1981 at my request to coach the first varsity women's basketball team.

When I arrived on campus as director of athletics in 1980, Georgia Tech had not begun a varsity women's athletics program. This meant that we were at least twelve years behind other institutions, and I had to move fast to prevent the NCAA and the federal government from heavily penalizing the school. I turned to North Carolina and selected Bernadette to be our first female director, asking her to develop the program to meet national standards. At the same time, she was to take on the duties of head women's basketball coach. Bernadette succeeded in handling both situations and was so promising that I promoted her to senior associate athletic director of administration.

From Georgia Tech, Bernadette joined another good friend and positive leader, John Swofford, who became commissioner of the Atlantic Coast Conference. From there, Bernadette moved on to become commissioner of the Atlantic 10 Conference. Needless to say, I am very proud of Bernadette. She has accomplished so much in a short time. At Georgia Tech she also handled the important responsibility of directing the Student-Athlete Total Person Program, which she elevated to national fame.

I've had a long association with many people from UNC-Chapel Hill. The past couple of years have allowed me to travel back to Chapel Hill, where I served for eight years as director of athletics. My right-hand person at UNC was Bill Cobey, who replaced me as director of athletics. I have stayed in touch with Bill and Nancy through the years, and we enjoy visiting each other just to get some good laughs about events we were involved in

Returning to Chapel Hill, NC, in 2010 where I served as director of athletics from 1968 to 1976. Pictured with close friends: Bill Cobey (replaced me as athletic director), Albert Long (former four-letterman at UNC), and Dr. Dan Lotz (son-in-law of Billy Graham and former UNC athlete).

during our time together. Bill has had a rewarding career, including service as a U.S. House Representative and leader in the state of North Carolina. He is a positive leader for sure. While visiting the Cobeys, I also had the opportunity to meet with old friends Dan Lotz, Albert Long, Moyer Smith, Eddie and Jo Smith, and Susan and Bud Strobel. Phyllis and I enjoyed our time in North Carolina immensely.

BILL LAM

I spoke at the Impact & Legacy Summit in Chapel Hill, North Carolina, on the campus of the University of North Carolina, in April 2012. Bill Lam, the host and developer of this program, extended the invitation for me to speak.

I had know Bill since my football coaching days at University of Oklahoma in the mid-1960s when Head Coach Jim MacKenzie hired me as offensive coordinator. The night I arrived on campus for the job, Jim took me to a collegiate wrestling match between No. 1 Oklahoma State and No. 2 University of Oklahoma. One of the wrestlers for the Sooners was Bill Lam. This young man's aggressiveness and grit impressed me so much that I logged his performance in my memory bank.

Bill Lam won his event, and Oklahoma defeated Oklahoma State to become the No. 1 team in the nation. Later on, when I became director of athletics at the University of North Carolina, I needed to hire a wrestling coach. I sought out Bill Lam. He accepted my offer and took over a losing program, producing several ACC champions and becoming National Coach of the Year. Many more honors followed because of his winning ways.

Bill Lam was a winner as a student/athlete and as a coach. I might add that today he is a Positive Leader in life. He teaches the principles of success that allow the pursuit of excellence to culminate in achievement. In other words, he is passing on to others what he became himself by teaching positive leader success techniques.

The program of the 2012 seminar that Bill Lam coordinated at University of North Carolina was fantastic. We all attended a banquet to cap off the day's highly interesting activities. The evening turned out to be quite different from what I expected. The banquet was in my honor, with Bill Lam and his guests recognizing me. What a surprise! I received the largest plaque of appreciation I have ever seen.

It was difficult to hold up during the evening because I was so touched by how many of my close friends and colleagues made the effort to come. My basketball coach from Georgia Tech, Bobby Cremins, came. I saw friends from my North Carolina days: Albert Long; Bill Cobey, my right-hand assistant; Susan Strobel, my former secretary; Danny Lotz, UNC great in basketball and football, our family dentist and a very dear friend; Eddie Smith, owner of the Grady White Boat Co. and another dear friend for many years and Moyer Smith, my long-time assistant at North Carolina. Even Woody Durham, legendary voice of the Tarheels came!

There were even more, including Bernadette McGlade, my top assistant at Georgia Tech, and Jack Lengyel, a long-time friend from the Naval Academy. John Swofford, commissioner of the Atlantic Coast Conference and Barry Switzer, who had been an assistant at Oklahoma with me, "attended" through video. Barry Switzer went on to become the head coach at OU, winning three national championships. As head coach of the Dallas Cowboys, he won a Super Bowl championship. The banquet was a grand evening and a real surprise to me. Bill Lam led the conference in admirable style and again demonstrated his talent as a true Positive Leader.

PEACHTREE ROAD UNITED METHODIST CHURCH, ATLANTA

Bill Britt serves as senior minister at the church. As a positive leader, he does a lot of good to make our world a better place. Our Sunday school class is named the Timothy Class. One morning as I walked into the church on the way to our class, an elderly couple stopped me and asked about a class for retired senior citizens. I promptly mentioned the Timothy Class. They looked at each other and turned back and said, "Well, Timothy was a young boy. Why do you have his name as your class?" That was easy. I said, "When the class began forty to fifty years ago, all the class members were young." That seemed to answer their concerns, and I led them to become members of our class.

Our Sunday school class at Peachtree Road United Methodist each Sunday always produces outstanding speakers. Ron Greer is a favorite, and I always look forward to his lessons. Ron offers a pastoral counseling service at the church. If you are interested in meeting someone who wants to lead a life of faith with integrity and character (and you should), then you must read and study his book *If You Know Who You Are, You'll Know What to Do: Living with Integrity.*

I have always been intrigued by Dot Addison another speaker who leads our class each year. In compiling information, I called upon Rosalie North Castleberry to assist in the research into the life of Dot Addison. Dot Addison is a graduate of Agnes Scott, and her age of ninety-plus would fool anyone. She is so active and "literally bounces around like a teenager," as one person who knows her said. She is a beautiful woman, full of life.

Her husband graduated from Emory University, but she must have a Georgia Tech connection somewhere. She is always ready to talk with me about the Yellow Jacket teams. She wants Tech to win, I am sure of that.

Her lessons are the best I have ever heard. You feel you are in a personal conversation with her even when she addresses the entire audience. She is able to captivate every single person in a class. She brings out the history of a topic so you feel that you are present at whatever time period she talks about.

Dot has taught each series of the Discipleship classes and almost every adult Sunday School class in the church. Her humor and straightforward speaking style keeps everyone on the edge of their seats. After each of her presentations, I always leave the room feeling upbeat and carry that attitude throughout the day. Dot Addison expresses a Positive Leadership personality.

My dear friend Bill Curry is a frequent guest speaker at the church. Bill Curry decided not to retire after his many years on the athletic coaching scene. Instead, he accepted the challenge of becoming head football coach at Georgia State University and to begin the first football program in the school's history. His work establishing the program for an urban university that has never had football program before will be a major story and accomplishment. He and his lovely wife, Carolyn, are both positive leaders.

I recommend that you read Carolyn Curry's book *Suffer and Grow Strong: The Life of Ella Gertrude Clanton Thomas, 1834-1907*, which was published in April 2014. Carolyn wrote a remarkable manuscript about the Civil War era by following the diary of Miss Thomas, from Augusta, Georgia. Carolyn was so inspired by her research on the diary that she founded Women Alone, a non-profit program for women who are on their own for any of a variety of reasons. An historian with a Ph.D. in history from Georgia Sate University, Carolyn Curry has taught at Westminster Schools in Atlanta and at the University of Kentucky.

THE DANIEL FAMILY

I am amazed how many people give of their time, service, and contributions to help others all over the world. A family that does so is Robert and Lee Daniel and their children, Maggie, eleven, and Griffin, nine at this writing. The Daniel family reported the story of their travels to Nicaragua to our Sunday school class recently. The family makes a one-week trip each year between Christmas and New Year's Day to the very poor country of Nicaragua with a mission group. Once there, the group from our church serves the country by building homes for Nicaragua families with electrical power and running water. They also supply the family members with medical care, personal hygiene supplies, science kits, playground equipment, and nonfiction books for their schools. In addition they supply workshops for the teachers, Bibles, and clothes, and they interact with the people in many ways. This demonstration of a young family's willingness to give up their Christmas at home and share their time with an extremely need family in the second poorest country in the world struck me. They belong as a family to an account tracking positive leaders.

CHICK-FIL-A AND TRUETT CATHY

Truett Cathy's life goal is to shape winners. Founder and CEO of Chick-fil-A, Truett has built a nationwide chain of more than fifteen hundred restaurants that are filled every day except Sunday with loyal, raving fans. Long before he achieved such business success, Truett was teaching Sunday school to thirteen-year-old boys. And when he recognized a child was at risk because of difficult life circumstances, he reached out to him.

In the book *It's Better to Build Boys than Mend Men*, Truett Cathy wrote, "A good child nearby is about to make bad choices that will have lasting consequences and needs for you to step in right now."

Truett founded his WinShape Foundation in 1984 to make a positive impact on the lives of young people. WinShape provides college scholarships, summer camps, and other programs that help young people succeed in life. Truett also opened twelve foster homes, each accommodating up to twelve children, with two full-time foster parents who provide long-term care in a positive family environment.

You don't have to know Truett personally to see his leadership traits in action. The operators he selects for Chick-fil-A restaurants reflect his commitment to shape winners every day, inspiring loyalty from their employees and their customers as well. Truett is a positive thinker and a positive leader who is making a tremendous impact for good in our world for generations to come.

Truett Cathy's Chick-fil-A Foundation produces the Chick-fil-A Bowl, and the effort is headed by GARY STOKAN, president and CEO of the foundation. The bowl is the number-one non-BCS bowl game in the nation. It also leads all bowl games in the nation in charitable and scholarship donations, giving more than $7 million in the last eight years.

Gary Stokan has more than thirty-three years of corporate sports management experience, and many of the major events that bring exposure and economic impact to Atlanta bear his fingerprints. He created the Chick-fil-A Kickoff Game, a BCS-type neutral-site game that matches top-ranked teams to open the annual college football season. The Chick-fil-A Bowl Challenge Charity Golf Tournament also provides $500,000 each year for scholarships and charitable purposes to participating universities. The Atlanta Sports Awards also recognizes and celebrates success in Atlanta sports.

Stokan's positive leadership efforts bring the National Football Foundation and the College Football Hall of Fame to Atlanta, but they do not stop there. Gary Stokan continues his magical leadership as president of the Atlanta Sports Council, helping to brand the city the "Sports Capital of the World" and drawing a range of international-caliber sporting events to metro Atlanta. Gary Stokan is a former star basketball player and coach at North Carolina State University, and he is considered one the most influential figures in the sports arena. His superb performances place him in the Hall of Positive Leaders.

GEORGE SCHISLER

Three times a week, I attend an exercise class at the Capital City Country Club in Atlanta. Our leader, George Schisler, accepted this position in August 1972. At the time, the class members were in their thirties and forties. The class is going strong in 2011. Although the age range now is more like sixties to seventies, with some like me in our eighties, George Schisler still is in charge of the class. That's nearing the forty-year mark. In 1972, George was in charge of the fitness class at the Life of Georgia, where he designed the workout area as well as a running track on the roof of the building. The class consisted of calisthenics, floor exercises, and a lot of stretching. One hour's participation is a real workout. For a single leader to stay in charge and keep these men returning time and time again is a remarkable feat. George Schisler's positive leadership is responsible for the success of a program developing strong fitness and health for these men. The program develops not only skills to stay healthy and fit but also camaraderie through the years of strong friendships.

BOBBY DODD

Georgia Tech has always been special to me. In the late fall of 1944, I received a call from Coach Bobby Dodd at Georgia Tech. He informed me that he would become head coach going into the 1945 season, and he was interested in my coming to the school as a quarterback. Assistant coach Ray Ellis visited me, and I signed a letter of intent to become a Yellow Jacket in the fall of 1945. However, soon afterward I received my orders from the U.S. Navy to report to the Great Lakes Naval Station. Immediately after boot camp, our ship sailed from Bremerton, Washington, to the

South Pacific theater for World War II action.

I did not make it to Georgia Tech until I received the call in 1980 to serve Tech in charge of the athletic program. In 1980, I became director of athletics and executive assistant to the president at Georgia Tech. Eight years later, and before Bobby Dodd died, I had the privilege to invite Coach Dodd to my office to inform him that the State of Georgia Board of Regents had approved the naming of our stadium the Bobby Dodd Stadium at Historic Grant Field. He was extremely excited, as were all the Tech fans.

After my retirement in 1997, I became a member of the Bobby Dodd Coach of the Year Foundation Board, chaired by Jim Terry and president Bill Curry. Each year the Dodd Trophy recognizes the coach of a team that enjoys a successful season while also stressing the importance of academic excellence, outstanding leadership, strong character, and high integrity. The first recipient was Vince Dooley, the legendary coach at the University of Georgia. Many great coaches have since then been inducted, including Tom Osborne, Joe Paterno, Bill Curry, Bobby Ross, Eddie Robinson, Bob Stoops, Mack Brown, and, recently, Gary Patterson of Texas Christian University and Chris Petersen of Boise State University. There are many more. Many outstanding positive leaders have led our young men and women, and the incomparable Bobby Dodd, who built a person's character from a foundation of integrity, began their path.

In 2014, I attended the Bobby Dodd Memorial Golf Tournament hosted by Jim Terry, Chairman of the Bobby Dodd Coach of the Year Foundation. As always, Jim and Kent Keasler, the marketing positive leader of the foundation, produced another successful program. More Bobby Dodd Coach of the Year winners were present: Jim Grobe (Wake Forest), Ken Hatfield (Arkansas, Clemson, Rice University), and Fred Goldsmith (Duke). It was a grand affair as I observed the leadership Jim Terry exercised in this challenge to further the cause of the foundation.

JIM TERRY

Jim Terry has been a close friend for many years. During my time at Georgia Tech he always supported my challenges to develop a class program at Georgia Tech from his executive position at the Coca Cola Company. When Jim retired, I called on him to assist me in my Leadership Fitness class. Like his other successes, he jumped in and proved his worth many times over. Jim certainly, in my observance, belongs in my Hall of Positive Leaders. Following is an excerpt an article from *The Buzz* magazine chronicling Jim's Coca-Cola Company successes and his devotion to Georgia Tech Athletics. He is a man of Integrity without any reservations.

Talk to Terry for a few minutes, and it's easy to tell that gold and white flows through his veins.

"My father loved Coach Dodd," Terry remembered. "He didn't think there was a better football coach or gentleman than Bobby Dodd. He cared more about the well-being of student-athletes than wins and losses. He had a deep admiration for Coach Dodd, and he instilled that in me."

In 1965, Terry's father retired from the military, and the family moved back to Decatur. He attended Southwest DeKalb High School, the same as his parents.

"I always knew I wanted to go to Georgia Tech, but I wasn't sure I'd be anywhere near Georgia by the time I graduated from high school," he said.

"I'm glad we were back here, because it was my first choice.

"It was very challenging and very competitive," he said. "I knew that if I got a degree from Georgia Tech, it would be a differentiator and help me get a job in the business world."

Terry graduated with a degree in industrial management in 1972. He was weighing five job offers and settled on Coca-Cola.

"I took the job because of the great reputation Coca-Cola had as a company in the U.S. and globally," he said. "The career opportunities we discussed in the interview process were endless. Plus, I would be selling the number one brand in the world. I knew if I did well, I'd end up back in Atlanta. So I walked right across the street."

His career at Coke saw him based in Charlotte, Cincinnati, Dallas, and Denver as he rose up the ranks and managed many of the company's major accounts across multiple trade channels and some of the largest bottling groups for Coca-Cola North America.

"Georgia Tech was really my springboard into the business world," he reflected. "If it hadn't been for Georgia Tech and that degree, I'm not sure what would have happened. The degree prepared me for the real world and taught me a lot about persistence and perseverance."

In 1985, he was transferred back to Atlanta ("Just in time for New Coke," he quipped), which allowed him to reconnect with Georgia Tech.

A senior vice president at Coca-Cola, Walter Dunn, knew Terry's passion for his alma matter and introduced him to athletics director Homer Rice, fundraising chief Jack Thompson (who calls Terry "the best on the planet"), and school president Pat Crecine.

From that point on until his retirement, Terry was the point person for every major contract development, sales and marketing promotions, and alliance partnerships involving Georgia Tech.

"Even as I moved into other jobs at Coke, I kept that

Jim Terry

role," he said. "It was important to me and very meaningful to me to steward that relationship."

Upon retiring from Coke after thirty-nine years, Terry
wasn't ready for a life of leisure, so naturally he turned
his attention toward Georgia Tech. He signed on as sales
and marketing consultant with the athletic department,
working with athletics director Dan Radakovich, assistant athletics director Wayne Hogan, and IMG general
manager Tom Stipes.

"Now it's all about how I can help Georgia Tech,"
he explained. "I want to use my marketing knowledge,
sales experience, and expertise to help grow the fan base
and sales revenues for Georgia Tech."

Terry also serves as the chairman of the Bobby Dodd
Coach of the Year Foundation, which annually honors
the coach "whose program represents the Dodd coaching qualities both on and off the field."

"There's not another award like that," he said. "It's
not based on just wins and losses. We want this award

to be the Heisman Trophy for coaches. We do the pre-sentations on campus, and we're the only ones who do that. It lets the fans, players, and the coach's family be a part of it. The base platform of the award centers on doing The Dodd Way with leadership, scholarship, and integrity at the center."

CHARITIES

Giving to and helping others makes us the most happiest we will ever be. I have contributed to several charities throughout the years, and I realize the truth of this fact. Most of my contributions are directed to the betterment of the lives of young boys and girls. The Mountain Top Boys Home in Sugar Valley, Georgia, is one of those causes that I assist. My friend Burt Bridges informed me about this organization, which he has been involved with for so many years. Listening to the story of Mountain Top, I became interested because of the opportunity to help young boys from dysfunctional families find positive direction. These boys have been maltreated and in disadvantaged situations. They have been through the foster care system and adopted families. When nothing is working for them, then the Mountain Top Boys Home is the answer. Young boys learn life skills to engage in healthy family lives and have the chance to become a success in society.

If we can save one boy each year, then the effort is worth every ounce of energy we can supply. I recently finished reading the book *I Beat the Odds* by Michael Oher. Like many millions of others, I had read the book and seen the film *The Blind Side*. It was good to read Michael's book and get the exact story of his life. He came from homelessness in the Memphis inner-city ghetto and a most difficult family life and found the opportunity to join a wonderful family. With the Touhy family (Sean, Leigh Anne, son S.J., and daughter Collins), Michael overcame his background and became an all-American at Ole Miss. He was drafted in the first round of the NFL by the Baltimore Ravens. Michael has not forgotten those who helped him, and his own interest lies in assisting young boys out of similar situations today. He gives back and inspires young boys to gain the confidence they need to break out of negative situations and become positive people. Michael Oher is squarely on the list of positive leaders.

Recently, as chair of the advisory committee for the Mountain Top Boys Home, I met with friends to join me in this important mission. Jim and Judy Dellinger, Coach Bill Curry, Charles Smithgall, Jeri Goldsmith, Terence Moore, Lillian Darden, Lee Shaw, Margaret McCamish, and others also believe that if we can save one boy a year and help him to become a quality citizen who contributes to society, then we have accomplished our goal.

FOOTBALL'S GENTLE GIANT: THE BLANTON COLLIER STORY

Tracking Positive Leaders has presented to readers many people I have known through the years who qualify, without reservation, as members of the Hall of Positive Leaders. These extraordinary individuals have made our country the *best in the land*. One dear friend who is also among those leaders is Coach Blanton Collier.

Blanton's daughter, Kay Collier McLaughlin, wrote about her father in a book entitled *Football's Gentle Giant: The Blanton Collier Story*. I wanted to check resources with her but ran into a stone wall trying to locate her. Serendipitously, friends from Kentucky I knew at Marco Island, Florida, where Phyllis and I lived in the winter months after my retirement, were able to assist me in my search for Kay. As we talked on the phone about her dad and leadership, I realized that just as her dad and I had been on the same page, Kay and I had much to share on the subject of leadership and she was also a part of what I was to write.

Kay is also a Positive Leader, and I am happy to include her in the Hall of Positive Leaders. She has an earned doctor of philosophy degree in counseling psychology with subspecialties in group development, life transitions, and bereavement. She is a human relations trainer with extensive expertise and spent twenty years as an internationally-known teacher of the Suzuki Talent Education method. A prolific writer, she has authored several works in addition to the book about her father. Her most recent, *Becoming the Transformative Church: Beyond Sacred Cows, Fantasies and Fears* uses the system of the Episcopal Church where she is deputy for leadership development as the model for effective leadership. Invited by the publishers to review the book and write a blurb for the cover, I identify it as important for any leader in any system.

Kay emphasizes focusing on those with potential for leadership rather than on negatives in a system; on honesty at all levels of the system; and on modeling and expecting healthy and effective behaviors. She believes these theories and practices are important in every aspect of both personal and professional life and carries them with her into other areas of her own life, such as her work as vice-chair of the board of directors of the Kentucky Pro Football Hall of Fame and a board member of the Blanton Collier Sportsmanship Group. Promoting ethics, excellence and education in athletics, she has taught and lectured in Japan, Germany, Russia, and Australia, as well as across the United States. She is an example of what Leadership Fitness is all about!

As I write about Blanton Collier, memories of our visits flow freely, fast, and lasting. Coach Collier had a profound influence on my life and career. He is one of the men for whom I have the greatest respect and admiration.

I first met Blanton at Great Lakes Naval Station, where he was on Paul Brown's Great Lakes coaching staff. I was entering boot camp in preparation for duty in the South Pacific Theater as a young seventeen-year-old apprentice seaman. World War II was in its last two years before President Harry Truman would order the atomic bomb to be dropped on the mainland of Japan.

Blanton had entered the service the year before at the age of thirty-seven. He had graduated from Georgetown College (Kentucky), been a quarterback on the football team, and then coach of all sports at his hometown of Paris, Kentucky, while teaching a full academic load. After seventeen successful years as teacher and coach, with a master's degree in educational administration and many hours towards his doctorate, he enlisted in the U.S. Navy. Little could he know that his decision would open a whole new chapter in his career!

Blanton was always a student of the game of football, and it was this attribute that led him to be "discovered" by Paul Brown while using every available moment he could find to observe and take notes about what the already-famous coach was doing. It led to a position on Brown's coaching staff at Great Lakes and after the war to his position as top assistant to Paul with the Cleveland Browns.

He was twenty years my senior.

In 1954 Blanton had been called "home" by the University of Kentucky to succeed Paul "Bear" Bryant as head coach of the Kentucky Wildcats. He always said it was the only position for which he would ever have left Paul Brown and the Cleveland Browns. After seven years at Kentucky, producing one of the best records in the history of the University, Coach Collier would return to the Browns, becoming head coach in 1962, succeeding another legendary coach. It is a tribute to his lead-

Kay Collier Slone and Blanton Collier in 1982.

ership abilities that he was able to succeed in both positions, not by trying to emulate the former leaders but by being himself—doing it "his way." In two short years he directed the Browns to a world championship. Those in the coaching profession who knew his work will all agree that Blanton was the *best* the game ever produced. He was so much more than a coach of football. He helped so many of us reach our goals in life because of his life teachings.

That was the year I was called back to my high school in Fort Thomas, Kentucky, as head football coach. Coach Collier and I became reacquainted when I traveled to Lexington to renew contact with him. That visit was the beginning of a long-term friendship. To be in his presence was a thrill I will never forget. He loved to talk football, and I hung on every word and phrase of that knowledgeable man. We could discuss one simple technique for hours. It was a fascinating time for me. I believe I picked up every word he said, not only listening but applying what he said to my life or my coaching approach. As I jotted down notes of the technical side of football, I realized that he was showing me parts of the game that I did not yet know existed.

Coach Collier did not just talk, however. He listened to me

share my thoughts, which gave me the feeling I was contributing to our discussions. He was a great communicator—not only giving information, but also receiving it from others. This back-and-forth exchange created a true friendship. Many others who came into contact with Coach Collier as a player or coach said that he was the greatest teacher of life. I will always remember a remark he made to me: "You can think your way though any circumstance." This advice has always given me hope in finding a way out of difficulties instead of giving up.

One area Coach Collier stressed in his technical repertoire was the use of his eyes. He often said that the proper use of eyes is a key factor in developing excellence in athletic performance. He would say over and over, "The eyes lead the body." He was obsessed with the idea that the proper use of the eyes could vastly improve athletic performance.

As little children playing sports, many of us were told to "watch the ball." However, I never realized the value of using the eyes to aid in controlling the body and muscular movement until I studied under Blanton Collier. Blanton told the story that when he was in the Navy during World War II, he gained experience on the rifle range under a chief petty officer. One day he was not doing well at the range. The officer in charge asked him what he was shooting toward. "The target, sir," Blanton replied.

"I want you to select a much smaller target. Look at the center of the bull's eye and keep your eyes on it until you pull the trigger," directed the chief. "Your margin of error will increase or decrease in direct proportion to the size of the target you select." From that point on, Blanton began using this theory in the passing game of football. It explained why a pass could be thrown so wide or so high that the receiver could not touch it. Subconsciously, the passer was throwing to the whole receiver— a six-foot-plus target. His margin of error was in direct proportion to that very large target.

A smaller target reduces the margin of error. For players that means one should pick out the numbers on the jersey, the chin strap, the belt buckle. Focus the eyes on a smaller target before the arm action starts and follow through until the ball is in the receiver's hands. This lesson carries over to every player's technique in his respective position. It carries over to every sport and even in other aspects of life.

As a student of Blanton's teachings I was able to train my quarterbacks and players at other positions over the years with this superior method. The four quarterbacks I trained in my collegiate coaching years were not only All Americans, with three drafted in the first round of the NFL, but also leaders in the nation or conference in offense. Coach Colliers' great techniques in teaching the game could become a library of books rather than this article. There is no doubt that Coach Collier was a genius in both technical football and life teaching.

One winter when Blanton and his lovely wife, Mary Forman, were vacationing in Naples, Florida, Phyllis and I met with them. Our dinner party at the Marco Island Country Club also included Ara Parseghian, the legendary Notre Dame coach and his wife, Kathleen. We three coaches got into a football discussion that lasted until closing time at the club. Interested, the other patrons at the club pulled their chairs up around our table to hear the discussion. Instead they got a football clinic. I don't think Blanton ever missed an opportunity to teach!

One day on the football field at Rice University, where I was head football coach and director of athletics, I looked up at a man who had come onto the field to watch our practice. To my surprise and excitement, it was none other than Coach Blanton Collier.

I could not believe that it was really Coach Collier. He and Mary Forman had built a home on Lake Conroe, north of Houston, to begin their retirement years. Phyllis and I also had a cottage on the lake, across from their new home. What a fortuitous time for the Colliers and the Rices! We would take our boat over to their place or we'd all meet for dinner. Selfishly, I was ecstatic with the time to visit with the greatest coach the game has ever known.

I used Blanton's techniques in my coaching at Rice. My quarterback at the time was Tommy Kramer. He led the Rice offense to a ranking of No. 1 in the nation. In 2012 he was inducted into the College Football Hall of Fame. Tommy demonstrated that the Collier techniques worked. While I was coaching at Rice, I received a call from Paul Brown, general manager and president of the Cincinnati Bengals. Coach Brown invited me to come to Cincinnati as head coach and in time to become a general manager. I met with Coach Collier about the call for what seemed like hours. He encouraged me to accept the position. I remember Blanton saying, "I understand why he wants you."

When Blanton was at UK he invited me to join his coaching staff. I was too involved with my Fort Thomas Highlands Football team to consider leaving them. I had invited Coach Collier to speak at our banquet to celebrate our team's 1957 state championship and he had been terrific. Later, he told me he understood why I would not leave my team. This time, it was an NFL offer and Blanton was advising me to accept. I had never coached on the level of the National Football League, although I had received offers from Tom Landry and others. If I accepted the offer, I would have coached on the three levels of high school, college and pro, just as Blanton had done.

Phyllis and I accepted and left for Cincinnati.

Years later Coach Collier passed away. It was a sad loss for the sport, but his teachings continue to aid coaches today and will in the future. What he gave to the game of football at so many levels is marked by excellence. I will always pay tribute to this great man. What an honor to place Coach Blanton Collier in my personal Hall of Positive Leaders.

Of course, what I have written tells only a small part of the Blanton Collier Story as I personally experience it. I am recommending that you seek the book *Football's Gentle Giant: The Blanton Collier Story* (Lexington, KY: Life Force Press, 1985) by Kay Collier-Slone (née McLaughlin), his astute Positive Leader daughter. She tells the whole story and the book is well worth reading to actually know and understand this great man. Blanton was a true giver on any level of friendship.

PAUL AND JANE MEYER

Paul J. Meyer, my great friend of more than forty years was kind enough to write the foreword to the first edition of *Leadership Fitness*, and he has been a tremendous inspiration to me from the day I first met him.

On October 26, 2009, Paul J. Meyer passed away. His death has been a huge loss to the millions who learned a positive approach to life and career success through his incisive and inspiring writings and presentations. However, Paul left each of us his success tools so that we can reach as high as we want to, moving upward through our life challenges and opportunities. Paul knew he was slipping away, but he did not focus on pity in his last days. Rather, in typical Paul Meyer fashion, he prepared his concluding thoughts in a brilliant book titled *Thirteen: A Collection Reflecting Thoughts and Memories of Paul J. Meyer*. He also prepared a book from his heart sure to touch ours, collecting favorite pictures, scripture, poems, and quotations in *My Peace I Give You*. These lasting documents are for us to carry through the rest of our own lives. Paul and his lovely wife, Jane, were the most giving couple I have ever known. I dedicate the addition of *Update 2010* to *Leadership Fitness* to Paul J. and Jane Meyer.

I also thank Karon Freeman, on the staff of Paul and Jane

Paul J. Meyer and Homer Rice meet at Paul's farm, the Summers Mill Retreat and Conference Center, for his annual leadership training seminar in 2005.

Meyer Success Motivation International, Inc. From Karon I was always able to get the information I needed to stay in touch with Paul and his latest research and teaching. I learned from Karon of her fight with breast cancer through her positive attitude toward recovery. She is a woman of strong faith, and I am convinced she will win this battle. Her positive attitude is a blessing to others in their everyday struggles.

JOAN CRONAN

Joan Cronan is one of the top leaders in intercollegiate athletics. Because of her past and present leadership roles and high integrity, she is a perfect candidate to be included in my Positive Leaders Hall of Fame in *Leadership Fitness*.

She has been an astute leader of men and women and has earned their highest respect. I met Joan during my involvement with the National Association of Collegiate Directors of Athletics (NACDA). This organization is the professional body for all levels of college sports.

A graduate of Louisiana State University, Joan Cronan coached women's basketball, volleyball, and tennis before moving into her collegiate administration role as women's director of athletics at the University of Tennessee. Her distinction includes expanding the Tennessee women's programs and taking them to the top. The Vols' women's basketball team and Coach Pat Summit made that program a perennial contender for the national championship. To name every honor and accomplishment of Joan Cronan would require me to "write another book," as my publisher would say.

Her reputation for integrity and success across the country stands out as her highest achievement. Joan Cronan is a true Positive Leader.

VINCENT (VINCE) DOOLEY

It is truly an exceptional privilege to add Vincent (Vince) Dooley to the *Leadership Fitness* Hall of Positive Leaders. I do not know of anyone who has accomplished as much in the collegiate sports world as Coach Dooley during his time as a football coach and as director of athletics at Georgia from 1964-2004. I doubt anyone will challenge his record in the future.

When I as director of athletics at the University of North Carolina-Chapel Hill from 1969 to 1976, our football coach was his brother, Bill Dooley. Bill always spoke of his sibling as "Vincent," and I came to know Vince Dooley by that full first name. I later learned that only three people call him Vincent: his brother, Bill; his astute and beautiful wife, Barbara; and me.

From the time that I was offensive coordinator for the University of Kentucky, I have known of Vincent Dooley. Our teams, Kentucky and Georgia, competed against each other in the Southeastern Conference. In the years since then, he has achieved every prominent award in collegiate coaching and administration.

Coach Dooley achieved a national football championship, won six SEC championships, and took his teams to twenty bowl games. He coached forty players who became first-team All American players and ten Academic All Americans. He was named national Coach of the Year and selected seven times as SEC Coach of the Year.

Only one coach in history (Vincent "Vince" Dooley) has accomplished these merits:

- President of the American Football Coaches Association
- Inducted into the National Football Foundation and
      College Football Hall of Fame
- Served as president of the National Collegiate Directors of
      Athletics Association
- Received its top award, the Jim Corbett Award
- Served as president of the 1A Athletic Directors Association
- Received its top award, The Homer Rice Award

This impressive leadership role and recognition is almost impossible for anyone to ever equal in the future.

Outside of collegiate sports, he has shown outstanding commitment to community service and charity work. And he is a prolific author. My favorite is his book *History and Reminiscences of the University of Georgia* (Looking Glass Books, 2012), illustrated with paintings by Steve Penley. Vincent tells the complete history of his university in manner that does credit to its long history and his association with the institution.

Vincent Dooley is not only an historian, but also an experienced gardener. It's difficult for an ex-football coach like me to fathom another football coach so skillful in the field of gardening. Yet Coach Dooley excels in all that he does. This positive leader is brilliant in every endeavor, from the locker room to the garden.

This Man of the Hour has provided tremendous positive

leadership at every venture he has undertaken and he has aided so many. He holds a position at the highest level in the Hall of Positive Leaders.

ROGER KAISER

Basketball jersey number 21 is retired at Georgia Tech, but the person who wore it probably never will retire. Bobby Dodd, famed football coach of the Yellow Jackets once said of him, "Roger Kaiser is the best all-around athlete in Georgia Tech history." Roger did not stop after becoming one of the winningest basketball coaches in the nation with four national championships. He went on to begin an athletic program at Mt. Bethel Christian Academy in Marietta, Georgia.

Roger Kaiser, an All-State high school player from Dale, Indiana, selected Georgia Tech as the school at which to exploit his athletic skills. He became Tech's first All-American as captain of the basketball team, taking Georgia Tech to its first NCAA playoffs. He was the Southeast Conference Player of the Year in

Roger Kaiser

1960 and 1961 and a consensus All-American in both years. Roger also was captain of and led the Georgia Tech baseball team. His multiple awards and records are unbeatable. I personally cherish that he accepted the Homer Rice Total Person Outstanding Alumnus Award from Georgia Tech.

Roger Kaiser is the Total Person. Beyond all his playing years—high school, college and professional and his fascinating career in coaching—his positive leadership skills have directed thousands toward becoming better people, due to his example and personal attention. Roger Kaiser is definitely a Positive Leader.

THE RICE GIRLS

Throughout my coaching career, from the level of director of athletics to adjunct professor, my dear wife, Phyllis, and I were fortunate to have three lovely daughters, only two years apart. Through those early years, the girls often were the center of attention. Everyone knew and talked about the Rice girls. Early in our career, we always took the girls on a fun vacation and this continued every year. As time went on our girls brought sons-in-law, grandchildren and eventually great-grandchildren to us so we could brag about them.

On November 15, 2013, my dear Phyllis died after a long illness with Alzheimer's disease. As she passed away, I huddled with the girls, who are now 62, 60, and 58, to say a prayer to God to take care of our dear Mom. She was in His hands now, reliever of all pain and able to be our Mom again.

Shortly afterward, I told the girls that we four were going on a vacation. This time, we went to Cambridge Beaches in Bermuda, where Phyllis and I spent our anniversary each year for more than twenty years. It turned out to be one of the best family vacations ever. I showed them places and events that Phyllis and I enjoyed

The Rice girls, Nancy, Angela, and Phyllis

during our times on the island. The visit brought about a renewed family love, with fond memories of the past. We felt connected to Mom in heaven and in communication with her in God's hands.

Each daughter has become a Positive Leader in the field of education, each with her own approach to the field: Angela Miller as the information specialist for Roswell High School, and Phyllis Ingle, a third grade teacher at Sweet Apple Elementary, both in Roswell Georgia; and Nancy Hetherington, the oldest daughter, as head of St. Mary's Episcopal School in Edmond, Oklahoma. Nancy recently retired and was honored with an endowed scholarship in her name. As I have placed so many into my Positive Leaders Hall of Fame, I could not leave the Rice Girls on the sideline.

After twenty-three years as head of school and more than thirty years working at St. Mary's, Nancy Hetherington will retire at the end of the 2012-2013 school year.

In her honor and to her surprise, the Nancy Rice Hetherington Endowed Fund has been established. Administered by the Oklahoma City Community Foundation and matched 3:1 by the Kirkpatrick Family Fund, the endowment will live in perpetuity, whereby only the earnings will be expended and restricted specifically for school-wide curriculum.

BILL SNYDER

Coach Bill Snyder is one of the greatest legends in the world of collegiate football. His record at Kansas State University is unparalleled. He took Kansas State from when it was down and out and became architect of the "greatest turnaround in the history of the game." He not only did it once, he also did it a second time, coming back to the school to do so. Bill retired after the first successful renewal but returned after the program dropped to the bottom, willing and able to bring it back again. In the 2012 season, he was named the Bobby Dodd Coach of the Year. The honor was his second, as he won the award after his first period of success in Manhattan, Kansas. Bill Snyder is one of the only two coaches in the history of the Bobby Dodd Award to be honored twice and the only coach to show such spectacular leadership during different appointments for the same institution.

I first met Coach Snyder in San Antonio, Texas, in the 1970s when he was the offensive coordinator of Hayden Fry's powerful program at the University of Iowa. I sought out Bill Snyder as a speaker for the Henry Frnka Football Clinic in Texas. A successful oil entrepreneur who gained fame as a coach of the University of Tulsa and Tulane University, Henry Frnka ran the most outstanding football clinic in Texas and nationally. Frnka asked me to speak annually to his clinic during my coaching career. Finally, he asked if I would help him bring in top coaches in the country for the program. I assisted my dear friend in this goal and brought Coach Synder, who gave an intriguing lecture on offensive football. I followed his career from that time on. Our next formal meeting was in his office at Kansas State University when

Jim Terry, chairman of the Bobby Dodd Coach of the Year Award Foundation, and I sat on each side of Bill Snyder as we announced on ESPN his acceptance of the award.

As we drove into Manhattan, Kansas, via the Bill Snyder Highway for that meeting, we gained a clear view of the respect in which the people of Manhattan and Kansas State's alumni and friends across the plains of the Midwest and the country hold this icon. Our vehicle approached the stadium, and a guide pointed out that the facility had been named the Coach Bill Snyder and Family Stadium upon the coach's insistence that the sign include his family and not simply his own name. Indeed at the banquet to present the Dodd Award, Coach Snyder, his lovely wife, Sharon, and their family all came for a presentation of the award to honor the man of the hour. More than a thousand people joined them for the event with a young John Currie, director of athletics at Kansas State and an emerging success story in his own right, making appropriate remarks to begin the program.

Bill Snyder certainly belongs in the Hall of Positive Leaders. His leadership is widely known throughout the sports world and beyond. On the campus at Kansas State University, Coach Snyder's philosophy and practices have been distilled in to a text for leadership studies.

Coach Bill Snyder is a winner on the field in the game of football. He also has produced thousands of winners in life through the players, coaches and others who have followed his advice. He is a master coach of the spirit of integrity in all of life's achievements.

MARY TIONG

Mary Tiong came from humble beginnings in East Malaysia on Borneo Island without running water or electricity in early childhood. Her family supported her at college as she pursued her vision of becoming an entrepreneur. She has become a Positive Leader by translating her skills from the world of commerce to the task of making the world a better place.

She showed leadership in high school and afterward worked a variety of jobs to save for college, attending courses for two years at Stamford College in Kuala Lumpur. After working in the insurance industry, where she became top sales agent for her company, she became the sole local distributor of computer equipment in 1990 for a Malaysian manufacture of international brands. Wildly successful at marketing those brands, she became know as the "monitor queen" in Malaysia.

Before the end of that decade, she shifted her focus to remanufacturing and refurbishing used computer monitors. Using her international experience, she has expanded operations into America, Australia, and Canada.

She also wanted to give back to communities in need. In 2001 she began to supply used monitors to local manufacturers to convert picture tubes for use by villagers in countries with very limited channel reception.

Mary Tiong arrived in Pittsburgh, Pennsylvania, in 2004 and has worked to coordinate e-recycling. Through her non-profit activity, electronic discards are used by local communities or sent to those in need, expanding access to computers and sharing electronic resources. She is a Positive Leader worthy of recognition.

BUD PARKER

Bud Parker passed away on August 10, 2012, following a massive heart attack. I was not prepared for such a tragedy. Our friendship was such a blessing. He had meant so much to so many. His wife, Robin, and family lost a devoted husband and father.

Bud Parker and General Ray Davis

The family asked me to speak at Bud's memorial service, and it was hard to speak of one who had given so much in his lifetime. But I also remembered his encouraging words to me so many times. I had to do my best. My comments from his service follow.

Bud Parker. I don't know where to start or how to finish. There is simply too much to cover at this moment. But I do know one special thing . . . he loved his family. He idolized his wife, Robin, the "head coach" of the Parker family. He was so proud of his granddaughter, "Mollie"—the miracle baby of a daughter, Emmy, son Robert and brother Bill, and his dear family. Bud also loved his country and was a strong believer in God and his faith.

I first met Bud when they presented me the keys to the director of athletics office at Georgia Tech in the name of his father, William A. Parker.

On Friday morning, August 10, 2012, came the shock heard around the world of the loss of our best friend. Just one week earlier, Bud, Robin, and I had met for dinner and reminisced about old times. Reminiscing with Bud was always with much love and laughter. We talked about our fun times when Phyllis and I would travel with Bud and Robin: Montana, Bermuda, Georgia Tech away football and basketball games and tournaments, and a "Bud-Project" trip. One trip was named by Bud, "Stops to the Top." It was Bud's plan to visit each location where I had coached. These were driving trips, and I always asked Robin to be our driver. Not that Bud was not a good driver, but when I was with him as a passenger, he had to be reminded to stay on the correct side of the yellow line.

The first stop on the route was my first job in 1951, in a small community in Tennessee. This is where I coached both the high school and the prison team. The warden provided equipment I needed for the high school team in exchange for my coaching the prison team. We were successful in locating one of my high school players just coming out of his garden with a big straw hat and wearing hook-up overalls. With his shotgun beside him, he invited us in for dinner serving squirrel stew (cooking on the wood stove). Bud made some quick excuse, and we drove away.

Bud was involved in many projects. One was rebuilding Georgia Tech athletics in the early 1980s, assisting me on several fund-raising adventures (and they were adventures). The most entertaining was with our friend Bill Moore (a Georgia Tech tennis great who became extremely successful). Bud had met Bill through Henry Thompson (another tennis great). Bill, Bud, and I had developed a three-musketeer team on numerous fishing trips either to Marco Island, Florida, or on Bill's ranch in Montana. Bill had donated the funds to help build the Bill Moore Tennis Center and the Bud Parker scholarships for our tennis program.

Now we needed funds to build what became the Bill Moore Student Success Center. This was a concept to make available the Student/Athlete Total Person program for all students on campus. We needed a large gift. I suggested we go for a certain amount, perhaps the largest personal gift in the school's history. Bud was somewhat skeptical. While fly-fishing the Sun River on Bill's ranch, I mentioned to Bud that I was going to pop the question. We were fishing close together at the time, and Bud just looked away. Because of the rushing current, the noise level of the fast stream made it necessary to shout to be heard. So I loudly asked Bill to consider a certain amount for the project. He thought it over for a moment and yelled back he could not do it in one year, but he would do it over five years. Almost simultaneously, Bud hooked a large rainbow trout and yelled, "Got it!" I was never certain if he meant the fish or the gift.

Bud had many attributes and successes both in school, business, and positive leadership. We know about his school (Georgia Tech): captain of the tennis team, SEC doubles champion, president of the senior class. lieutenant in the U.S. Navy for three years, a business leader in the family's Beck and Gregg Hardware and Genuine Parts, and an investor. But the main story is his love of his family, friends, and people from all walks of life. And his laugh! Bud was full of love and laughter. His positive energy was catching! For every occasion Bud brought gifts for everyone.

In the 13th chapter of First Corinthians, Paul's letter says faith, hope, and love abide, these three; but the greatest of these is love. This love leads to becoming a True Giver.

My father, a Methodist minister, once told me as a young lad, "Son, do not judge others. The Divine Power will be the Judge. Love all people regardless of color, race or creed." However, he went on to say, "You will need to recognize the *grabbers* from the *givers*. You be a *giver*." I followed this advice through the years, and as time went on, I could see a huge difference. Then I met and became a close friend with the truest giver, Bud Parker.

I have never known a person to give so much to others.

In this book I asked Bud to furnish a chapter. Titled "Freedom Is Not Free," Bud shares the inspiring story of his father-in-law, a captain in the 507th Parachute Infantry Regiment and their contributions for the Allies winning World War II, in the European invasion at Normandy. From that and more, Bud developed a passion to aid the military in numerous ways.

Bud's passion with the real ability to bring about laughter connected with thousands. Through laughter he stimulated others to receive a positive reaction (free from negative thoughts).

Someone once said, "Success is not measured only by your climbing the latter to success, but the number of people you have helped climb the ladder." If this is true, and I believe it is, then Bud Parker is one of the most successful leaders I have been privileged to know.

I know Bud is up There looking down. He may be laughing! I can almost hear him say, "The best is yet to come."

Recently I arranged to have Bud speak to our Sunday school class. As an introduction, we sang as a class, "Onward Christian Soldiers, written by Sabine Baring Gould in 1864. Bud told me, "That may be my favorite."

Onward Christian soldiers, marching as to war—
With the Cross of Jesus going on before.
Christ, the Royal Master, leads against the foe,
Forward into battle, see his banners go!
Onward Christian soldiers marching on to war
With the cross of Jesus going on before.
Bud always closed his presentations, "God bless America!"
Following is a lesson on Freedom that Bud wrote for *Leadership Fitness*:

FREEDOM IS NOT FREE

As Expressed by Albert "Bud" Parker

Albert "Bud" Parker has been my friend and close aide in directing the Leadership Fitness class through many years. Each semester I assemble a roster of prestigious speakers who address the need for ethics in the business world, and he is included among them. Bud always delivers a terrific message. Recently, he changed the angle of his approach and spoke about the 507th Parachute Infantry Regiment. The unit made a crucial contribution to winning World War II by its actions during the invasion of Normandy.

Leaders come from all walks of life, and the military has produced its share. Many military people have made personal sacrifices that have paved the way for the freedoms we all enjoy. In class, Bud shares the inspiring story of his father-in-law, an American paratrooper who helped ensure the success of Allied forces on D-Day. In 1971, Albert "Bud" Parker married Robin Rae and became a son-in-law. His wife's father was fifty-six years young, and Bud and his father-in-law became tennis partners whenever their families came together in Birmingham, Alabama.

"I had never focused on the fact that he participated in World War II until by accident I came across his Purple Heart and the Distinguished Service Cross awarded to him by Gen. Omar Bradley," Bud said. The Distinguished Service Cross had been earned during the early days of the invasion of Europe in June 1944. The Purple Heart came from action in the Ardennes during the Battle of the Bulge.

The 507th Parachute Infantry Regiment, which included Capt. Robert D. "Bob" Rae, was assigned to the 82nd Airborne Division for the night drop in the early hours of D-Day. As fate would have it, he was given the assignment of launching an al-most suicidal assault across a fully exposed causeway more than five hundred yards long. He was charged with securing the other side of the causeway, a task vitally important in ensuring that the troops from the beach could come inland rapidly. Without hesi-tation, he led his men across despite a great loss of personnel, and they accomplished their mission.

In a phone conversation with Gen. James Gavin, who had been the commanding officer at the time of the battle, Bud learned firsthand of the general's great respect for his father-in law. He appreciated even more the sacrifice that had occurred that day. "I was, and have continued to be, humbled by his and his fellow veterans' sense of duty and devotion to their unit and country," Bud said. "Having walked the LaFiere Causeway, I am convinced it is a miracle that he made it across without being killed." Bud's appreciation was personal as well. "I am glad he did, though, or I would never have met his daughter."

With that background, Bud did not hesitate to honor Bob Rae's request in the fall of 2000 for assistance in raising funds to construct and dedicate a memorial in Normandy to the veterans of the 507th Parachute Infantry Regiment, or 507 PIR. The unit had taken heavy casualties in securing every objective assigned to it. After Normandy, it was reassigned to the 17th Airborne Division, and after the war ended, the unit was disbanded. As a result, histories of D-Day make little mention of the fact that the 507 PIR had ever been to Normandy, much less fought there. The memorial would help correct that historical oversight. The memorial's location and design were agreed upon and funds se-cured for the project.

On July 23, 2001, in Amfreville, France, the U.S. ambassador dedicated the memorial. Filmmaker David Druckenmiller, who had once worked at Georgia Tech, was commissioned, along with Phil Walker, to document the video as a gift from Bud's family to Bob and his veteran friends. The resulting film became their gift to us as well as all Americans.

The film proved so compelling that PBS arranged to show it nationally in primetime in June 2004 during a television tribute to the sixtieth anniversary of D-Day. Millions rather than hundreds were now familiar with the 507 PIR and profited from the message of their sacrifices.

"As a youngster, I was advised never to judge men by their balance sheets or their headlines," Bud explained, "but instead by how their lives have benefited others. Over the past months, I have gained an even greater respect for not only the men of the 507 but also for all who have gone into harm's way to ensure that I have the opportunities I have had. I salute them every day."

He appreciated most those who were willing to volunteer to be there so that he and others could be here today, enjoying precious freedoms and opportunities that are the envy of the world. Will the rest of us and the generations to follow always remember that rich heritage and resist becoming apathetic to the lessons of history? Bud hopes so. He hopes we all will never fail to be grateful for the blessings we've inherited. By just being born in America, we have won the lottery.

"We must never forget one of the significant lessons of history," Bud concluded. "No great nation has ever endured forever. Hopefully, I, along with a growing number of Americans, will come to appreciate how very valuable and precious our citizenship in the United States of America truly is. And hopefully it will be many generations before America ceases to be the great nation it is."

The men of the 507th were truly successful, positive leaders. They made it possible for each of us to have abundant opportunities now and in the future in this country.

Help us never to forget the sacrifice made today and in the past that make it possible for us to live in America with unsurpassed opportunities, freedom, and liberty. Help us to never forget that freedom is not free!

Bud goes on to write more about our true freedom:

"Freedom!"

It is great to live in the Land of the Free.

For most of my life I have largely taken for granted my freedoms and the opportunities provided by my country. It wasn't until in 2000, when I was introduced to the World War II veterans of the 507 PIR who had jumped into Normandy on D-Day that I became passionate about my heritage and my love for America. So many have sacrificed so much for me and preserved the freedom and opportunities I have enjoyed. Those who know can attest that since 2000 I have lived with an "attitude of gratitude" for the blessing of being an American!

It is amazing what happens when you realize what a very different nation America is from others. America was founded on self-evident principles proclaimed in our Declaration of Independence. Those principles are protected by our Constitution. They include the rights to life, liberty, the pursuit of happiness, free speech, and freedom of religion. America is truly the bright light of liberty among all other nations. If opportunity exists anywhere in the world, it exists here.

Initially when I was asked to share my thoughts on freedom, I was emotionally concerned about the direction in which our country was headed and was proactively involved in the midterm elections of 2010. A national political debate was boiling and dividing the country over our growing national debt, increasing entitlements, our economic recession, and the growing size and encroachment of government into our lives. A liberal Congress and administration were using every tactic to enact legislation that polls indicated the people of America did not wish to see enacted. Both in style and substance, the governance of our country disturbed me. Frankly, it still does.

History reminds us that over time *every* great nation of the past has ceased to exist for many and varied reasons. I felt I was about to witness the collapse of the America I loved.

History reminds us that our founders gave us a participatory republic. The recent 2010 midterm election demonstrated to our national leadership that "Main Street" America cared and was willing to fight to prevent government encroachment in making decisions Americans felt were their responsibility to make. Standing up for freedom is not easy, but it is our responsibility to do so! Freedom requires sacrifice to protect it.

Our Constitution limits our federal government's ability to intrude into our day-to-day lives. Through enumerated powers, our founders intentionally left most governance to those closest to each of us: to our elected officials in state houses, county court-houses, and in our school boards. We are the beneficiaries of a remarkable inheritance of freedoms that no other nation has ever known. To retain our freedoms, each of us must participate in the process to the utmost of our ability. We must truly educate ourselves about the political process, work to help worthy candidates, and care about our country. We must *vote* in every election!

It is the natural inclination of those in control to seek more power and to *impose* their version of social justice. Regulations that control us are *imposed*. But *values* that guide us are *inspired* by those we respect. Basic and solid values that have made us exceptional must be better conveyed to all of us by moms and dads, our media, teachers, coaches, religious leaders, those who lead at every level down to our youth, and each other. We must return to those values.

Thomas Friedman in an editorial in the *New York Times* remarked that the cause of poor performance in our schools may well rest in the reality that our students are not motivated. He pointed out that a growing number of students today, from all

Bud and Robin Parker receiving an Emmy for one of their
National Public Television documentary awards.

economic backgrounds, don't like school and don't work hard.
As a result, they don't do well.

In a 2008 survey of public school teachers, 21 percent judged
student absenteeism and 29 percent felt student apathy were serious problems. Dropout rates continue to be a growing concern.
According to Friedman, we are experiencing a *values breakdown*.

If we are to maintain our freedoms and prosper as a nation in
the future, we must stop assigning blame for our problems and
those of our youth and start assuming responsibility for them.

"America is still by its life span in history just a big, talented kid," according to a quote I once heard, and "with its
self-reliant freedoms and blessed by the environment of the
free enterprise system, it still has so much positive potential
ahead." If "Main Street" Americans are willing to sacrifice to
protect the values that have led to us becoming exceptional, it
will remain so.

In 2000, when I visited Normandy, a World War II veteran

pointed out to me as we entered a somber military cemetery, that our country has sacrificed its blood and resources to preserve freedom.

Many fine Americans may view history differently and disagree with me about the appropriate role, size, and mission for our government. Some may even disagree with the motivations provided by our free enterprise system. Few, however, will disagree that we live in the greatest nation on the planet.

Artist Steve Penley summed this up best. "The list of contributions the United States has made to the world cannot be measured. We provide basic necessities to keep children alive and healthy all over the world. From agriculture to medicine, we have given greatly to the quality of human life. Americans have followed their dreams and in doing so have made the world a better place. We sent men to the moon and in doing so discovered new technologies which have helped all the world. Capitalism has given men and women the incentive to create for the good of Americans and everyone else."

Where would the world be without America? Those who criticize our nation should imagine the world without us to protect them. What power would rise to the top? I doubt our critics would be happy with the alternatives.

Show me a better place! *God bless America.*

BILL CURRY

I have often said, "Look in the dictionary for the word *respect*, and you will find a picture of Bill Curry."

Bill is highly respected because of his positive giving to others. We know about his honors as an All-American football player at Georgia Tech, an All-Pro center for the Baltimore Colts (Super Bowl champions), and his leadership as the National

Bobby Dodd and Bill Curry

Football League Players Association president.

We've seen his impact on hundreds of young men as he coached at Green Bay, Georgia Tech, Alabama (winner of the Southeastern Conference), Kentucky, and Georgia State. We've celebrated his many Coach of the Year awards, including the Bobby Dodd Coach of the Year Award.

We've watched him mesmerize and then challenge audiences of thousands with his powerful message as a speaker. And we've been touched by his willingness to give credit to the mentors in his life who helped shape him.

Bill Curry's caring and kindness have touched countless lives. It seems whenever I talk with former Georgia Tech athletes, they praise Bill for the positive impact he had on their lives. He was like a father to so many of his players, and he lived a life before them that they respected and could follow as a true positive role model. One player told me, "To be around Coach Curry is to become a better person."

During my time in presenting the Total Person Program, I can say without a doubt Coach Bill Curry is the top of the class to absorb the concepts and become the ultimate Total Person.

FINAL WORDS

As I close the *Leadership Fitness* manuscript, I am compelled to think back on my long and exciting career. I have strived to make it a career of giving. Through years of practicing and teaching Positive Leadership, I have gained a great deal of knowledge

My life's work sprang from my father's advice on how to live. My father, Samuel Cecil Rice, was born in 1890. He lost his parents as a young boy and was a self-made man. A relative with a farm provided him with a spot in the barn, and my father worked to earn his keep. He did other jobs to move himself forward, purchasing books so he could read them to educate himself. At age sixteen, he was awarded a scholarship to attend Berea College in Kentucky.

He walked several hundred miles to begin college life. He continued working to support himself while in college, and his academic success at Berea enabled him to gain scholarships for advanced degrees. He attended Syracuse University and Columbia University, then earned a doctor of divinity degree from Boston Theological University. After serving in World War I, he returned to Berea College to teach English. There he met a pretty brunette who caught his eye. He would marry my future mother, the beautiful Nancy Grace Wilson. They lived together for sixty-six years until my father's death in St. Petersburg, Florida.

My father was an outstanding athlete. At Berea, he was captain of the rugby team, a stellar shortstop on the baseball team, a tennis star, and an outdoorsman who enjoyed hunting and fishing. He faced a career decision of whether to accept a contract to play professional baseball with the Cincinnati Reds or to become a minister in the Kentucky United Methodist Church. He chose the ministry.

His lessons to me were critical in shaping my life and the decisions that I made along the way. He taught me not to judge other people. He taught me to love and respect all people, regardless of color, race, or creed. My father told me that there are two types of people: the grabbers and the givers. He emphasized the importance of being a giver.

He also talked to me about having a positive faith and the meaning of believing in the God of the Universe. When I was twelve years old, he presented me with the book *I Dare You!* by William Danforth. Danforth insisted on the importance of setting a plan—of writing down goals in every area of your life. That book started me in writing about a positive lifestyle and becoming a leader in sports. The goals that I set and wrote at that young age all came true. I became a believer early in life in positive thinking.

In 1933, my father was appointed superintendent of the denomination's southeastern Kentucky district. We moved to Pineville, Kentucky. My older brother, Robert Cecil Rice, attended Pineville High School, and I was enrolled in the first grade. My brother was a star athlete on the high school sports teams when I was eight or nine. Football was my favorite sport, so I would watch each practice from the sideline. Head Coach Walter Grabruck, himself an All-American quarterback from Centre College, noticed me each day. At one point he decided that I should be the team's mascot. He found a uniform to fit me, and playing football became my passion. I was so impressed with Coach Grabruck that I decided I wanted to be a football coach.

After six years living in Pineville, my dad was appointed to a Methodist church in Middlesboro, Kentucky. I continued to play all sports, but the biggest decision in my life was to recognize that a pretty girl stood out in my seventh grade class: Phyllis Callison Wardrup. Also at the age of twelve, I decided that she would be the girl I would marry.

Eleven years later, after I served in World War II in the South Pacific theater and finished college, we married. Phyllis and I were married for sixty-four years. My dearest companion for those years, she passed away on November 15, 2013, at the age of 86. We had a wonderful, loving life together. She lived with the positive attitude that allowed us to achieve so much together in our family and career.

From Middlesboro, Kentucky, my father was appointed superintendent of the northern Kentucky region. We lived in Fort Thomas, Kentucky, a community in the greater Cincinnati area. I attended Highlands High School starting in my sophomore year and met Coach Ewell "Judge" Waddell. Although not eligible to play in varsity games due to a transfer rule, I practiced with the team each day. Practice during the semester I was ineligible to play after transferring paid off. I was a starter the next two years, an all-state quarterback, and on conference and state championship teams. Most importantly, playing under Coach Waddell and being captain my senior year was probably the best situation I could have imagined being in. My relationship with Coach Waddell was almost like father and son. He mentored me, and his positive leadership example has stayed with me my entire life. I give him credit for shaping my attitude toward what makes for a successful life and career.

Early in my coaching career, I took on extra off-season jobs to make ends meet for my family. One was selling life insurance. I had luck early on in selling one company a salary savings plan for $1,000,000. At a rather early age, this made me a member of the Million Dollar Round Table, where I met Paul J. Meyer, the organization's top salesman. He took an interest in me, and we became life-long friends. His concept of the Total Person Success Plan gave me the idea to develop the Total Person Program for student-athletes, helping them become a success across every area of their lives.

Paul founded Success Motivation International, Inc., encompassing more than forty worldwide companies. When I was putting this book together, he graciously agreed to provide the foreword. Paul J. Meyer became a *New York Times* bestselling author. This friend, Paul J. Meyer, was another strong influence in my life whom I credit with developing my desire to become a Positive Leader for others. I have come to the conclusion that the only true happiness we will ever have in our lives lies in helping others. Paul J. Meyer may be the happiest person I have known.

After high school, serving with the U.S. Navy in the South Pacific theater in World War II, and college, I completed twenty-seven years as a high school, college, and NFL football coach. Another twenty-seven years as a collegiate director of athletics came next, and a decade as an adjunct professor has followed. At the age of eighty-seven as of this writing in June 2014, I am still working on the program that I began at age twelve. That program is to become a Positive Leader.

My ambition has been to develop others for this same goal in life. I named it the Total Person Program, and it is my silent ministry. The Total Person Program begins with an Attitude Technique Philosophy. This technique requires changing your negative thoughts into positive thoughts. When a negative thought enters your brain (the human computer), stop and take one minute to change the negative into a positive response. It works. Over months and years, this technique will reshape your entire attitude. You will gain unbelievable benefits. This change in yourself can be instilled by reading, studying, and practicing how to become "fit" as a Positive Leader. God has given each of us a brain with both conscious and subconscious aspects that enable us to apply this simple technique. The book *Leadership Fitness: Developing and Reinforcing Successful, Positive Leaders* is the tool to make it happen!

I have looked back over the years and picked out eight people for this closing who made a significant impact on my life. Many more are mentioned throughout *Leadership Fitness*. Even more are not listed whom I should have mentioned, including fellow coaches, players and friends.

My list of eight starts with my father, Samuel Cecil Rice. I add William Danforth, author of the book *I Dare You!* My older brother, Robert Cecil Rice, and his football coach, Walter Grabruck, are included. My dear wife for sixty-four years, Phyllis, entered my life early, also. My high school coach at Fort Thomas (Kentucky) Highlands High School, Ewell "Judge" Waddell, and Paul J. Meyer of Success Motivation International, Inc., are listed. And the eighth is Grant Teaff.

Grant is executive director of the American Football Coaches Association and the American Football Coaches Foundation. He is the legendary former football coach and director of athletics at Baylor University. Grant has been successful in every situation and often demonstrated his positive leadership. I believe that as an author, coach and administrator, his leadership has had an impact on more coaches and athletes than any other person in our profession. His latest book, *A Coach's Influence: Beyond the Game*, will change the lives of thousands of coaches and athletes, and should affect the way people should think and act throughout our great nation.

Recently, Grant called to make me aware of an award that will be presented to me at the 2015 American Football Coaches Association Convention in Louisville. Hearing about this honor struck me like a bolt of lightning, because the name of the award is The Spirit of Giving. The executive director gives it as a special presentation, and it is awarded sparingly by the Board of

Directors and Board of Trustees, under the director's guidance. I am a fortunate person to have received many awards through my lifetime, including fourteen Hall of Fame citations and numerous others. The Spirit of Giving Award is special. It takes me back to the words and influence of my father, who taught me to be a giver since my early years. As I close in on the age of eighty-eight, a man I have respected for more than half of my long life provides this high honor from the American Football Coaches Association.

If you believe in miracles, count this moment as one. This is a miracle from a life of giving. God has directed the path I chose so many years ago. Believing in Him has brought forth this recognition, made possible by all those who aided me throughout my lifetime. I can only thank them.

In closing, I would like to share seven words for life to live by.

FAITH

Faith is a belief in something bigger than myself. It is trust in and loyalty to God without doubt or question, an inner certainty that there is a plan for my life. With faith, I do not need all the answers. I can enjoy the journey, knowing that with God all things are possible. What is impossible for mortals is possible for God, according to Luke 18:27. As Matthew 21:22 says, "If you believe, you will receive whatever you ask for in prayer." And if you had faith the size of a mustard seed, you could say to that mulberry tree, "Be uprooted and planted in the sea," and it would obey you. (Luke 17:6)

HOPE

Always have something positive to look forward to. St. Paul gave a message to the Philippians stating that we have the strength to face all conditions by the power that Christ gives us. (Philippians 4:13) We can look to the future with a positive knowledge.

FORGIVENESS

You will never be happy until you can forgive others. Remember Louis Zamperini's story told in Lauren Hillenbrand's book, *Unbroken: A World War II Story of Survival, Resilience, and Redemption*. You can face your enemy, and forgiveness has a great, life-changing power.

LAUGHTER

The medical secret for life with no pain is laughter. Norman Cousin wrote so well about this in *Anatomy of an Illness*. The benefits of laughter are well documented.

INSPIRATION

God is the source for filling all our needs, and we can gain inspiration from studying the Bible. Mathew 7:7-8 says, "Ask and you will be given what you ask for. Seek and you will find. Knock and the door will be opened. He has said I will enter and will never abandon you." The architect of the universe did not design a ladder leading to nowhere. A carpenter from the plains of Galilee gave us the inspiration we need when He said, "As you sow, so shall you reap." (Galatians 6:7)

ENERGY

Good health habits are the foundation for a life of energy. A healthy life is essential to achieving success in all areas.

INTEGRITY

Always do it the *right* way!

To this, my Phyllis added, "Lord help me to admit when I am wrong, and make it easier to live with when I am right!"

I close with this prayer for young people. *Father in Heaven, direct us and guide us as we accept the all-important responsibility to give toward positive training of young people the very best we have within us, that they may become a mighty fortress in the years ahead. We give thanks for all our blessings, for the power that is vested in each of us, and for being a servant unto you. We pray this in your name. Amen.*

NEVER SAY NEVER

It all started years ago on Marco Island when my dear wife, Phyllis, lost her favorite dragonfly pin and Karen found it (see story on page 288). That event began a close friendship between Rices and the Powells—Karen and her husband, Josh.

Several years later Josh and Phyllis both passed away after extended illnesses. Karen and I kept our friendship, and both of us made the statement, "I will never remarry."

God had other plans for us, bringing us together in marriage on May 20, 2015.

So many people have told me, "Karen is beautiful, not only on the outside, but beautiful on the inside."

My daughters agree, and have added, "Dad, you are getting your life back."

Our happiness is blessed by our Father in Heaven.

Karen Sue Rice

UPDATE 2017

Leadership Fitness: Developing and Reinforcing Successful, Positive Leaders has entered its ninth printing.

From 1997 through today in 2017, *Leadership Fitness* has been an outstanding instrument for training young people to become Positive Leaders in our society.

I began teaching a course called "Leadership Fitness" in 1998 at Georgia Tech, encouraged by Georgia Tech's Dean of the College of Sciences Gary Schuster and President G. Wayne Clough. The course contains the Total Person Program, which I developed for the NCAA initiative CHAMPS (Challenging Athletes' Minds for Personal Success). The Total Person Program makes it possible to become successful in every area of your life by setting goals about personal self-image, health and fitness, career, and financial independence, with a program to obtain these objectives.

The program requires a study of the brain and its two minds, the conscious and the subconscious. Controlling your thinking process will change negative thoughts into positive thoughts. I call this approach the Attitude Technique Philosophy. To become Positive Leaders, we must be fit in all areas of our lives.

Lessons 1-9 of the book *Leadership Fitness* are the text for the course I teach. Each semester's course finishes with a session producing a Personal Life Blueprint for every student.

As new printings of this book take place, I have added interesting personal notes for the reader. The ninth printing in 2017 adds these topics:

- My 90th Birthday
- Todd Stansbury, Director of Athletics of Georgia Tech
- "Leadership Fitness" Course and Annual Alumni Luncheon Reunion
- Dr. Steve Usselman—Class Rating
- The Unknown Story of Greg Page
- Jack Markwalter—The Lee Candler Fund Committee
- Closing Remarks

MY 90TH BIRTHDAY

I have to admit I have never been big on personal birthday parties but when my 90th year came about on February 20, 2017, I have admit that I felt the excitement. My wife, Karen, and the three Rice daughters put on a major show.

Thirty-five daughters, sons, grandchildren, and great-grandchildren came to Atlanta for the occasion, with the Capital City Club our destination. What a blast! After a wonderful meal, we all gathered in another room for a program. I sat in a big comfortable chair as each of the children spoke, saying what their grandfather had meant to them. Their stories brought back positive memories for me. Karen got people to participate in a trivia session about my life. My granddaughter Leigh Hetherington of Culver City, California, sang songs from my earlier life to close out a day that I will never forget. It was a fun time.

We had so many people from the Rice and Allen families who came or sent gifts. They included Nancy and Steve Hetherington, Ryce, Leigh, Kaya Rose Curcio, Drew, Lisa and Brooks. Phyllis Ingle and Brian, Jamie and Kane Keeling, Jack and Homer, Jordan Evans. Angie and Jeff Miller, Dave and Andrew. Bob Allen and Laura, Aidan and Emily. Mike Allen and Heather, Drew and Brooke. J.J. Allen and Kathryn, Carter and Caroline. David Allen, Lisa, Rob and Bryson. Jenny and Clay Compton, Alexis Williams, Michelle and Nick Kilby. Mark Allen and Leslie, Connor, Lillian and Lauren. Steve Allen and Sarah, Everett.

That's not all. The next day, Karen and I attended a Georgia Tech basketball game. Jim Terry, my dear friend and associate for the class I teach at Georgia Tech, approached me regarding presenting a plaque to someone during a basketball game time out.

I agreed to help in the presentation, so Karen and I together left our seats and headed down to the playing court. Todd Stansbury, Director of Athletics, was waiting and ushered us onto the court. The crowd was standing, and they began singing "Happy Birthday" to me. I really did not catch on at first, but then I realized they were applauding and cheering me. Todd knew I would not have agreed to be the center of attention, so Jim Terry had to be the one to escort me onto the court for a service opportunity. I have to admit that I was honored and appreciated the occasion.

I am 90 and still in good health, keeping busy doing a lot of meaningful activities like teaching, speaking and writing, along with exercising every day with Karen. This keeps me upbeat and allows me to continue to contribute. Karen and I take our breaks to Marco Island, Florida, and to Montana, as well as other trips.

It is Karen, my beautiful and energetic wife, who makes sure I am up and running each day. God has blessed our lives with an important message be Givers.

TODD STANSBURY
DIRECTOR OF ATHLETICS OF GEORGIA TECH

The school year of 2016-2017 was exciting and interesting for Georgia Tech Athletics. I had stepped down as Director of Athletics in 1997. Dave Brain, Dan Radakovich, and Mike Bobinski had followed. In 2016, it was time to select the next Director.

Georgia Tech's strongest attribute is its passion for integrity. Georgia Tech people believe in doing it the right way. President "Bud" Peterson appointed Todd Stansbury on September 22, 2016, to the position of Director, with the aid of a search committee chaired by Al Trujillo. President Peterson had hired the person who would undertake the position in the right way! The Georgia Tech nation applauded the selection.

Todd Stansbury is a Georgia Tech graduate and former football player who served Oregon State University as Director of the Academic Center before he became Director of Athletics at that school. In 2016-2017, he came home to Georgia Tech, gaining instant success.

Georgia Tech President G. P. "Bud" Peterson hires Todd Stansbury
as Director of Athletics, September 22, 2016

Football Coach Paul Johnson defeated the University of Georgia "between the hedges" and took the team to the TaxSlayers Bowl (formerly the Gator Bowl), defeating the University of Kentucky. Men's Basketball Coach Josh Pastner was named Atlanta Coast Conference Coach of the Year after taking the team to the finals of the National Invitation Tournament Championship in his first year. Women's Basketball Coach MaChelle Joseph took her young team to the Women's National Invitation Tournament Championship finals. All sports and Georgia Tech athletes had exciting and successful seasons.

As a football player at Georgia Tech, Todd played under Bill Curry. Todd was a strong believer in the Student Athlete Total Person Program.

In his career journey, he has directed the Total Person program everywhere he has had a leadership role in intercollegiate athletics. I believe Todd will take his work to an even higher level as a Positive Leader at Georgia Tech.

It is a great pleasure to welcome Todd and Karen Stansbury home again.

BLAZING A PATH

*From Rice to Stansbury, Georgia Tech's groundbreaking
Total Person Program continues to provide student-athletes
with opportunities to succeed in life*

By Jon Cooper

How do you improve on something that has shown the
kind of prolonged excellence and staying power of Dr. Homer
Rice's Total Person Program?

We're talking about tinkering with a visionary program
first implemented in 1981, which has become the road map for
student-athletes' success in life away from the sports arena and
has even been adopted, repackaged and renamed CHAMPS
(Challenging Athletes' Minds for Personal Success)/Life Skills
by the NCAA.

Putting athletics director Todd Stansbury in charge of the
renovation is a good start.

Stansbury (Class of '84) has a sure grasp of the program's
mission, having gone through it as a student-athlete, has an
undying passion to see those in it succeed, having implemented
its principles at every stop he's made in his 29 years as an administrator (East Tennessee State, Central Florida and Oregon
State), and has great vision for strong additions to benefit future current and future student-athletes on The Flats.

"I was fortunate enough to be a freshman Dr. Rice's first
year here as athletic director so, as a student-athlete, I benefited
from his leadership. I became an administrator on his staff and
was actively engaged in working to develop aspects of the Total
Person Program," said Stansbury, who was named Georgia
Tech's director of athletics on Sept. 22, 2016. "For me to come
back to Georgia Tech, where it all started, and expand the Total
Person Program and really take what he started and make it the

center of Georgia Tech Athletics and what our brand is, is something that is incredibly gratifying and humbling."

At least one expert feels it's also a perfect move.

"He's put the program in everywhere he went throughout his career. He probably did a lot better with it than I did," said Dr. Rice, who not only was A.D. when Stansbury came to The Flats as a linebacker from Canada in 1981 but also hired him as academic counselor for football in 1988 (Stansbury would eventually work his way up to assistant athletic director for academics). "I can't think of a better thing for Georgia Tech than to have him in charge of the program."

Leah Thomas, who has run the Total Person Program since 2008, feels that Stansbury offers a unique perspective.

"You can't appreciate [Total Person] like he can," said Thomas, who first came to Georgia Tech in 2003 as director of nutrition. "Even myself, I didn't go through it, I wasn't a student-athlete here. He would tell you that [the Total Person Program] is why he is who he is today, so that's huge for Georgia Tech athletics and huge for our current student-athletes, because there's going to be so much more focus and effort and resources that go into it. With him coming along, it will be nothing but positive for our student-athletes."

The Total Person program has introduced Georgia Tech to important initiatives such as the Student-Athlete Advisory Board (SAAB), Career Development and Placement, a series of self-help seminars that take on such areas as stress/time management, financial planning/wealth management, sexual assault and violence prevention and awareness, drug/alcohol use as it relates to health and athletic performance, etiquette training, and sports nutrition/dietary supplements. It's also instituted a massive community outreach effort in the local community, led by SAAB. The Georgia Tech Sports Nutrition Center and Homer Rice Center for Sports Performance have been duplicated in colleges all over the United States.

Stansbury believes that a key in expanding Total Person is keeping the wants and needs of the student-athletes in mind.

"The program offers our student-athletes programming they can get excited about and it helps them figure out who they are, what they're passionate about and, ultimately, what their purpose is," he said. "If we can push those buttons and help our student-athletes find out what their purpose is, then we're not going to have to worry about their motivation and their ability to work hard because we already know that they're motivated and they're willing to work. So the secret sauce is finding something that they're really passionate about.

"We offer a wide palette of experiences and opportunities," he continued.

Among the opportunities that Stansbury plans to roll out are Jackets Without Borders, an international service organization for student-athletes, and industry-specific pipelines that will connect student-athletes with professionals in related fields (e.g.—connecting student-athletes interested business careers with business partners or those interested in going to medical school with medical professionals).

"The idea is to have our student-athletes kind of gravitate to where their interests are and provide them programming that they can get excited about," Stansbury said.

Thomas likes some of the things Stansbury has in store.

"He has a lot of ideas that we will start to implement here," she said. "For example, we've settled into a series of community service projects that we do every year and we do well but it's always been kind of here in Atlanta and here in our community, which is important. He wants to send kids overseas and give them that experience of seeing a third-world country and working there for a week. That's positive for them to see how good we actually have it here.

"There's a Junior Achievement partnership that he's interested in, there's a big networking and connecting with our letter-winners part that has existed on a small level, but I think will just explode and create a much bigger network for our student-athletes to tap into. I think we're just going to enhance some of the phenomenal opportunities." Stansbury eagerly awaits the maiden voyage of Jackets Without Borders, tentatively scheduled for Costa Rica in August.

"I'm incredibly excited about that because seeing the results of what happens when student-athletes go into other communities overseas as a group and work on projects and do service to others is a total game-changer," he said. "It changes their lives, changes their whole perspective on things. Getting that up and off the ground here this summer with our first trip is something I'm very excited about."

The importance of Total Person is one thing Thomas stresses from the first day freshmen come to Georgia Tech.

"Every year when our freshmen get their orientation, Total Person is one story that I make sure they understand," Thomas said. "We take a lot of pride in that history. Homer Rice, who implemented this program, was incredibly visionary and innovative. He was determined that this is what we will be about. It has evolved tremendously over the years. I make sure the kids understand that this is a big deal and something we should be proud of."

Rice is proud of where his program is and in whose hands it rests.

"I think they will continue to expand on it," said Rice, who still teaches a course, "The Leadership Fitness," which is open to all Tech students. "The results have been unbelievable—how many people that feel that it has changed their lives or helped them in some successful way. It's a positive thing, and we don't live with the negatives. We live with the positive things to make this a better place. I think what you'll see is that Todd will take it to a higher level than it's ever been, and I can see it really developing and being good for Georgia Tech. The timing's good right now. It's a good time to take it to at a higher level."

Taking it higher and keeping the Georgia Tech brand out there and ahead of the curve are tops among Stansbury's goals.

"There are so many things that we were on the front end of, or the first at, that are now commonplace in intercollegiate athletics," he said. "We need to be the place that anybody with an idea as it pertains to sport—whether it's a budding entrepreneur, whether it's one of our student-athletes or whether it's somebody who works here—we are a test-kitchen that can help them incubate that idea into an actual product.

"My vision is that Georgia Tech becomes the center of innovation as it relates to intercollegiate athletics," he added. "I'm really excited about the elevation of the Georgia Tech athletics brand. I really want to emphasize, as I tell the Georgia Tech story, what makes us different. I know that we'll be judged on wins and losses and graduation rates, but the ultimate success of our program, I believe, is what our student-athletes are doing five and 10 years after graduation. My plan going forward is a program that focuses on developing market-ready graduates that are ready to take on the most competitive postgraduate challenges. The idea is to move our paradigm from looking at graduation as the end of the road to it becoming the beginning of the road."

Reprinted by permission of Georgia Tech Athletics. It originally appeared in The Buzz magazine, spring 2017.

ADVANCING THE TOTAL PERSON

*Former Gridder Sam Bracken Bent on Reviving
the Bedrock Initiative of Tech Athletics*

By Adam Van Brimmer

Homer Rice's Total Person Program has changed many young lives over the better part of the past four decades. Ask Sam Bracken, a Georgia Tech offensive lineman among the first participants in the early 1980s, and he'll tell you the initiative literally saved his life.

Bracken came to Georgia Tech a broken young man, one abandoned by his single mother three years earlier and carrying the baggage of a "primal, primitive background" marked by neglect, abuse, drug and alcohol use and a dearth of adult role models. He found his center on The Flats thanks in large part to the influence of his coach, Bill Curry, and Rice's initiative, which promoted a balance of excellence in academics, athletics and personal well-being.

"I really should be dead, in prison or insane," Bracken said. "Georgia Tech and Dr. Rice's program are the reason I'm not."

Bracken found incredible success in life instead. He's an inspirational speaker, author and professional development consultant who spent a decade as an executive with FranklinCovey, the acclaimed training and leadership organization.

And now Bracken is back at Georgia Tech, hoping to change—maybe even save—lives by leveraging the same principles that put his life on track. He's helping one of his old Yellow Jacket teammates, athletic director Todd Stansbury, in an effort to make Rice's Total Person Program the core of Georgia Tech athletics again.

"The Total Person Program is still part of our DNA," Stansbury said. "It hasn't been the focus, but it's still a part of our history, our story and what we stand for, which is the over-all development of the student-athlete. Sam and I were fortu-nate to be among the first to go through the program. My freshman year was Homer's first year, so I was literally in the first class. To be the ones who bring that back is a great honor."

FULL BUY-IN

Stansbury is new to his job. Hired in September and on campus only since late November, he's spent much of his early tenure "fact finding." He found a department full of passion and pride in the Georgia Tech brand.

"They realize Georgia Tech is unique, a place that repre-sents excellence," he said. "Everything we do is at such a high level and by hanging our hats on the development of the student-athlete—a belief that already exists—we are going to differentiate Georgia Tech from the other schools in the Atlantic Coast Conference and around the country."

Enter Bracken. He's teamed with Stansbury to instill the Total Person Program principles in Stansbury's previous career stops, including Central Florida and Oregon State. Stansbury had to rebrand the program "Everyday Champions" and he's evolved it along the way, but at the core, what Bracken and Stansbury have built elsewhere is the Total Person Program.

The first step to re-emphasizing the initiative at Georgia Tech is to educate and secure buy-in from the administration, coaches and staff. Bracken is leading workshops and projects to foster that culture. His passion quickly wins over skeptics, just as it did in his FranklinCovey days, when one of his big suc-cesses was to deliver leadership principles to prison populations.

"His personality is so infectious because of the fact he truly cares about what he's trying to accomplish and the people he's working with," Stansbury said. "They know he's not making it up or just repeating stuff he's been told to say. This is what he believes. This is what he stands for. It's hard to come out of a meeting with Sam and not be pretty energized and enthusiastic."

'GO-TO GUY'

Bracken's given off that energy and forthright attitude since the day Stansbury met him at a Georgia Tech football practice. Bracken was far from a household name with fans during his Yellow Jacket tenure—he was an offensive guard on a team that featured stars like Pat Swilling and John Dewberry—but he was the "go-to guy" when a teammate was struggling with life off the field.

Such a role would seem appropriate, given all that Bracken had overcome. Only no one knew about his background, even his roommate Stansbury.

"I didn't know until I read his first book," said Stansbury of Bracken's memoir, 'My Orange Duffel Bag, a Journey to Radical Change.' "Back then, he was just one of those standup guys who, when you are 18 or 19 years old, kind of stands out."

Bracken's book outlines his personal journey, which was troubling from the start: He was conceived when his mother was raped. He was abused by his stepfather and stepbrothers, who introduced him to drugs and alcohol. As a teenager living in Las Vegas, his friends included a mobster's son.

His mother moved in with a motorcycle gang and abandoned Bracken when he was 15, leaving him homeless. Only then did his life take a positive turn: He was taken in a by a friend's family, and a stable home life allowed him to excel academically and athletically, leading him eventually to Georgia Tech and the program that would save his life.

BUILDING A REPUTATION

Bracken's standing as a living, breathing testimony to the power of the Total Person Program represents the future of

Georgia Tech athletics.

Stansbury foresees the personal development piece of the Yellow Jacket brand attracting more top-level talent. As the culture takes hold internally, with the staff and student-athletes, it will begin to project outward. The plan is to target letterwinners, staff and students beyond the athletic department and ultimately the public.

Once prospects and their families around the country begin to associate Georgia Tech with producing leaders, innovators and ready-made professionals, that reputation will raise the Yellow Jackets' profile.

"Georgia Tech is going to make you pro-ready, market-ready and life-ready," Bracken said. "If you are among the few who get to the pros athletically, you are going to be a better pro because you are driven by character, passion and purpose. That has the potential to be a huge strategic advantage for us."

Stansbury has the time and devotion to Georgia Tech to make it happen. He's just 55 years old, is the first "Tech man" to lead the athletic department since William Alexander, and he makes no bones about the fact that this is his dream job.

"To be back where it all began," Stansbury said, "is awesome."

Reprinted by permission of Georgia Tech Athletics.
It originally appeared in The Buzz magazine, summer 2017.

"LEADERSHIP FITNESS" CLASS
AND ANNUAL ALUMNI LUNCHEON REUNION

As I am writing the 2017 update to *Leadership Fitness*, I have decided at the age of 90 to continue teaching my course "Leadership Fitness" for the 20th year. The class has produced outstanding students who have become Positive Leaders in our society.

Each fall during Homecoming weekend, the former class members meet for our annual reunion luncheon at the Downtown Capital City Club. Each student stands and shares his or her success story. It is amazing how these students have accomplished unbelievable results in their careers through goal setting. With their achievements, these students have developed a High Purpose in life. In every case, this involves giving to others. They understand that this is what brings true happiness.

During the 2016 semester, our class was featured in an article by Steve Hummer in the *Atlanta Journal Constitution*. Steve personally sat in on some of our classes to get a clear picture.

RICE'S WHISTLE
STILL LOUD AND CLEAR

By Steve Hummer

Almost certainly this once-a-week class is called to order like none other at Georgia Tech.

Commanding the front of the room is a trim man of modest height, looking appropriately scholarly. He claims to be 89, but looks no part of it. Maybe there really is something to his working-out-every-morning thing.

He goes by the title of adjunct professor. "When I got that title I asked what did that mean. They said it means we don't pay you anything," Homer Rice likes to say.

There are 16 students in this semester's class—a cross section of the Tech populace, upperclassmen mostly who have signed up early and beat the rush to claim one of the rare seats inside this nook of Tech's Global Learning Center. Generally, none of them require the three credit hours to get over the scholastic hump. They take the course because, well, they want to. And, as a bonus, it comes with dinner after every late-afternoon Wednesday session.

They know it is time to settle in when Rice pulls the little tin whistle—the one he bought for a quarter from a traveling sporting goods salesman 65 years ago when there was nothing else he could afford to buy—and lets loose a shrill blast. "Leadership Fitness" is in session.

"What kind of day are you having?" asks Rice.

"A great day," his class answers as a chorus.

"How many made your bed today?"

Hands rise, but not unanimously, around the room.

"Getting better. Getting better."

Today, as he has for the better part of 20 years, Rice is teaching the young, non-football-playing population at Tech, with the help of Tech alum Jim Terry. Between 1980-97, Rice was far more involved with the broad-shouldered student body as the athletic director who inspired something of a renaissance on The Flats.

His fingerprints are all over the place. He is that Homer Rice, of the Homer Rice Center for Sports Performance, located just off that big stadium on campus.

And with the news Thursday that Tech had hired Todd Stansbury as its new athletic director, the connections between the former AD and the present-day department gained another strand. For Stansbury is a Tech man. And Rice was the fellow who hired him to his first job in sports administration, as the Yellow Jackets' academic advisor, in 1988.

It took nearly three decades, but the mentee finally has succeeded the mentor. And the mentor couldn't be happier.

"(Stansbury) has all the ingredients that he needs to lead this school for the coming years. I feel very fortunate that Todd is the new director of athletics," Rice said.

In any of the three roles that have dominated Rice's life—coach, athletic director, adjunct professor—teaching always has been at the core.

He was first a coach, following a timeout for WWII and service in the Pacific. Everywhere from high school in the 1950s to a season and a half posting with the NFL's Cincinnati Bengals.

(A quick detour here. There are too many stories to tell, but some demand to make the cut.

Like the one about Rice's first coaching gig, at tiny Wartburg Central (Tenn.) High. Back when he barely had enough money to buy a tin whistle. Back when in order to outfit his team he had to strike a deal with the nearby prison: If he coached the inmates, too, the warden would let him have some equipment for his high school kids.

"I used to say that was the best job I had—all home games, no problems with alumni, and you'd hear a siren go off and say, 'I sure hope the sheriff picks up a good tight end.'"

Karen Rice works alongside her husband in the Leadership Fitness class.

He retired undefeated as a prison coach, at least by his count. "The first three we won. The fourth game, the other team got way, way ahead. But we got in a big fight, so I didn't have to count that as a loss. They canceled the game.")

He moved into athletic administration in 1969, first at

North Carolina, then Rice (no relation), where he also coached, and then after much cajoling from the folks off North Avenue, came to the administrative rescue of a struggling Tech program.

Before he retired as AD in 1997, Tech had returned to national championship prominence in football (1990), won its first ACC basketball championship, made it to its first Final Four and built up its women's programs.

(OK, *another story: "I hired Bobby Cremins (for whom Tech's basketball court is named) and everybody said Appalachian? Where in the world is that?" Rice said, referencing Cremins' previous posting.*

"When I was at North Carolina we were playing South Carolina in the ACC tournament. We get behind in the last two minutes or so, Bobby was their point guard and captain. He dribbled all over the place. We would foul him, he goes up and shoots 12 straight free throws. And I never forgot that, how cool he was. When I came here, I had to hire a basketball coach and I thought of Bobby.")

And now a teacher. But that always was a component of whatever Rice did. As the athletic director, he implemented the Total Person Program at Tech, a personal development curriculum for athletes that has become a model for other universities.

(*One last story: In his 19 years teaching Leadership Fitness, Rice has had only one kid fail his class. That young man kept to himself behind dark glasses, didn't contribute in class and skipped the end-of-class interview with Rice.*

Coach Rice—he prefers his students call him that, rather than Dr. Rice—doesn't have too many demands. The rules are simple enough. The students receive a roster of 10 of them, ranging from "No cellphones" to "Never say, 'No problem' and always say, 'You're welcome.'"

Oh, and there's No. 3: "No dark glasses.")

When he is not teaching or out on a speaking engagement,

Rice might be found at his Marco Island, Florida, retreat.

Which begs one question: Why not curl up in a hammock strung between a pair of palms and just relax? Like for the duration?

Such a thought is repugnant to Rice. He's someone who still lives the tenets that he teaches—with emphasis on enthusiasm, positivity, energy.

Even at 89, he did as he asks his students and composed a list of personal goals for the upcoming year.

Here is the ultimate definition of an optimist: Someone who gets remarried at 88. That's Rice, who took Karen for his bride in May 2015. His wife of 64 years, Phyllis, died in 2013.

The theme of his life, as well as his classroom, has been built around the power of positive thought and action.

"That's what I turned around when I came here," he said, remembering 1980. "Everything was down, negative. The city. The campus. Everything. We talked about what a great opportunity we had to build this thing, and it worked."

He and his roster of guest speakers—academic, business and athletic leaders—apply that same thinking to the lessons for the college kid about to launch into the real world.

"We work on being a positive person, a good person, and go from there," Rice said.

They're teaching a little Homer at the Technical school downtown, seeing as the classics never seem to go out of date. And Rice said he'll keep blowing the cheap tin whistle to call class to order for just as long as he has the wind.

Reprinted by permission of The Atlanta Journal-Constitution

I invite key Positive Leaders to speak to the class. The speakers embody ways of becoming a Total Person. For the last class of 2016, I was fortunate to bring in my good friend Jim Host from Lexington, Kentucky. Jim founded Host Communications, a college sports marketing and association management company with an international reputation. His firm became part of IMG, which is active at most colleges and universities in America.

Jim became one of the most influential businessmen in the history of college athletics, but he is more than a businessman. He has had an impact on the lives of young people and on people throughout the country. He is a true Giver. A former outstanding baseball pitcher for the University of Kentucky and Chicago White Sox, Jim is a man who gets things done, whether it be building a coliseum or any other important matter. Karen and I always look forward to visiting with Trish and Jim. Jim will always be in my Hall of Positive Leaders.

As I continue the course each year, I am indebted to my staff, which makes all of this happen: Jim Terry, Bill Curry, Leigh Thomas, Lauren McDow, Anthony Bridges, and Karen Sue Rice.

DR. STEVE USSELMAN
CLASS RATING

My "Leadership Fitness" course at Georgia Tech is rated annually, as required by the Board of Regents. Dr. Steven W. Usselman, Professor and Chair of the School of History and Sociology at Georgia Tech, sends me the report each year.

The class is open to students in all disciplines across campus, with students who are majoring in engineering, business, pre-med, industrial engineering, history and sociology, and many other areas. Each year, we have scored 5.0 in evaluations, achieving the highest rating.

Many students have recommended the course of study and noted that implementing it has changed their lives. In 1997, Dean Gary Schuster of the College of Sciences approached me

Georgia Tech | School of History and Sociology
Ivan Allen College

March 20, 2017

Dr. Homer Rice, Adjunct Professor
P.O. Box 422298
Atlanta, GA 30342

School of History and Sociology
Ivan Allen College

Dear Homer:

Thank you for your contributions to our instructional mission during 2016.

An annual written review by the respective unit head of each faculty member's performance is required by the Board Regents and by the policies for Georgia Tech. For further details, see these sections of the policy manuals: BOR 8.3.5 and GIT 3.1.2. The criteria governing these evaluations are the same as those used for promotion, tenure, and salary decisions.

Based upon my observations and available information, my evaluation of your performance is as follows:

Teaching:
Your instruction for HTS3813: Leadership Fitness was rated 5.0 for "overall course effectiveness," with an interpolated median on CIOS Item 21, "overall teaching effectiveness," of 5.0.

Beyond these numerical scores, I had the opportunity to address your students, share a meal with them, and read their summary journal reports, all of which convince me that this well-conceived and well-executed course is making a significant impact on their lives.

Summary:
We very much appreciate your willingness to continue providing this experience for Georgia Tech students and are pleased to have the course offered through our School of History and Sociology.

We are currently planning next academic year's course schedule and have you again slated to teach this course, with me as co-instructor, on Wednesday afternoons and evenings in the fall.

If you would like to discuss this evaluation, I would welcome the opportunity. Please contact me at steve.usselma@hsoc.gatech.edu to schedule an appointment.

Thank you for your contributions to the School of History and Sociology and to Georgia Tech.

Sincerely,

Steven W. Usselman
Professor and Chair

In accordance with Institute policy, please acknowledge receipt of this annual performance review for calendar year 2016 and return to the School of History and Sociology, retaining a copy for your own records.

Homer C. Rice   4-1-17

(Signature and date)

regarding teaching a course related to Positive Leadership. He said that he had witnessed how the Student Athlete Total Person Program improved the lives of our athletes at Georgia Tech. I named the course I wanted to teach "Leadership Fitness."

To become a Positive Leader, you must be fit in every category of your life: the type of person you become, health and fitness, career, and financial planning for the future. Each student learns how to set goals to accomplish these steps. Being successful in all areas of your life is vitally important. If you do not achieve success in this way, you will not be the kind of leader that people listen to and follow.

THE UNKNOWN STORY
OF GREG PAGE

Greg Page was one of four African-American players who played at the University of Kentucky in 1966-1967, but he also gained a claim to fame as the first African-American football player to be recruited to that university. He was recruited to the University of Kentucky in the 1964 and 1965 school years.

I have learned in recent years from Karen's son J.J. Allen that a sports writer's column mentioned another person being the first recruit, and I have put together the Unknown Story of Greg Page so that the record is as accurate as possible. This correction ensures that we understand the story as it unfolded, without taking away from the accomplishment of others. Greg Page passed away before he was able to play his first varsity game, but he rightfully should be regarded as the first African-American recruited to play at the University of Kentucky.

After the end of the 1965 season, I left the University of Kentucky to coach at the University of Oklahoma. All the papers of Greg's signing, grades and commitments were deposited

Greg Page

with the football office before I left for Norman, Oklahoma. Unfortunately, the former coaches and players I have talked with have not been able to furnish any information. Outside of Greg's own family, I have not been able to find people still living who knew details of his recruitment or about what happened between my departure and when Greg called me at Oklahoma.

In late November 1961, as head football coach at Highlands High School (Fort Thomas, KY.), we finished our fifth undefeated season and won another state championship.

Ninety miles south of Fort Thomas, The University of Kentucky was in the process of changing its football coaching situation. Head coach Blanton Collier was stepping down and returning to the Cleveland Browns to join Paul Brown. The combination of Collier and Brown outcoached their opponents winning several World Championships. Coach Collier was the best teacher the game of football ever had.

Kentucky was seeking a new coach. To my surprise, I was contacted by the Wildcats director of athletics, Bernie Shively, to meet with the search committee to discuss the opportunity to lead the football program. The committee was comprised of UK President Frank Graves Dickey; Dr. Ralph Angelucci, UK Board Chairman; W. L. Matthews, Dean of the Law School and Faculty Chairman of Athletics; and Athletic Director Bernie Shively. During the interview Dr. Angelucci compared me to Paul Brown, noting that Paul had gone from the successful Massillon High School to Ohio State University. I would be making a similar move. It was an incredible compliment, however, I decided I was not ready for the position. The group then asked me if I would consider the top assistant's position. Of course, that would depend on the person they selected as head coach. I told them I would be interested.

The following week, Charlie Bradshaw, an assistant on Coach Bear Bryant's staff at Alabama, came to Fort Thomas to speak at our Highlands Banquet. Charlie, as other coaches visiting on recruiting trips to the area, stayed at my home.

Charlie wanted the UK head job, and I called Bernie Shively and recommended Coach Bradshaw. He was accepted as head coach and he and the search committee asked me to become the offensive coordinator. I accepted the offer and moved to Lexington with my wife and three daughters.

In my fourth year (1965) at UK, our offense led the Southeastern Conference and the nation in passing yardage. (Quarterback Rick Norton was selected second overall in the AFL draft by the Miami Dolphins.) The season before we were also successful as an offensive unit.

During the 1964 season my wife's (Phyllis) father, Leo Wardrup became ill. We made trips to his home in Middlesboro, Kentucky, to check on him. He was in the Middlesboro Hospital where his nurse, Wilma Jean Page (the first African American nurse in Middlesboro) was taking care of Mr. Wardrup. Mrs. Page learned I was a UK football coach, and she told me her son Greg was a football player at Middlesboro High School. I took the opportunity to visit his practices and games and concluded this young man was an outstanding football player. I discussed at length Greg's potential and character with his coach, Walt Green. Everything was beginning to come together.

We did not have a single black player on our squad at UK. If he was interested and would sign a letter of intent and later the grant-in-aid document to attend the University of Kentucky, Greg would be the first African American to join us at the University. As time went on, going into 1965, Phyllis's father was in need of major medical attention. I asked Dr. Angelucci if he could help. He did arrange to bring Leo Wardrup to the University hospital in Lexington. However, it was too late, and soon we took him back to the Middlesboro Hospital in Middlesboro.

He would pass on in a short time. During my trips to Middlesboro I continued to visit Greg and his family. I will never forget a meeting in the Pages' home with Greg; his mother; father, Robert Alexander Page, a coal miner for Consolidated Coal Mines; and younger brother Mel. It was time for Greg to commit to UK, which he did. He signed all papers. I explained, this would be similar to Jackie Robinson becoming the first black player in the Major Leagues with the Brooklyn Dodgers. Greg actually committed in the spring of 1965 with the signing taking place in September of his senior season and the verification to take place in December.

With that all settled, I left UK to take the position as offensive coordinator at the University of Oklahoma. Jim MacKenzie became the head coach at OU following Bud Wilkinson and Gomer Jones, after serving as defensive coordinator and top assistant for Frank Broyles at Arkansas of many years. Jim played for Coach Paul Bryant at Kentucky.

During our spring practice in May 1966 at Oklahoma, I received a call from Greg Page. He indicated he had not been contacted by UK and asked if he could come to Oklahoma. My answer was yes but I told him I would call UK and tell them he had called. I called Bernie Shively and explained the situation. Bernie said he would check on this and get back to me. In a couple of days Charlie Bradshaw called and said they had contacted Greg and he was coming to UK. Greg called again and asked what he should do. I told Greg he should go to UK. He was their first black player to sign and should stay with his commitment.

I do not know what happened in the period of our first meeting 1964 and the mix-up with Kentucky not contacting him after I left for Oklahoma. Greg made a visit to the UK campus during the time his team was playing in the state play-offs (late November 1965) and I was able to meet with him and also see him play again. He was going to be a great player for the Wildcats.

In the upcoming season of 1967, Greg, in football practice before UK played their opening game was involved in a freak injury. His back was crushed and he never recovered. Greg Page died 30 days later. What a tragedy! When I learned of this information I called Mrs. Page and talked to her regarding the unfortunate situation.

Here was a young man, to become the first African American not only of UK football, but in all sports in the Southeastern Conference.

During the 1965 season at UK, I was not aware of another African American being recruited by assistant coach George

Boone. In fact, I did not learn of Nate Northington and Greg being roommates until 50 years later. After my dear wife Phyllis passed away (with Alzheimer's) in 2013 I was remarried to Karen Powell in 2015. Karen and her husband Josh were our dear close friends. After both Phyllis and Josh had passed away after extended illness Karen and I stay friends but both of us said, "we would never remarry" but God stepped in and changed our thinking. It was Karen's son, J.J. Allen from Lexington, Ky that told us about the recognitions of the four African Americans:

Greg Page, Nate Northington, and a year later Wilbur Hacket and Houston Hogg being the first to open the way from the University of Kentucky.

All of this led to catching up with Greg's younger brother Mel Page and to replay the beginning of the saga in 1964. Regardless of how this story plays out, it is important to pass along a "Thank You" to Paul Karem and Paul Wagner as they present the University of Kentucky's role in integrating college athletics.

I have been in contact with Greg's younger brother Mel Page many times. The Page family knows that Greg was the first to sign and would like for the story as I knew it, before I left the University of Kentucky, to be made public.

Paul Wagner with Paul Karem are putting together a documentary about Greg Page, Nate Northington, Wilbur Hacket and Houston Hogg, the four players who came to Kentucky in 1966-1967. They were the first African-American players to sign with the University of Kentucky, with any Southeastern Conference team, and with almost any university in the South. In the fall of 2016, Karen and I were guests of Mel Page and his family for the unveiling of the four players' statues at the University of Kentucky football facility. The documentary "Black in Blue" about the four will be aired nationally in spring of 2018.

JACK MARKWALTER
THE LEE CANDLER FUND COMMITTEE

Jack Markwalter is chairman and chief executive officer of CIBC Atlantic Trust Private Wealth Management, holding these positions since January 2004. In addition, he serves on the CIBC Operating Committee as a member of CIBC's executive leadership team.

He joined CIBC Atlantic Trust in 2002 as head of business development and has more than 31 years of experience in the private client and investment industry. From 2005 to 2013, Jack also served as senior managing director of Invesco and as a member of the Invesco Executive Management Committee. From 2008 to 2010, he was head of Invesco U.S. Institutional Sales, Client Service and Consultant Relations as well.

Prior to joining CIBC Atlantic Trust, Jack served as managing director and national director of the client strategy group for Morgan Stanley Private Wealth Management.

Jack earned a Bachelor of Science with highest honors from the Georgia Institute of Technology and a Master of Business Administration from the Harvard Graduate School of Business.

Jack serves in various leadership roles for numerous community organizations. Among other positions, he is a member of the board of directors for Children's Healthcare of Atlanta Foundation, the board of directors for the Georgia Tech Foundation, the board of directors for the Marist School and the board of directors at the Atlanta History Center. He serves as co-chairman for his Harvard Business School Reunion Fund Campaign and is a member of the Big Brothers Big Sisters board of directors and Capital Campaign Committee.

Jack has been featured in various publications and other media outlets, including *The Wall Street Journal*, *Barron's*,

Jack Markwalter

CNBC, *Private Asset Management* magazine and *Family Wealth Report*.

Jack graduated from Georgia Tech in 1981 before going to Harvard Business School for his MBA. I hired this young man to work for our Georgia Tech Athletic Association, and this is the story why:

In his senior year at Georgia Tech, Jack was actively involved and served as the student body president. During that time, many students were forced to live off campus in unsafe neighborhoods surrounding the campus. Students went to the Georgia State Board of Regents for funds, only to learn that the Regents had already allocated their entire annual budget. The only option left was to get money through the Board's supplementary funds. In order to do this, Jack organized a huge publicity campaign in which parents of every in-state student were called and asked to write letters to their representatives and other important legislators in the state of Georgia. In addition, he was able to get free television time from a local news station.

His efforts eventually resulted in $18 million in state funds to build the new Woodruff Dormitory.

After Jack graduated from Tech, he worked for the Alexander-Tharpe Fund through the Georgia Tech Athletic Association to raise money for scholarships for athletes. During the time, Georgia Tech was rebuilding its athletic association. In order to make it one of the best in the nation, Tech needed to provide better opportunities to the athletes it was recruiting. While Jack worked with the Alexander-Tharpe Fund, the second largest amount of money for athletic scholarships in the nation was raised.

Through these experiences, Jack learned the following:

- Set high goals—anything is possible.
- Power of teamwork
- Surround yourself with great people.
- Reward, recognize, and motivate
- Lead by example.
- Power of positive thinking

He also included these thoughts on leadership:

- Vision
- Ethics and integrity
- Service orientation
- Communication skills
- Self awareness
- Teamwork

Jack is also a member of the Lee Candler Fund that I chair, providing revenue for the Student/Athletic Total Person Program at Georgia Tech Athletics. The fund also supports the Academic Center, Sports Medicine Center and facilities related to these programs, as well as the "Leadership Fitness" course. Other members of the Committee are President "Bud" Peterson, Ray Jones, Jere Goldsmith, Charlie Hurt, Charlie Moseley, James Terry, and Marvin Lewis. Stephanie Swant serves as Secretary of the group, and Jack Markwalter is slated to replace me as Chairman when I step down or can no longer serve.

Randolph Thrower was an original member of the committee instrumental in aiding me in soliciting the gift from Lee Candler. I was introduced to Mr. Thrower, former United States Treasurer and a prominent lawyer in Atlanta, by his nephew Bill Cobey. Bill was my right-hand assistant when I served as Director of Athletics at the University of North Carolina. I met Randolph when he was Chairman of the Board of Emory University. Mr. Thrower passed away at the age of 100.

CLOSING REMARKS

It is time to close another update of *Leadership Fitness: Developing and Reinforcing Successful, Positive Leaders.*

It has been one pleasure after another to continue adding to the original manuscript. The feedback from so many people keeps me motivated year after year.

On May 20, 2015, Karen Sue Powell and I were married, after having lost our loved ones years earlier. We have become not only man and wife but also partners in contributing the wisdom of *Leadership Fitness* to Georgia Tech students and others through our writing and speaking.

Our speaking engagements include many audiences, such as orthopedic doctors at The Johns Hopkins Hospital, American

Football Coaches Association conventions, the Amway lecture series (sponsor of the College Football National Championships' "Glass Football Trophy"), Bill Lam's Wrestling With Life seminars, alumni events for several schools, Hall of Fame banquets, the Timothy Class at Peachtree Road United Methodist Church, Billy Graham Training Center, and leadership classes at the University of Alabama in Tuscaloosa with Jack Markwalter and at Centre College by President John Roush.

Through these and too many opportunities to mention, we are spreading the positive word of *Leadership Fitness*. I look forward to more positive reactions from those who say their lives have been changed for the better and that they have achieved true success.

After I add a book update, I always think it may be the last one. However, as each year goes by, I think about how Karen and I are blessed to receive such happiness by giving.

Thank you for reading *Leadership Fitness*. May it be as beneficial to you as it has been to many others.

Karen Sue Rice works alongside her husband's "giving" and
"contributing" to Homer Rice's Hall of Positive Leaders.